SHIPPING
and
the 800-lb
GORILLA

First published in paperback in 2017 by Futurenautics Books
43 Berkeley Square, London W1J 5FJ

ISBN: 978-0-9574325-5-0 PB

Typeset in 10.25pt Garamond

WWW.SHIPPINGANDTHEGORILLA.COM

INTRODUCTION

Back in 2013 a report was published. It was called *Global Marine Trends 2030*. And it made me angry.

The report was created by a variety of worthy organisations which between them had used all sorts of clever modelling to decide what the shipping industry would look like in 2030. That wasn't what made me angry. What made me angry was that in the whole sweep of this very expensively produced report the foundational driver of disruption—technology—was almost completely sidelined.

The 2030 report dedicated one of its 145 pages to technology, and decided that it was simply too disruptive to model. In the report it rates alongside global economic collapse in its unpredictability.

That's what made me angry. It made me angry because I spent my time identifying, contextualising and explaining to large organisations exactly where the technology was going, the effects it was likely to have, and how they should anticipate and prepare to both defend against, and capitalise upon them.

It was becoming clear to me however, that this kind of information was something that should not be confined to companies who could afford it. I believed that the industry—in common with every other—was on the cusp of profound and destabilising change and it needed all the help it could lay its hands on if its incumbent companies were going to thrive, and in many cases, survive.

Our response came in October 2013 when the first issue of the Futurenautics magazine, *The Maritime Future*, was published.

It covered autonomous, unmanned ships, Big Data, analytics and predictive analytics, Millennial mindsets, gamification and even warned that Amazon was a potential competitor shipping should look out for.

It appeared shortly after the inaugural London International Shipping Week, where none of these subjects were discussed. They failed to make the agenda to such an extent that we included a cartoon about it. Two shipping folk in black tie having a conversation whilst the 800-lb gorilla named 'technology' squatted outside and regarded them through the window.

What I and many others knew back in October 2013 was that whether you called it the elephant in the room or the 800-lb gorilla, technology was about to start tearing up the shipping and maritime industry and reshaping it into something unrecognisable. But that's not the whole story. As those who have heard me speak or read me in the past will know, I am fond of making the point that technology is rarely the competitive advantage on its own, but it almost invariably enables the competitive advantage.

Technology isn't the only driver for change in shipping, but in combination with global megatrends, changing demographics and new mindsets it is busily reshaping the world in a variety of ways that makes a careful study of it—and the combinatorial and orthogonal effects on the status quo it's causing more generally—essential.

What the shipping and maritime industry really needs to find is a vision for its future—a digital vision. Together with Roger Adamson, and a whole host of other disruptive, clever, driven people both inside and outside the industry, I wanted to help it do that. And I have a feeling we're getting close.

People have been asking for a while now if we could collect some of the best of the articles of the past three years into one, handy, easily accessible format.

Turns out that's called a book. And thank you for buying it.

K D Adamson
Singapore, December 2016.

CONTENTS

1

KISSING THE FROG

Every winter around this time, in an expensive building opposite Dirty Dick's pub in the City of London, a group of senior managers gets together to thrash out their 10-year investment forecast.

I expect there'll be coffee, and two kinds of water. And considering these senior managers work for Barings—which as I write has around $275 billion in assets under management—probably some really good biscuits. You know the ones I mean; covered in chocolate and wrapped in gold foil. Or perhaps not. Because when things start going pear-shaped it's the little extravagances like really good biscuits that tend to be the first casualty.

Remember three months ago when I introduced you to the new Seaconomics? When I pointed out as I have been doing for several years, that the historical link between global GDP and shipping volumes was decoupling and the entire globalisation paradigm of endlessly rising trade volumes was looking dodgy? Well, looks like Barings agrees.

"We believe globalization has probably reached its peak," says Marino Valensise, head of the multiasset team at Barings. "The market won't like it." That's why at this winter's meeting Barings will be considering reducing or perhaps eliminating altogether what they call their 'globalisation premium'. And that's awfully significant.

The globalisation premium is a big deal because to date it's meant that U.S. stocks collectively traded at a price/earnings ratio about one whole number higher than they otherwise would have. But rather like the link between GDP and shipping volumes, that link has been decoupling. Over the last ten years Barings has cut that premium by 50 per cent, and if—having relentlessly pored over all the data it can lay its hands on—Barings decides to do away with it altogether, the outlook for stocks is going to head south along with it. Particularly in those sectors viewed as most likely to suffer from the slowdown.

Enter Hanjin. Or should that be exit? Barings might be reassessing the biscuit budget but Hanjin have already scraped the bottom of the barrel. The heat and light of its implosion has been spectacular, and my sense is that by providing a cold, hard light of day example of the industry's problems it has finally given people the opportunity to start saying out loud what they've been suspecting for some time. That shipping's in trouble. Big, big trouble.

But despite the fact that everything from the Danish Maritime Forum to IHS and Lloyd's List seem to have finally woken up to what's going on, that really is only part one of what needs to happen. Acknowledging there's a cliff edge coming up only helps if you're then capable of doing something to stop your company strolling into the void.

I've come to the conclusion that what this is boiling down to is scale. To paraphrase Douglas Adams, shipping is big. Really big. For most people it is so mindboggling big they're happy to walk away and leave it to others they consider 'qualified' to manage it. But as big as shipping and its problems is, the scale of the solution to its problems is actually several magnitudes larger. And that's what we're having a problem with.

I've said many times that the companies which don't stroll over the edge into the digital abyss won't necessarily be the ones with the best technology, the deepest pockets or even the best ideas, they'll be the ones with leadership of the correct mindset, and probably blessed with a little bit of luck too. The luck you can't do so much about, but that mindset you can have a shot at changing. If you understand where it came from.

While Hanjin was busily going bust IMO was celebrating World Maritime Day with the slogan, "Shipping: indispensable to the world." Although it sounded to a lot of people as though it was IMO that thought it was indispensable to the world. That slogan tells you a lot about the shipping industry. There's no doubt that ships have been absolutely indispensable in getting us to where we are today, and that led to an embedding into the global consciousness of a shipping-centric view of the world.

Perhaps the clearest example of that comes from the Mercator Projection, which reimagined the earth as the surface of a cylinder then laid it out flat to make it nice and simple to steer a ship across an ocean. For almost 450 years that map, developed by a Flemish geographer in the 16th century as an aid to shipping, has been one of the standard maps of the world. What Gerardus Mercator gave shipping, shipping then enforced on the global consciousness. But in recent years we've begun to realise just how narrow a view that map has given us, and the effect it's had on the way we think the world actually looks.

On the map lines of longitude are parallel, but in reality lines of longitude converge at the poles. Which means that the closer you get to the poles the more distorted the map becomes and the bigger everything looks relative to its actual size. Hence countless generations have gone out into the world with the idea that Africa—weighing in at a land mass of 30.4m km2—is pretty much the same size as Greenland, at 2.2m km2. That Europe and other countries in the western hemisphere are actually much larger in comparison to the vast countries they colonised—like India and Africa—than they really are.

You can debate the extent to which the received wisdom of that shipping-centric map of the world has distorted policies and even morality over the centuries if you want to, but the important point is that we don't need to rely on a map drawn up in the 16th century any longer, particularly not one which is demonstrably suspect. And actually, a very similar thing has happened to shipping. I've mentioned the decoupling of the link between global GDP growth and shipping volumes, but there's another link that's been decoupling for many years that I'd argue might have been even more significant.

In English law there's a test that the courts apply when they want to decide whether or not a party has acted reasonably. It's called 'the man on the Clapham omnibus', a reasonably educated, intelligent but nondescript person against whom the defendant's conduct is measured. Ask the man on the Clapham omnibus, or the New York subway, or the woman in the nail bar, or the housewife in the supermarket to define 'shipping' and they'll most likely tell you that it's when something is sent from one place to another.

The bottom line is that shipping is no longer a noun, it's a verb. It has come to mean, in everyday parlance, the conveyance of a good from one place to another, and that conveyance may include ships, trains, aeroplanes or trucks—or even drones—but that doesn't matter. It refers to the activity, and if you'd like evidence of that fact then just google the word and see what you get.

What the man on the Clapham omnibus is telling you is that shipping isn't about ships. But he's telling you more than that— something really, really vital and valuable. It isn't about ships. It's about MORE than ships. It's about the end result, not about all the links in between.

There's an old Chinese proverb about a frog sitting in a well. The frog that sits in a well—it reads—only sees his piece of the sky. For centuries shipping's dominance and relative importance to world trade has mean that its sky became everyone's sky, to the extent that it has skewed everyone's view of the world we live in. But that just isn't the case now.

When your industry has genuinely been at the centre of the world, it's not hard to understand why adjusting to the fact that you don't even own your own name any longer is tough. That's why IMO's assertion is beginning to look more like a plea. Shipping is becoming less indispensable to the world for all the reasons I outlined last issue—the new Seaconomics is seeing to that. But the industry is still resolutely refusing to look outside its piece of the sky. I read one analyst talking about ship operators needing to concentrate on realising 'marginal gains' from digitisation and the role of the maritime press in raising the profile of the industry. Well, Hanjin has delivered awareness of the shipping industry that the Ruperts at IMO's PR agencies overseeing the annual World Maritime Day offensive could only dream about.

It's been accurate, informative and devastating. Because what it shows—from the tearful mother interviewed on the BBC whose seafarer cadet son was stranded on a vessel with no supplies off Singapore, to the frantic manufacturers and suppliers with no idea where their stuff was, when it might arrive or where—was that the world is still too reliant on a dysfunctional industry that isn't fit for yesterday, let alone tomorrow.

I am sorry to be the one to tell you this, but shipping has no divine right to exist anymore than trucking or aviation does. And it doesn't matter how many times you trot out the weary stat that it delivers 90 per cent of everything, increasingly the man in the street is going to tell you that trucks do too. And in a few years drones might. And after that hyperloops or heavy-lift airships.

So marginal gains aren't enough. They aren't even a start. You have to think bigger. Much, much bigger. What shipping has on its hands is a need for wholesale digital reimagination—it needs to understand that shipping's problems aren't big enough. And that requires genuinely blue-sky thinking, which is just about impossible for a frog that won't leave its well.

But seeing the big problems at all is often hard, and that's not something that shipping has a monopoly on. The investor and founder of start-up incubator Y Combinator Paul Graham describes the phenomenon as 'Schlep blindness'. A schlep is a Yiddish word for an unpleasant or difficult task usually an intrinsic part of solving a really big problem. The magnitude of the schlep involved can subconsciously stop you from even seeing the problem in the first place.

Graham cites the example of Stripe, which has become a massive global payments platform. He points out that for more than a decade every hacker he knew who'd had to process payments online knew it was a pain in the backside, and yet no one created a start up to solve the problem. "They decided to build recipe sites, or aggregators for local events," writes Graham on his excellent website. "Why? Why work on problems few care about and no one will pay for, when you could fix one of the most important components of the world's infrastructure? Because schlep blindness prevented people from even considering the idea of fixing payments. Though the idea of fixing payments was right there in plain sight, they never saw it, because their unconscious mind shrank from the complications involved."

And you know what, that's exactly what's happening in shipping. In fact I think this is somewhere between schlep blindness and a Somebody Else's Problem—let's call it a Some-Schmuck Else's Problem (SSEP)—because the real problem isn't shipping. The real problem is that the global trade and logistics system is still massively inefficient, and that's such a huge problem, such a massive, humongous, monstrous problem, that just like the online payments problem, shipping can't even entertain it.

Ask yourself why we have vertical markets. I think at least part of the answer is because you had to silo things off to make them manageable. Because the human brain simply couldn't cope with the complexity of managing ecosystems in the way that the power of computing now enables us to.

That's why this is a mindset thing. Because what the digital age of exponential computing power allows us to do is to stop thinking at a functional level and begin looking at delivering an end result from a strategic perspective.

The end result of shipping is for the customer on either end to get what they want. Shipping is just one small part of a trillion-dollar global circulatory system for trade which has the potential to operate far, far more efficiently. But until now the schlep required to attack that problem has been too much for anyone. Until now.

"Global trade is no longer a human scale problem," says Matt

Tillman, chief executive officer and co-founder of the Singapore and San Francisco-based ocean freight rate platform Haven. "It's a machine scale problem." You've heard of Haven, right? And Clearmetal? And Xeneta?

Or what about Flexport? It just raised $300m-odd in a funding round. Someone described it thus: "Can you imagine what the world would be like if international trade was made easier, the way software has made our work and personal lives easier? Flexport is where 'software eats the world' meets international shipping." That someone is Y Combinator founder and Flexport investor Paul Graham.

These are the people who are busily schlepping away to solve the big problem that should forge shipping's new place in these hyper-intelligent digitally-enabled trade flows. So can we all please shut up about the dearth of innovators in shipping, because we've got them. The industry's problem is that it's been looking for them in the wrong place. People with big titles in legacy shipping companies aren't showing any signs of the kind of transformative thinking the industry urgently requires, but we're still wringing our hands trying to persuade them to look at a different piece of sky.

Possibly the most shocking thing I heard out of Copenhagen's Danish Maritime Forum was that the Vice Chairman of CMA CGM sat on a stage and said he had no idea what a Millennial was. That on its own should bar him from taking part in a discussion on the future of the industry. But it won't. Because he's *important*. Yeah? Come see me in a few years and we'll discuss who's important.

I have very different ideas about who's important than the organisers of the Danish Maritime Forum do. The very first Futurenaut we ever featured was Xeneta CEO Patrik Berglund, and I told every last one of you that what he and his team were doing was transformative. Finally, three years late, he's just won the Lloyd's List award for something or other. Like my other poster boy for disruption Adam Compain at Clearmetal who's just got given a gong by Lloyd's List Intelligence. Fantastic. About time. But the real trick is to find these people and encourage them fast. Not wait until they've got the money to spend advertising in your magazines or buying tables at your awards dinners. Or indeed, buying your awards.

That doesn't get the frogs out of the well. But we do. And you know what, when that happens, the results can be astonishing. We took a variety of really very senior frogs—from ship operators to bankers, connectivity experts to insurers, cyber experts to cutting-edge ship designers and engineers and most importantly, customers—and stuck them in a room in north Norway while I poked them with sticks. What started life as a discussion around autonomous ships soon developed into a wholesale reassessment of shipping's role as part of the new intelligent global transportation systems that Industry 4.0 is creating.

"Sitting here today we've already redesigned the port infrastructure, redesigned and simplified the ship, integrated haulage companies into the maritime logistics chain, and addressed cyber security value," said Futurenautics Maritime CEO Roger Adamson summing up the day.

"We've started to discuss how we engage our customers better, asked how we get ship owners out of asset plays and into the business they should be in which is moving stuff around the globe at a profit on time, on behalf of happy customers, questioned where we need people and where we don't, and whether a more distributed physical network is required."

That's the kind of big thinking that needs to happen if we're going to develop into what I call the blue logistics channel that shipping has to become. We need a digital vision for this industry, and it needs to be shared and engaged with and built upon collaboratively, with passion and belief, by people who think far bigger than boats.

Transparency is what's really driving this, because once you get transparency and visibility you can start to measure things. That's data. Big Data, and using analytics turns that into information and intelligence, which in turn delivers efficiency on a scale we could only dream about in the past. There have long been those who held that shipping simply couldn't be disrupted in the way other industries had been because it's so physically rooted in meatspace. But the cyber physical systems are already changing that. Machines and humans are merging so fast it's dizzying and it's allowing us to shrink the physical world the same way we've used the Internet to shrink the digital one.

That's why the disruption and the opportunity has barely started for shipping, if it thinks big enough. Right now there is no value created on the ship. All anyone can focus on is reducing cost and that's just not enough. This is the reason that everyone's struggling with the concept of autonomous ships, because taken in isolation they don't save money. Because you're looking at them solving your current problem, which is making money, as opposed to the real problem, the huge SSEP you're struggling to even see, which is making global trade more efficient.

Maersk Line global sales head Michael Hansen recently warned that the industry had to change otherwise it would be disrupted by new entrants. "Someone once said—and excuse my French—if you have an industry with shit service then you deserve to be disrupted," he said. "It's no coincidence that an industry like this has got a number of start-ups knocking at our doors and at the doors of our customers."

He's right, the opportunities are so huge they are mouthwatering. But what he's missing is the motivation, the Big Hairy Audacious Goal I'm always banging on about. "Flexport is one of that small handful of startups that are going to change the world," says Paul Graham. That has to be the ambition. Changing shipping, or changing your loss into a profit just isn't enough. And that's where the big incumbent companies are struggling. As one of the audience in a session on 3D printing I moderated in Copenhagen observed, it's very difficult indeed to get new ideas or projects off the ground when they're being evaluated in terms of legacy ROI. How do you put a price on changing the world? I think the very fact that companies are trying indicates they are destined to fail.

Chat with Patrik Berglund as I do and you'll hear a genuine passion for the industry in which he works. Have a walk around Hyde Park with Adam Compain as I did recently and he'll tell you how he sought out a position at OOCL because he was absolutely fascinated by the industry. These men, and so many others running these disruptive companies are simply not motivated by the almighty dollar alone. "The platform comes off as a bit idealistic. But that's kind of the point of technology," says Haven's CEO, Matt Tillman. "It's here to create something new." Not shore up something old.

Shipping isn't indispensable, and instead of finding big problems it can solve it's focussed on managing dissatisfaction in an atmosphere of learned helplessness so pervasive that most of it isn't even sure it's possible to do anything different any longer. Technology is allowing us to see things we couldn't before and it's encouraging more people to change things they don't like.

Take the new global hot spot maps to illuminate how what we buy pollutes the planet and where. "What we are trying to do is to connect economic activity and global supply chains with environmental impacts. That has not been done before," said Daniel Moran, a postdoctoral researcher at NTNU's Industrial Ecology Programme, who was one of the lead authors. "We tried to spatially locate environmental impacts on the production side and link that to global supply chains. The idea is to help governments, industries and individuals target areas for cleanup."

Or what about that shipping-centric map of Mercator's, which the website True Size is challenging by allowing you to compare the size of any nation or U.S. state to other land masses, just by moving it around on the screen. These are whole new pieces of sky that shipping has to get excited by if it's going to reimagine itself.

The bottom line is that we need to move from shipping's traditional zero-sum game to a hero-sum game. That's one where individuals and companies do things not because it's good for them, but because it's good for everyone. Heroes are those who are sometimes prepared to sacrifice their personal concerns for a greater goal and a greater good. It may sound fanciful but transparency really can drive that.

Here's an example: received wisdom would suggest that those customers using the Xeneta platform to benchmark their freight rates would be desperately pushing to make sure they were paying the least possible, right? Wrong. What Xeneta has discovered is that customers don't want to be paying the lowest rates possible, because they know that means their business is worth the least to the carrier, which means they're probably getting the worst service and have the highest likelihood of their cargo being rolled. Makes sense doesn't it? Value versus cost. If shipping can start harnessing that kind of thinking then the evidence is that profitability beyond its wildest dreams could well follow.

But is it going to happen? As the old fairytale goes, could the kiss of digital transform the shipping frog into a prince? To be honest the evidence isn't looking too promising. The Digital Infrastructure Investment and Transformation study we're currently running with Ericsson has shown up some interesting interim results. So far the average maritime company thinks it's undertaking digital transformation on around $100,000 a year. So, yeah. About that.

That doesn't apply across the board, and if there's anything that's heartening then it's the fact that enquiries to Futurenautics Maritime from companies wanting to get a handle on what the digital shift means for them and how the heck to take advantage of it are up 150 per cent year on year. Show me a ship operator who can say the same.

That we're getting so busy trying to help answer those questions has to be a good sign. But there are still too many people who want the future to turn into the past. It's an attitude that seems to be gaining traction in a lot of places.

From Trump's desire to make America great again to the UK's Brexiteers wanting to take their country back, there's a sense that the past was a far better place than where we're heading. And I don't think that's got a lot to do with politics. It's to do with vision. Because at the end of the day, despite all the technology, connectivity and globalisation, there are still a lot of frogs in their own little wells, rigidly focussed on their own pieces of sky.

Shipping can rightly claim to have broadened the minds of the world in the past. But if it's going to do it again it needs to find a vision of its own. I've been kissing this particular frog for a while now; in fact I've had my tongue down it's throat for the thick end of three years, but I'm beginning to wonder if it's crossed the line into mouth-to-mouth.

No amount of snogging seems to be turning the shipping frog into the handsome digital prince—or princess—we all want to see, and the truth is that the time for transformation is fast running out.

Before long it'll be time to forget the frog, put your head between your legs, and kiss something else goodbye.

London, October 2016.

2

THE EMPEROR'S NEW CLOTHES

COP21 is still reverberating. If you're worrying about it then I've got excellent news for you. You can stop right now. Just take a chill-pill, bunker-up with the thickest sludge you can lay your hands on and steam off into the sunset.

Impressive though the accounting sleight-of-hand employed by the ICS in order to make everyone believe that shipping's emissions were falling was, it wasn't necessary. It doesn't matter what shipping's emissions are at the moment. What matters is the measure everyone's using to work out what they'll be in the future.

The IMO GHG report was created by Dr Tristan Smith, whom I know personally, and also like, respect and admire in equal measure. His probity and accuracy I do not question for one moment. But he's wrong on this. And for a very simple reason, not of his making. Coincidentally, it's the same reason underlying the quiet equilibrium in most of shipping, the companies which supply them, the banks which finance them and the individual investors who buy shares around the world in their publicly-listed companies.

When you dig right down, way down into the detail of where and how shipping's share of global emissions are going to grow to

6-14 per cent by 2050, it's dependent upon one small fact. That shipping volumes will continue to grow at a rate a percentage point or so above global GDP. Except it isn't a fact. It isn't even a strong hypothesis any longer. It's just plain wrong.

That link is in the process of decoupling. As I write today the multiplier has dropped at least to parity, and it's still falling. Considering the monumental implications of climate change and the angst around suggestions that shipping may be included in the final COP21 wording it seems almost inconceivable that no one in IMO or the ICS picked this up. It's the equivalent of a 'Get out of jail free' card, and no one's played it.

Why? Well, it's possible that these powerful representative bodies genuinely haven't realised that the age-old multiplier on which everything from COP21 to shipping loans are calculated isn't fit for purpose any longer. But what's more likely is that even if they did, well, everything from COP21 to shipping loans are calculated on this multiplier. And if it isn't fit for purpose any longer, the implications for the industry go way, way beyond emissions targets or legislation.

Well, it isn't. And they do. And there are people who know that. Remember last year when I told you you weren't going to like what I said about the culture and cognitive diversity of the industry? Well, that may have upset you—I'm afraid I remain unrepentant—but if that was upsetting, what I'm about to outline may just act as the greatest laxative known to man.

Because the detonation of this apparently small and unremarkable little article of faith, which everyone seems to have forgotten they've built all their projections around, represents a chillingly alternative near-future for the shipping industry. So it's no wonder those in the know are keeping very quiet about it indeed.

The impact of this decoupling on the underlying projections for shipping's future growth could be—at least for some overextended operators or suppliers—terminal. But this is about more than projections, although that's a part of it. The reason the decoupling is happening is the really important part. The shift from the global consumer economics which have held sway for the best part of a century, to something radically different. Something which will usher in a new era for shipping—what I call the new Seaconomics.

Projections have always been problematic things. We have to have them in order to function, but their accuracy is always open to question. We've come up with some incredibly sophisticated models to help us, and in the pre-digital age where linear growth was the norm, they worked fairly well. But not any longer.

The prefix for everything digital tends to be 'e', and that's generally taken to mean 'electronic'. But in this new digital world 'e' stands for exponential. Understanding the difference between the linear growth we're used to and the exponential growth we're experiencing now is at the heart of the speed and scale of the change we're seeing.

You already know about exponential growth, Gordon Moore of Intel encapsulated it in the eponymous Moore's Law—namely that the power of computing will roughly double every 12-18 months. But as the world becomes digital, as industries, sectors and technologies become powered by information flows their price and/or performance also begin to double approximately annually. And it seems that once that doubling starts, it doesn't stop.

Dubbed the *Law of Accelerating Returns* this exponential growth means that forecasting the way we're used to—using past experience to extrapolate future performance—doesn't work any longer. In fact it makes predicting growth and change incredibly challenging, for a very simple reason.

As David Frigstad, CEO of research firm Frost & Sullivan once said, "Predicting a technology when it's doubling is inherently tricky. If you miss one step you're off by 50 per cent."

Using linear models to predict technologies and industries growing exponentially led McKinsey to advise AT&T not to enter the mobile phone business. Its models predicted that by 2000 there wouldn't be 1 million mobile phones in use worldwide. And there weren't. There were 100 million. McKinsey's prediction was off by 99 per cent, and it meant AT&T passed on one of the most lucrative business opportunities of modern times.

But this isn't an isolated example, and it isn't the same as the guy who turned down signing The Beatles. What we're seeing isn't incompetence or poor data. It's the fact that the rules have changed. You can have excellent data and clever people, but if you insist on applying linear growth models to exponential technologies you are going to end up looking stupid.

But there's another problem with these breakthrough technologies. They aren't sitting nicely in their boxes on their respective shelves. They're playing with each other, inserting bits of themselves into other technologies and giving birth to newer technologies and disruptive scenarios.

The combinatorial effects are creating disruption on an unprecedented scale. And it's happening everywhere. Right now modelling what the future is going to look like is probably one of the most challenging jobs on the planet. Believe me. And the technology is only one part of it.

Global businesses are about to integrate their operations into a seamless, digital whole—a process called Industry 4.0, or the fourth industrial revolution—and that's disruptive enough. But that shift is running up against, and in some cases combining with, a range of powerful megatrends which are busily reshaping the global economy.

Between 1970 and 2015 seaborne trade volumes increased by an average of around 3-4 per cent per annum, driven by a demographic 'sweet spot'. Between 1970 until around 1990 the global population expanded fast, with the working-age element increasing significantly. The addition of Eastern Europe and China to the world economy in the 1990s and 2000s supercharged everything, accounting for most of the expansion of world trade volumes.

But that's over now. What we're facing is a period where demographic growth is going to slow significantly. Between 2015 and 2030 population growth is expected to account for only a quarter of global consumption growth.

The world's population is ageing—average global life expectancy was 71.4 years in 2015—fertility is dropping and the population decline which we've already seen in Japan and Russia is now spreading to Germany and other European countries and even to

China where it's already forced a re-think of the 'one child' policy.

The implications of all this are massive. We have ageing populations in developed economies and a digital industrial revolution delivering productivity and efficiency via technology and automation, but not creating jobs for the huge young populations in India and Africa that will pull them up the economic ladder.

But the impacts aren't limited to the young in the developing world, they're already hitting the developed economies. Using data from a range of surveys carried out over decades one study examined the disposable incomes and wages of young families in eight of the 15 largest developed economies in the world which together made up 43 per cent of the world's GDP in 2014.

It found that in the US, France, Germany, Italy and Canada the average disposable income of people in their early 20s is more than 20 per cent below national averages. In France, for the first time the recently-retired generated more disposable income than families where the head of the household was under 50.

The average under 35-year-old in Italy was poorer than the average pensioner under 80. Looking at the US data, it found that in 2013 the under 30-year-olds had less income than those aged 65-79. That's the first time that's ever happened, at least as far back as there's data to analyse.

Why is this important? Because older people don't spend the way younger ones do. Their money goes on tourism and healthcare, but not on commuting, kids toys and houses. Tourism and healthcare doesn't translate into seaborne trade volumes, and the people whose spending traditionally does, are watching their economic clout evaporate.

A recent report by the Resolution Foundation in the UK found that the Millennial cohort, or Gen Y, spent their twenties earning on average £8,000 less than their parents' generation did. Many can't afford to buy houses any longer—the traditional British rite of passage. Many have struggled to get jobs at all.

Is it then so surprising that this generation has markedly different concerns and expectations. The desire for access over ownership isn't just a response to the altruistic concerns around sustainability you could argue is an inevitable result of a generation growing up with the threat of climate change hanging over it. It's also a pragmatic response to the fact that owning things isn't as easy or as cheap as it used to be. Unless they're digital. Or, increasingly, created by digital means.

I had a conversation with a futurist the other day who said he could see no way in which 3D printing was a more sustainable choice for a Millennial mindset. But it is, on many levels. Not only does 3D printing enable a level of personalisation which can make an item more valuable and useful, and lead to it having a far longer life-span, it also enables individuals to maintain items and equipment which in the previous paradigm were simply uneconomic to fix.

How many of us have chucked out an otherwise perfectly serviceable item because something simple like the handle broke off? Now the opportunity exists for that handle to be printed on demand, on your high street or in your back-bedroom, not in batches of 5,000 in Asia and shipped halfway across the world.

At the most fundamental level one has to understand that 3D printing goes by another, far more instructive name, for a reason. It's also called additive manufacturing. Traditional manufacturing takes a chunk of material, often scarce, virgin material, and chips away at it until it gets what it wants. Additive manufacturing as the name suggests takes the opposite approach. The item is built up using only what's necessary. Little or no waste.

What we're observing is the combinatorial interplay of technology, demographics and mindsets, and it's all moving exponentially. This is something every citizen of the world should be focussed on. But the shipping industry should be all over it like a cheap suit.

"Most long term outlooks are anchored in the historical relationship between population growth, urbanisation and increasing seaborne demand. The emergence of the fourth industrial revolution redefines the recipe for economic growth by opening the gates for long term gains in efficiency and productivity. The outlook for the shipping industry is deteriorating accordingly."

That's a quote from the most recent Shipping Market Review

by Christopher Rex and his team, Mette Andersen and Ninna Møller Kristensen, at Danish Ship Finance. What they are eloquently and powerfully outlining in that simple paragraph is the emergence of the new Seaconomics.

If you want more detail then I can't recommend highly enough that you subscribe to their free reports. Because there are still far too many people who don't.

Here's another quote, this time from the Greek Minister of Shipping and Island Policy, Theodore Dritsas, when he visited Posidonia last month.

"The shipping sector has faced great challenges over the past years, which are related to the excess tonnage, combined with short term reduction in the demand side for transported cargo volumes, lack of funding from bank institutions, sharp decline in vessel values, uncertainty in oil prices and acute competition," said Mr Dritsas. "The gradual recovery of the world economy will certainly lead to the reduction and hopefully the elimination of those phenomena." Dritsas added.

Oh dear. That's not it at all. Which reminds me, talking of oil prices, did I mention that the cost of solar and other renewables is plummeting? The cost of solar power has fallen from $30 per KWh in 1984 to under $0.15 per Kwh. That's a scale of 200 times in 20 years. Another little 'amuse-bouche' for the shipping folk who are gaily trumpeting the tanker segment at the moment.

Except none of this is funny. At all. Because this is an industry with an awful lot of people and money depending on it. And there are at least some who are beginning to get jittery.

"You see a real nervousness about the reliability of the industry and the sustainability of the business model," said Joost Sitskoorn, Special Envoy for the Global Shipper's Council. "The predictability of cargo flows is becoming more and more difficult," said Robbert van Trooijen, Chief Executive North Asia for Maersk Line. "As an industry we are reacting to trends we did not see coming."

Nowhere was that more evident than a place where you might have reasonably expected to hear some serious and measured discussion of just how the hell we're planning to deal with what's on its way. You might have done. But you would have been disappointed.

That place was the 5th Capital Link Analyst and Investor Forum, also held at Posidonia. "The majority of owners reiterated the importance of taking advantage of second hand ship prices and their optimism for better markets to come," Capital Link reported. "During the event, shipowners vocalized their interest in India and Africa as the new markets of opportunity and advised on a bullish view of traditional shipping values, advocating a countercyclical investment play into the secondhand market. While others differ in opinion, the overall sentiment was warm in the dry bulk and tanker sector."

Yes, you read that correctly. Let's have a listen in on what those 'traditional shipping values' are shall we? This is from Lloyd's List describing one panel discussion about whether it was time to buy second hand tonnage. "Hamish Norton, president of Star Bulk Carriers, tended to agree. He said he was, last night, on a boat of a "very wise man", who "is much more motivated at this point in the cycle by greed". "It was a very big boat," he responded when asked how to justify the man as "wise".

"Ignore the analysts, buy anything that floats that is cheap," said George Procopiou, the Chairman of Dynagas LNG. "The market will come back on any ship type and you must be there."

But that doesn't appear to be the mood music coming from the banks, who are kicking each other's legs out trying to get to the top performing loans, whilst jettisoning operators who just a few years ago were solid prospects and are now struggling to get any debt finance at all.

And what about the capital markets? "Investors are looking to invest in sustainable companies," according to Christa Volpicelli, Managing Director of Citi Investment Banking. And do shipping have those? According to Christa, no, it don't.

Perhaps most depressing was the assertion by Kristin Holth, Global Head of Shipping, Offshore & Logistics, DNB. "Maybe shipping will never be an investment grade industry like others," she said. And she's probably correct. Not as long as traditional shipping values are apparently centred around greed and wilful disregard of market analysis, anyway. So the message appears to be that we need to all shut up and leave it to ship owners to place their bets as they see fit. Because that's actually what the industry is all about.

"People say that shipping is a volatile business. That's not the case. Shipping is the most stable business because it's stable in its instability," said Dynagas' Procopiou. "The volatility is how you make profits and timing is the key." Not customers then? No. Thought not. That'll come as no surprise to the many I speak to who are exasperated with being the collateral damage in a game of tonnage speculation where the ships are worth money and the customers aren't. Those kind of comments are really going to go down well. According to Capital Link Mr Procopiou was apparently making, "a rare public appearance this Posidonia as a show of support for the Greek industry during difficult times." Rare. But perhaps not rare enough.

But if he's right, if volatility really is how you make money in shipping then where is it? You couldn't ask for a more volatile global economic and business environment over the past few years, so—to paraphrase Jerry Maguire—show me the money, George?

It certainly isn't in evidence in the container sector, although that doesn't seem to have made the radar of some people. Here's my personal favourite quote from Capital Link at Posidonia,

"George Youroukos of Poseidon Containerships and Technomar did leave room for some bullish opportunities for those with "balls big enough" to invest in larger secondhand boxships on the market." Balls big enough, eh? For those of us who operate outside shipping, just listening to this stuff is jaw-dropping. What's even more astonishing is that the whole event was supported and funded by the NASDAQ, the Big Board and EY.

That's EY, whose latest marketing campaign is all about digital transformation and the exponential technologies changing the world, and how they can help companies profit from it. Maybe they should divert a tiny fraction of the millions they're spending advertising it towards explaining it to their shipping division. Because judging by this performance, they don't seem to have any idea.

Here's the thing, individual greed and big balls is a poor basis for an industry, and in a world turning faster and more transparently than ever, it's no wonder things are beginning to fall apart.

The tragedy is that shipping could be an investment-grade industry. The family ownership structures could enable risks to be taken that would be harder elsewhere, and enable new relationships and partnerships that could transform things.

There are those who have seen the writing on the wall. Danaos CEO John Coustas for example, who was a lone voice at the Capital Link forum.

"For many years, world trade volume had grown about twice as fast as global economic output, but that multiplier dropped to less than one in 2015, Mr Coustas pointed out," reported Capital Link. "As a result, this structural shake up in the correlation between trade and GDP growth means the latter can no longer be taken for granted as a practical indicator of shipping."

People know. People like John Coustas, and Christopher Rex, and even Hamburg Süd. Take a look at their recent annual report and you will find buried in the executive summary an acknowledgment that the link between volumes and GDP can't be relied upon any longer. MSI's Adam Kent wrote recently that it was likely for "shipping market cycles to become shorter with lower peaks." So not cyclical any longer then?

Because if that's the likelihood, then why not stand up and tell all these people we're advising that the old chestnut about shipping being inevitably cyclical, like that link between global GDP and shipping volumes, is a busted flush?

Maybe because ship owners don't seem to like analysts, at the best of times. Or that analysts have been wrong about a lot of things.

What about the analysts in Seoul who were still tipping Hanjin Shipping to outperform Seoul's main bourse in the same month that it finally began to seek creditor approval for restructuring? According to financial data provider Wise FN, only 0.1 per cent of reports expressed sell opinions. 86.6 per cent gave buy recommendations, with 3.6 per cent of those strong buy recommendations.

Apparently there's going to be an investigation. But I can save them some time. I know exactly what the problem is, and how you fix it. There's a certain Danish gentleman who wrote something very instructive which should be required reading for the shipping industry. And I don't mean Christopher Rex—although he should be too.

The Dane they should be reading is Hans Christian Andersen. Specifically his short story called the *Emperor's New Clothes*. It's about a couple of weavers who tell their emperor they've weaved him a suit of clothes which is invisible to anyone who is stupid, incompetent or unfit for their positions.

Once they've dressed him in the non-existent clothes he parades amongst his subjects, none of whom dare to point out that he's naked. Apart from one small child.

It's a tale of the blindness of powerful men, how those who depend upon their favour will collude with them. And the importance of speaking truth to power.

The shipping emperor is naked. And when the emperor is parading around naked it's hardly surprising that he has an unhealthy preoccupation with the size of his balls. But the truth is they're shrivelled and wizened just like his balance sheet. And it's about time that the people funding him took a long hard look at just how unappetising a sight he's become.

It's about time they started asking the hard questions, about where demand is coming from in the future? What the projections for growth and profitability in his companies are actually based on? What kind of vision for the future there really is?

Because until we all begin to accept the reality of the new Seaconomics, shipping has no chance of righting itself in the digital age. And being prepared to stand up and say that really does require substantial *cojones*.

Instead of throwing more money at him, it's time you grabbed that emperor by those balls of his. Because then, and only then, will hearts and minds follow.

London, July 2016.

3

CORE ISSUE

I t's a curious fact that—in the Western tradition at least— apples have a long-established association with disruptive change and innovation. For a start, the apple which Eve consumed in the Garden of Eden was from the Tree of Knowledge. Contrary to what many assume, it wasn't the disobedient act of eating the apple which caused Adam and Eve to be banished by God, it was the knowledge they gained by eating it. Part of that knowledge was an awareness of their nakedness. Once they were no longer innocent of that, they couldn't remain in the garden. And the rest, as they say, is history.

Fast forward to the 1660s and possibly one of the most famous moments of innovation. Sir Isaac Newton, sitting under an apple tree and watching an apple fall to the ground conceived his theory of Universal Gravity. Some like to think the apple actually struck him on the head, a metaphysical representation of how random and how powerful Newton's idea was.

29th June 2007 and another Apple changed everything—at least in the mobile phone ecosystem. The introduction of the first iPhone catapulted Steve Jobs from leading a floundering company to pride of place in the global pantheon of history's great innovators. These days it's easy to forget that Apple had its toes hanging over the edge of the precipice before Jobs saved it with the iPhone and turned it into America's richest company. But Jobs never did. "Innovation distinguishes between a leader and a follower," he once said, and continually reinforced his status as the genius innovator at the core of the company.

It's the way we all like to think about innovation—one individual having a sudden and blistering insight which fundamentally changes everyone else's perception. In an age of global media and connectivity acquiring that kind of reputation can get new ideas funded and products bought. It can grow global brands and create cult-like status. But it cuts both ways. Jobs has been gone a while, and without him people are watching closely to see what's left. The news hasn't been too good.

Apple recently announced weaker than expected second quarter results which included its first year-on-year decline in profits in thirteen years. What followed was eight straight days of share price decline which saw it close last Friday at a level last seen in 2012. In eight days Apple has lost all the share price gains it made in the last four years.

At the heart of this is the concern that Apple has stopped innovating, and started renovating. Steve Jobs undoubtedly was an innovator, but new CEO Tim Cook is an operations guru. Although he's talking about all the cool stuff they have up their sleeves, the thing they've been adorning people's cuffs with recently—the Apple iWatch—hasn't been an innovative game-changer. In the crowded field of wearables it was nice, but not transformative.

But this is a company with US$233 billion cash in its back pocket, and a price-to-earnings ratio of 10—lower than IBM (11), Cisco (13), Google's Alphabet (31) and out of sight of Facebook's (92). And yet investor confidence is dwindling and the market is pricing it as a company in long-term decline. Now just stop and think about that. Because it's the most tangible measure I can point to right now of just how central and crucial innovation is to a business. It's always been important because—as others point out this issue—it's part of human evolution. What we've experienced so far has been a mixture of incremental innovation, and some intense periods of disruptive innovation.

As an example of incremental innovation may I suggest the toilet. Water-flushed toilets appeared in Knossos and Akrotiri in the ancient Minoan civilization from the 2nd millennium BC. Although we now have those which heat the seat, shoot temperature controlled water jets at you from unexpected places, and come with a control panel which wouldn't look out of place on the bridge of the Star Ship *Enterprise*, it's taken quite some time to get there, and the basic concept hasn't really altered. Disruptive innovations are fewer and farther between, and interestingly they often come in batches. Roman technology still underpins infrastructure today, whilst the flowering of the Renaissance and the industrial revolution all saw major scientific and technological disruptions that changed lives.

What's happening now is that both kinds of innovation are speeding up, and that's due to the exponential growth of a range of technologies which are combining together to create what's described as combinatorial disruption. As they do so they're spreading horizontally across business and society, breaking down the vertical markets we're used to and eroding the power of domain knowledge and expertise.

This exponential growth is leading to dramatic falls in the cost of a range of technologies—from solar to robotics to biotech—which are bringing them within the reach of smaller, less well-resourced companies. These new companies are building on the technology platforms which have gone before, iteratively using them to experiment and test out their own innovative ideas, using them as the foundation for the next leap forwards.

This presents a real issue for incumbent companies, burdened by cumbersome legacy structures, operational silos and—crucially—domain myopia.

Some recognised the limitations of that model many, many years ago. For example, the origins of the Lockheed Martin Skunk Works—whose compact nuclear fusion reactor project I wrote about last year—go back 70 years to 1943 when the US Army needed a jet fighter, and they needed it yesterday.

Lockheed's Kelly Johnson set up his Skunk Works based on an unconventional organisational approach, breaking rules and challenging the bureaucratic system that stifled innovation and hindered progress. For 1943 his philosophy was truly revolutionary, but Johnson and his team proved it was sound by designing and building the XP-80 in only 143 days—seven less than the US Army had demanded.

There are many more skunk works around today—which in some respects is a measure of how little company structures and limitations have changed and how much they're likely to soon—but they're just one part of a much larger arsenal that organisations focussed on innovation are deploying.

Google famously has its R&D factory "Google X", where Chief of Moonshots Astro Teller's mission is to invent and launch 'moonshot' technologies that could make the world a radically better place. Some of their publicly known projects include the self-driving cars, the smart contact lens, high-altitude wind-power generation, and Project Loon, to name a few.

That's all great, but spinning out an R&D skunk works is by definition separating that innovation from the core business of the company. What's increasingly required is to harness and drive innovation within the company itself. And there even Google is having a problem. You may assume that anyone who was prone to having good ideas would want to work at Google, but the reality is those highly motivated employees also have a habit of getting great ideas and then leaving to make them happen.

The result is—reportedly—Google's 'Area 120'. Google already allows employees to work on '20 per cent projects', personal ideas they can spend a fifth of their working day on. Successful 20 per cent projects have included services like Google News, AdSense and Gmail.

But now Google is going further, creating a startup incubator that will allow employees to work on personal projects full time. Employees will pitch the company for a place in Area 120 and if accepted will access funding and support with Google becoming an early investor in successful projects.

Of course, you might say that tech companies like Google would do that, wouldn't they. But here's the thing. It isn't just technology companies that recognise the importance of innovation.

The Boston Consulting Group has spent the last ten years undertaking an annual global survey of the state of innovation, and in 2015 79 per cent of respondents ranked innovation as either the top-most priority or a top-three priority at their company. That's the highest percentage since the survey started in 2005.

The survey shows that science and technology continue to be seen as increasingly important underpinnings of innovation. The data has led BCG to identify four attributes that many executives point to as critical to innovation success—an emphasis on speed, well-run and very often lean R&D processes, the use of technological platforms, and the systematic exploration of adjacent markets.

The importance of technology to successful innovation means it's no surprise that BCG's list of the 50 most innovative companies over the last ten years has included those closely associated with that capability. The likes of Apple, Google, Microsoft, Samsung, Amazon, and IBM have made the list in nine out of the ten years, but that doesn't tell the whole story. As the years have gone by technology companies have not elbowed their more traditional counterparts aside as you might have expected, there are still plenty on the list. In fact five of the top ten companies in 2015 are non-tech companies. On the longer list of 50, 38 (76 per cent) are non-tech companies.

That's important. Because as I've said many times technology can enable a competitive advantage, but rarely is it the advantage in itself. What the non-tech companies on that list have done is to understand the scope and the power of exponential technology growth and leveraged it.

So what's this telling us? Clearly building an innovative company is a complex challenge, but there appear to be some basic ingredients. Technology is important in two respects. On a tactical level it's key that the organisation has the correct technology infrastructure to allow it to take advantage of data and analytics, collaborate, secure itself, connect and share ideas inside and outside. But what's also necessary is a much wider strategic grasp of the big technology trends reshaping the world, and how they will impact on traditional economics, markets, consumer demand and value chains.

That, plus domain expertise and data should allow you to identify the big problem that you should set about solving. But there is a fundamental prerequisite to all of this, which is that your company must have both the desire and the intent to innovate.

And in the shipping and maritime industry we fall at that first hurdle. Everyone in the industry seems to be talking about innovation—a point universally acknowledged by the contributors to this issue—but very, very few are doing anything about it. At this stage it's important to separate out the maritime supply side and the ship owners and operators, because while there is clear desire and intent amongst some of the supply side, that's in shorter supply amongst shipping companies themselves.

In most industries suppliers create products to meet the needs of customers, but we've reached a situation in the maritime industry where shipping companies buy so much kit and services to ensure compliance with regulations, the link between customer need and product development has all but decoupled.

Maritime suppliers have learnt to look towards the next set of regulations, creating products that IMO wants—and they know shipping companies will have to buy—rather than identifying the real problem and innovating to address it.

But it gets worse. Take ECDIS for example. Speak to any shipping company and there is almost universal despair at the bugger's muddle ECDIS has become. IMO's mishandling of the affair is one thing, but what it did provoke was a very rare agreement amongst ship operators that the plethora of different ECDIS systems and user interfaces was complex and potentially dangerous. What ship operators wanted was an 'S' mode, something that would provide a common view across all systems.

In what one hopes is the low water-mark for maritime manufacturers, they blocked it. In fact one maritime electronics manufacturer association actually trumpets its part in preventing ship operator customers getting what they wanted—on safety grounds—lobbying heroically against 'S' mode in order to protect the profit of its members.

Is it any wonder that so many ship operators just don't trust technology suppliers in maritime? And is it any wonder that suppliers are endlessly renovating their products and services, rather than innovating. The reality is that too many of them just don't know enough about what their customers actually do day to day to identify the problems they might be able to solve for them. Wedged into their silos—HVAC, catering, pumps, navigation, paints, broadband—none of them are trying to understand the interactions across those silos which new technologies are driving and which are changing how ships will be operated in the future.

But the ship operators are no better. If you're part of a shipping company which is genuinely innovating around your business model and customer requirements then, congratulations. Help yourself to a biscuit and shut the door on your way out.

As for the rest of you, let's be clear that reducing your emissions and giving your seafarers access to broadband is not innovating. Nor is ordering more ships, or bigger ships, or slow steaming. I have a lot of conversations with shipping people and on the subject of innovation they are almost universally a bit helpless. I think there's a simple reason for that. Great innovation comes from solving big problems, and shipping—in its usual, self-obsessed way— has picked the wrong problem.

Shipping thinks that the big problem is no one is making money. But that's not the problem, it's actually just a symptom. The real problem is that shipping isn't providing an adequate service to its customers. But shipping can't see that. It's too busy doing anything it can to make money, and just to compound the problem, it's doing it at the expense of the customers it serves.

Let's take bigger ships. Huge, expensive boxships which allow the liner companies to get even better economies of scale. Customers hate them. They hate them because they can only get into a handful of ports, which means that customers are then faced with a variety of new surcharges—high-tide surcharge, low-tide surcharge, etc. On top of that the customers then have to grapple with port infrastructure creaking under the weight of coping with tens of thousands of containers being discharged—if of course you're fortunate enough to have your container arrive at all, or vaguely on time, which is close to an even chance. Then the customer has to truck that cargo from the only port big enough to accommodate your behemoth of a ship, adding emissions to the customer's tally rather than yours.

And whilst we're on the subject of emissions let's look at the great innovation of recent years, slow steaming. We're all very smug about that. Look at the emissions and cost we've saved and the market we've propped up. And what has that meant for customers?

According to an analysis by McKinsey, slow steaming adds three days to the supply chain between the United States and Asia. The additional annual inventory and obsolescence costs for US importers can reach $415 million. Worldwide, that same three-day delay could cost about $5.7 billion.

That's without factoring in the environmental impact of manufacturing that additional inventory. But at least these big cargo owners benefit from their own economies of scale. Don't they? Apparently not. According to research by our friends at Xeneta, big cargo owners making long term deals with container lines are getting worse rates than the little guys booking stuff on the fly. Still think shipping oils the wheels of world trade?

It isn't even as though customers aren't queuing up to tell shipping what's wrong, but they aren't listening. Henry Ford famously said that if he'd asked his customers what they'd wanted they would have told him a faster horse. Shipping doesn't even have that excuse. Shippers are begging for a Model-T and they're getting an emphysemic donkey.

Access to the kind of intelligence, research, data and information about what's happening globally to disrupt markets and economies is there for the taking. It's so prevalent that one wonders how shipping can really avoid knowing what's going on, but they're doing a marvellous job. One commentator, a ship operator writing for a popular shipping website, plaintively asked recently if anyone had a 'big idea' for shipping, before going on to make the following statement.

"Consider the 3D printer," he wrote, "– at the moment, not much more than a toy, but capable of very much more." Tell GE it's not much more than a toy; they're 3D printing everything from transducer probes to aircraft engines. "The real problem," the commentator continues, "is working out how to make a lot of money in a non-expansionary shipping market." No. Wrong problem.

But whilst shipping companies and maritime suppliers are by and large still flogging their dead horses to their respective customers, there are others who are working together to create some real disruption. At our Autonomous Ships roundtable late last year we brought together ship operators, customers, technology suppliers, insurers, lenders and cyber security experts at Rolls-Royce's technology centre in Aalesund.

The result of that morning was a fascinating arc of disruptive innovation which encompassed everything from the design, size, propulsion, maintenance and autonomous operation of the ship, to regulation, ports, sea traffic management, smart logistics and intelligent transport systems, new ownership ecosystems encompassing lenders and insurers, and new seafarer skillsets.

So to that commentator I say, there are ideas. Big ideas. The kind that have the capacity to sweep things away very, very quickly. And they are slowly taking shape in maritime suppliers, class, flag states, ship operators, and customers. What at the moment I think we're missing is the link between them all that's going to hook everything together. But that's on its way.

When asked about his multiple achievements, innovations and contributions, Sir Isaac Newton said, "If I have seen further it is by standing on the shoulders of giants." The disruption, when it comes, may feel to those like our friend trying to get to grips with 3D printing, to be an unexpected bolt from the blue. But the foundations for them are being laid down now. And for some of us they won't be any surprise at all.

Kirsi Tikka of ABS writes this issue about the need for an innovation infrastructure for the shipping industry. It's a genuinely good idea. I'd like to see it start with a new kind of innovation event, one that is truly collaborative, instead of pulling in ship operators for free and then pimping them out to suppliers whose only interest is in flogging them stuff.

We need a space in which shipping, its suppliers and its customers can come together to identify what the big problems are and go about solving them together. We need to gather, showcase and connect those big ideas whether they're from seafarers, start-ups or Silicon Valley in a big, bold way. Not for fear of the potential threats, but in search of the huge opportunities.

Of course you can only take the shipping horse to water; you can't make it drink. At the moment it isn't thinking big enough so those identifying the big problems, and with the thirst to solve them, aren't shipping companies.

As Martin Kits van Heyningen says in his article this issue, there's no point in trying to solve the little stuff. It's the big, hairy audacious goals that innovators like him, and Walter Hannemann, Oskar Levander, and Tero Hottinen, and Constantine Komodro-mos want to get their teeth into. And that also goes for the people outside shipping that these guys are helping to draw in.

In the meantime most ship operators remain oblivious to everything other than their own sticky situation, delivering a marginally faster horse, that eats a bit less and farts a bit less, but will ultimately end up as glue.

London, April 2016.

4

AI, AI CAPTAIN

When I first started working in offices in the late 1980's desks were already groaning with chunky word processors, big switchboards, fax machines and huge printers. And they were always going wrong. At one ad agency in London there was a sign in the photocopying room which read, "Remember—if the photocopier won't work it's probably because you upset the fax machine—they're all in the same union." I've made that joke ever since, but I'm going to have to stop soon. Because shortly it won't be so funny.

I don't know how many of you recognise this issue's cover image. For those that don't it's a still from what was voted in 2010 by the Moving Arts Film Journal as the greatest film of all time. *2001: A Space Odyssey*, directed by Stanley Kubrick features a couple of astronauts en route to Jupiter on a spacecraft which is controlled by a sentient computer called HAL. Problem is that HAL goes haywire and kills the crew, aside from Dave, the astronaut whom he traps outside the spacecraft pod-bay and refuses to let back in. Dave eventually does get back in and deactivates HAL which gradually loses its mind as its various circuits are removed. There was some discussion here about using the image of HAL's glowing red light on the cover, but I won. My argument being that *2001* is widely regarded as one of the most influential films ever made. So whether you've actually seen it or not you will most likely have seen something that was made because of it, and all those thousands of depictions and repetitions have shaped and influenced the public—and therefore probably your—view of artificial intelligence.

That influence has extended far beyond movies. Back in 2011 it was revealed that users who ordered the iPhone 4S's intelligent assistant Siri to 'Open the pod-bay doors' would be met with the chilling response, "I'm afraid I can't do that, Dave." Just the same as HAL does. On one hand it's a great engineer-planted joke, but it's also a recognition that Siri isn't just a cool gadget on your phone. It is artificial intelligence. And it demonstrates how pervasive and deeply embedded into society that fear of being outwitted by something that is more intelligent than you, but isn't human, has become.

It's activated when we hear the term driverless car, drone or unmanned ship, but is that reasonable? When people talk about the future of shipping and its SmartShips is that what we're heading for? Is some Master somewhere sometime soon going to get maritime's first 'I'm-afraid-I-can't-do-that-Dave' moment? I don't think so. Not because we won't have the kind of artificial intelligence which is capable of outwitting us, but because of the reasons why, and the global context in which, SmartShips are developing, and how they'll operate.

The recent World Economic Forum in Davos took as its theme the 'Fourth Industrial Revolution', and you can read a very concise description of what that means from this issue's Futurenaut, Christopher Rex. If you want to understand what Industry 4.0 means for shipping, well, we covered that back in April 2014, pointing out that as the world digitised, manufacturers—shipping's customers—were profoundly changing the way they operated, that highly integrated supply chains were going to be pivotal to sustaining competitive advantage and that shipping was the weakest link.

I argued back then that shipping had to recognise and close the digital competence gap between the way it did business and the way its customers and the rest of the logistics channel did. Failing to do so would mean it couldn't integrate with the cyberphysical systems that were going to be the engine of this new industrial revolution.

The concept of the cyberphysical system was somewhat challenging for shipping when I used to talk about it in 2014. But now the ramifications of the Internet of Everything is beginning to hit home for people, the idea of a component which knows what it is, where it needs to be, what it needs to do and can communicate all of those things to other components around it, isn't so mind-boggling.

That's because the roadmap which gets us to the cyberphysical systems of Industry 4.0 can sort of be broken down into about 4 steps. Shipping is currently wrestling with the first two steps: Connectivity, and Sensors and Data.

Unlike our shore-based counterparts, the availability of cheap ubiquitous connectivity hasn't extended to the deep sea, and it probably won't ever be as cheap and ubiquitous as on land. But it is getting far, far better. The broadband offerings now are solid and affordable and the advent of the high throughput satellite services over the coming few years will provide previously unthinkable bandwidth at sea. So that's one part.

The other is the Sensors and Big Data wave that shipping is surfing. Newbuilds are being delivered with virtually all the sensors you could want, and retrofitting them isn't expensive. As an industry we're beginning to appreciate how the application of sensors—and in the case of GE's Direct Write, sensors you can ink onto components—changes the game. Because sensors generate data. Big Data. Class Society DNV GL admits it's been taken by surprise by the growth of Big Data, but it's catching up fast, as are other Class societies like ClassNK, featured this issue launching its Ship Data Centre.

These are the first couple of building blocks along the path to Industry 4.0 and shipping has woken up to them. Data is now being generated in massive quantities and a good proportion of it is being transmitted ashore. But that's where we've got a bit bogged down, to the extent that a lot of the industry is still asking what Big Data is for and querying how much data it really needs.

Not everyone is asking that of course. It's always dangerous to talk about 'the industry' in a homogeneous sense, because it contains a very diverse set of organisations, and, particularly on the supply side, many of those operate not just in maritime and shipping but across a variety of other verticals.

Rolls-Royce is one, and it's transferred its years of data expertise in aerospace to maritime. You can read more about what they're doing with it in *Buying the Cow* elsewhere in this issue, but the bottom line is that what Big Data needs—the next building block of the cyberphysical system, the next step on the roadmap—is analytics, and the algorithms behind them.

In order to generate value data needs to become information and that's where analytics and algorithms are essential.

Sensors attached to big oily bits of machinery, by and large, shipping gets. Algorithms not so much. Data analytics and algorithms require sophisticated and specialist expertise that shipping and maritime has not routinely employed or encountered, but it does exist, and it is turning data into information.

However, whether it's via ABB's newly unveiled Integrated Operations Centre, Maersk's in-house monitoring centres or Wärtsilä's condition based maintenance, in order to bring those analytic algorithms to bear on the data, it has to be brought back to a central processing centre ashore.

The data has to be crunched by algos and—perhaps surprisingly—still considered by human engineers before it becomes actionable information. And importantly, once that information is actionable the action is being taken by the human rather than the system.

It's up to the guy in the control room at Maersk, Wärtsilä, ABB etc., to pick up the phone or send an email to the Master or the Chief via that comparatively expensive satellite link, and tell him to go and turn something up, down or off. And of course, it also requires someone on the vessel to immediately carry out the instruction. That might differ where remote support is enabled and the ship operator has either implemented its own, or signed up to a manufacturer's remote support package. In that case the action will be taken directly from the shore-based control centre. But it still requires a human to intervene.

Despite all the technology, we're still operating with humans very much in the loop. Which is why even though it might not feel like it right now, the journey from step one to three has been fairly straightforward. The next part is likely to feel like less of a step and more of a leap. Not because of the current limitations of technology, but because many of us haven't yet understood its power and the changes that intelligent networks are going to drive globally.

The entire Big Data and SmartShip debate has revolved around technical, engineering data delivering optimisation and efficiency, which is very important, but not the whole story.

I always talk about Big Data being mistaken as an IT transformation wave when in fact it's a business transformation wave and that goes to the heart of the SmartShip. For several years now the buzz word has been Ship Efficiency, which is cost control by another name. Leaving aside the fact that operating an expensive asset efficiently should be a basic requirement of any shipping company, it focusses totally on cost. Big Data is about cost containment in real time, but it's about other things too. It's about tracking of physical items, real-time forecasting and reinventing business processes.

Finding value in Big Data when you restrict its use to operational efficiency is challenging. As Inmarsat Maritime COO Trond Leira said at the Futurenautics roundtable on the subject, "It is very difficult to get good business models just around engineering data, I know companies have tried for a long time to make some monetary value out of it."

Despite all the manufacturers and Class societies talking about efficiency, that is not the part of the equation that adds value.

That's going to come from step four, when the ship becomes a cyberphysical system—unmanned or not—and able to operate as part of the much wider intelligent transport system developing now. Step four on the path—the SmartShip as an autonomous, cyberphysical system—is underpinned by the falling cost of microprocessors and the development of distributed networks powered by edge or fog computing, where instead of bringing data to the centre to be processed, it is analysed and turned into actionable information by the individual component or system. And instead of waiting for a human to intervene, that component or system will take action itself via actuators, based on the decision its algorithm makes.

That cyberphysical system is the essence of an autonomous ship, one which could sail unmanned. Now shipping has got itself very bogged down about unmanned ships arguing that they wouldn't offer any benefit over manned ships. But that's not surprising when you only consider the unmanned ship in the context of cost saving.

Class societies and engineers are myopically focussed on the efficient operation of the asset itself and how much everything will cost, but no one yet has understood the value the autonomous ship brings as part of a much bigger intelligent network.

That value isn't just monetary, it extends to safety and welfare too. Fears about drone ships floating about the ocean having to take impossible decisions in drastic situations are the same as those being raised about autonomous cars. And the answer to both is that these autonomous vehicles aren't developing in isolation, and are designed to operate as part of this far wider, intelligent system.

The Internet of Everything will see hundreds of billions of intelligent devices thrown online in the coming years of which autonomous cars, trucks and ships will be just be a part. What is being created is a vast, globally distributed cyberphysical system of intelligent, connected objects that will eventually develop into an external brain, or perhaps more accurately, an external nervous system.

At the moment shipping has a lot of less than satisfied customers, and what an awful lot of them are frustrated with is shipping's inability to integrate its operations with theirs. A survey of INTTRA members identified digital interaction over cloud platforms as number one on their wish list. A brief look at the number of start-ups piling into the transport and logistics space trying to get a piece of what they correctly see as gross inefficiency in maritime operations is instructive. It puts the discussions about autonomy, and the opportunity it creates, into perspective, and it clarifies the roadmap that much-pilloried innovators like Oskar Levander at Rolls-Royce have laid out.

The SmartShip reflects shipping's experience of a wholesale transportation disruption. The way they'll create value is by allowing us to become part of the Industry 4.0 cyberphysical systems and wider intelligent transport systems, and that will move us up the value chain for our customers.

It may seem like a giant leap to get there, but as I indicated before, technologically, it's not far at all. The Sea Traffic Management systems developed by the MONA LISA project are pretty much ready to be deployed, and Rolls-Royce is already utilising a degree of edge computing in its condition monitoring solution.

But perhaps the most overt signal as to where the industry is going came from the signing of a strategic agreement between Inmarsat and Ericsson late last year. The two companies intend to jointly develop services, solutions and applications to drive industry standards for satellite connectivity and applications integration in the maritime industry. Their shared intent is to facilitate the sharing of cargo, logistics and vessel operational data to streamline the entire maritime supply chain.

In practice what that means is integration between the Inmarsat network and Ericsson's Maritime ICT Cloud—an end-to-end managed cloud solution that connects vessels at sea to shore-based operations including maintenance service providers, customer support centres, fleet and transportation partners, port operations and authorities. "Enabled by Inmarsat, the Maritime ICT Cloud will ensure that trucks will spend less idle time at ports, cargo will spend less time in transit, and producers will be better able to plan their shipments," say the companies. That, in a nutshell, is how you add value.

Maritime connectivity has acted as a brake on technology adoption in the past, but now it's the bridge. And according to Mike Mitsock, VP of marketing at KVH, that's being recognised. "Since we launched KVH mini-VSAT Broadband 2.0 at London International Shipping Week last September, some people's eyes seem to have been opened," he told me. "We're now at the point where speeds are increasing and costs are declining, and the next step—HTS—will be a quantum leap in the potential for both. Bandwidth will always be a precious commodity at sea, but the wider availability and falling cost have opened the door to different conversations, around strategic, value-based adoption—satcoms as a value-enabler, instead of just being considered a cost centre."

The reality is that the vertical markets we're used to are beginning to converge, driven by the enabling technologies via which we are integrating our operations and creating new collaborative ways of working. We need to talk not about shipping, but about Blue Logistics—a phrase you're going to hear from me much more during 2016. I believe that's important because it focusses us not on the insular shipping market, but on the world beyond, and the customers and suppliers—and the consumers—that we have to get to know and serve better if we're to survive.

"I think Big Data will be applied to shipping in different ways with information coming from across the supply chain rather than just from the ship. It will come from the end users of shipping, the consumers, who may look very different in years to come," agreed Warwick Norman, CEO of RightShip at our Big Data roundtable.

That end-consumer's influence is only going to grow. They are insisting on transparency, accountability and security from the companies and products they interact with and purchase, and those preferences will have a major impact on the supply chains of which shipping is an integral part.

Blockchain technologies based on the principle of distributed ledgers are likely to form the basis of secure transactions in the Internet of Everything, and already start-ups are building applications which enable a consumer to digitally investigate the entire lifecycle and journey of the product they're going to purchase.

That kind of transparency has been anathema to shipping thus far, but it's going to have to become second nature in the future. Because it's likely we're going to be rated for everything from emissions to cyber-security to underwater noise. And that will take a SmartShip and a smart network to deliver.

We're creating a smart world, a world where artificial intelligence is everywhere. So why don't I think we'll end up with an M/V HAL? Well, because the trend is not towards one, clever, all-powerful device, but the intelligent network. A massive grid of individual smart devices each with its own objective but able to negotiate in real-time with each other to achieve the safest, most efficient delivery. The likelihood is that a few devices will go tonto now and again, but the distributed system will cope.

Kubrick's terrifying vision of a psychotic artificial intelligence killing humans has a twist. At the end of the movie Dave discovers that he and his fellow astronauts have not been given the whole truth about the mission on which they've been sent, and why. HAL, however, has known all along. It is being forced to lie to the astronauts by mission control which has been the cause of HAL's breakdown and malfunction.

SmartShips are coming, but they aren't threatening. Because they will be what we make them. The most dangerous and unpredictable thing we have to deal with is the same as it's always been. And that's us.

London, January 2016.

5

PIGS WILL SING

There's an American sitcom called *Two and a Half Men*, you might have watched an episode or two. In one of them the main character, a dissolute womaniser, has just tried—with disastrous results—to persuade his fiancée that although she's moved in with him, she shouldn't get rid of her apartment. His logic is that, just like the Titanic, you have to make sure you've always got access to a lifeboat.

Having watched the fiancée storm out in fury, he is congratulated by his brother for ferociously defending an unwinnable position by comparing his relationship to the Titanic. To which the womaniser replies, "Oh, come on, who remembers the names of boats that don't sink?"

I suspect that those of you who can name any number of ships still afloat will now be snorting with bitter laughter at the unfairness of it all. Thinking once again how the great invisible workhorse of the world, the global shipping industry, is constantly dealt the worst of hands. Roundly ignored whilst it goes about its vital business, and then roundly abused when the worst happens.

Situation comedy is funny when it tells the truth, and the truth is that shipping is remembered for Titanic, Exxon Valdez, Costa Concordia and Sewol, and whole host of other disasters. But that situation isn't funny. And in an industry where consensus is hard to come by—on anything—that's something we all seem to agree on.

The 'image of shipping', is one of the industry's favourite chew toys. Just in the past few months the issue has been raised at conferences at London International Shipping Week, and at the Danish Maritime Forum, and it has been highlighted in the new UK maritime growth study.

Coincidentally, or not, during the same period there have been a series of hard-hitting pieces in the New York Times about the lawlessness of the high seas, and the resurfacing of an article from 2009 about shipping's unacceptable emissions that catapulted us to the top of the Internet.

The bottom line is that at the moment shipping just doesn't appeal to people. At best the general public is ambivalent about it, and reading some of the vitriol expressed in relation to the story about shipping emissions in the British Guardian, we should be grateful for ambivalence. Which is astonishing when one considers how intimately connected most human beings are to the sea. We love beaches, boats, cruises and watersports, but when it comes to the shipping industry, awareness of it and the prospect of engaging with it or working in it, everything changes.

At this stage the question to ask is why, and here's the first big problem. Shipping has decided it already knows why. This is a failure of image, a failure of public relations, and a lack of strong branding.

Not only has the industry already identified the problem, it is already busy delivering the solution. IMO has appointed 'maritime ambassadors', and launched a series of open mornings where it frogmarches captive schoolchildren to IMO and points out to them that the shipping industry is IMPORTANT. Apparently the magic is working.

According to reports the kids at IMO were inspired by presentations from the Institute of Chartered Shipbrokers, the Merchant Navy Training Board, and an educational activity booklet entitled 'The World of Shipping' containing puzzles on trade routes and ship types and with a foreword by—wait for it—Koji Sekimizu. The 'shipping is great, you just don't realise it yet', bandwagon is on a roll.

While IMO explains shipping's importance, patiently, using paper booklets and international bureaucrats to engage the digital native generation, one child at a time, the UK maritime growth strategy is even more gung ho. It too has identified that the solution to shipping's image problem lies in that unholy trinity of branding, public relations and marketing. According to its report what's required is big ad campaigns, branding agencies and public relations, that can take our Cinderella industry and spin it into the hearts and minds of the public.

Now if you were reading one of those other nice, comfy maritime industry magazines, written by proper journalists according to the Maritime Foundation—read *Both Barrels* for more on that— you'd probably get a thousand words quoting some maritime marketing agency about how your company can join in by getting onto Twitter, and making your CEO write something for your blog. Oh, and go into your local school and tell the eight-year-olds what great fun it is working in shipping.

Unfortunately that is hogwash. And, as nothing about this magazine is designed to be comfortable, I'm going to explain why. You aren't going to like it, in fact of all the things you've read in Futurenautics you really didn't like—of which there are many I'm sure—this is going to take the cake. Because in shipping we don't like people who disagree. We don't like people who rock the boat. That's not the way shipping raises us. And that, actually, is our problem right there in a nutshell. But we'll come back to that.

There are a couple of reasons why thinking better PR and branding will save shipping is stupid. One of them is pretty straightforward, the other less so.

Patriotism may be the last refuge of the scoundrel, but marketing and PR has become the first port of call for everybody with a business problem to solve. It has worked hard to cultivate its own stereotype as a magic bullet, using gravity-defying sleight of hand to turn pedestrian products and companies into world beaters. And it can't. So that's number one. When it comes to stereotypes, branding, public relations and marketing—in which I include adland— is in a league of its own, and that's hardly surprising. Creating stereotypes and broadcasting them loudly is its stock in trade, and there's a very good reason for that. For a very long time they have worked extremely well. But the megatrends, generational mindsets and technologies that are disrupting every other industry are disrupting marketing and branding too. And that's number two.

But in order to understand either of those reasons you first have to actually grasp what the purpose and function of marketing and branding is and why it has developed in the way it has. I have a nasty suspicion that a lot of the people calling for shipping to brand itself better actually mean they'd like a pretty logo and a strapline they can put on a nice, thick, classy brochure. Preferably with a foreword by Koji Sekimizu.

If you want to chart the social history of the world, and particularly the Western world, over the past fifty or sixty years then a trawl through the advertising archives is basically a colour coded guide to the changing attitudes, tastes and aspirations of the general public. The globalisation of consumer markets went hand in hand with the explosion of broadcast television channels, the dominance of that medium in the life of the average consumer, and our increasingly sophisticated understanding of the way that individuals respond to visual and aural messaging about products.

As the drive to sell things to people gathered pace and the time in which to do so contracted, efficiency became all-important. If you've got thirty seconds to make someone want something badly enough to go out and buy it then efficiency is key. In search of that efficiency those in advertising began to take a closer interest in the psychology of what makes people buy stuff.

As far back as the 1960s the much beloved Sesame Street changed everything by recognising that the way to sell children numbers and letters was with big purple monsters with googly eyes that repeated the same, simple message again and again. What adland instantly realised was that this approach isn't something that just works for children, it works for adults too. There are hundreds of excellent books that will give you exhaustive detail on all of this, but there are some very simple things that every marketer knows, and in my view anyone who leads a business should know.

The first is that the mind is a limited container, and it's very, very busy with important stuff like work, remembering its mother's birthday, and breathing. As a result minds hate complexity: complexity equals confusion, so the most efficient way to enter the mind is to oversimplify the message.

But even if you manage to get into people's minds, staying there is an even greater challenge. According to Al Ries and Jack Trout, two of the world's greatest marketing strategists and their "22 Immutable Laws of Marketing" (read them) the mind creates its own 'product ladders' for categories of product it encounters, from toothpaste to ship management software. The mind can generally only remember around seven items even in high-interest categories, and in general most people will only recall about two or three. That's why when you ask someone to name a ship, the answer they come back with is, 'Titanic'.

That may sound like an interesting little fact that's useful to trot out during a lull in the conversation at the next interminable reception, but it's far more than that. Because as it exhaustively researched how it could sell us things more efficiently, what marketing realised was that those top two or three positions on the product ladders in our minds also happened to be the only profitable ones. In fact positions one and two on that product ladder account for around 60% of all sales in that category.

Getting to position number one or two on that ladder means creating an incredibly powerful proposition that not only cuts through the noise, but delivers the lasting emotional resonance necessary to maintain its foothold. That's a tough challenge. And it got tougher with the death of the salesman. No longer did you have a guy turn up on the doorstep and point out all the features of the vacuum cleaner, or the brush set, or the encyclopaedias.

Housewives no longer went to a grocer who told them what was the best deal of the day and picked the produce for them and put it into a bag. Now she glided around supermarkets and made her own choices about what she picked up and put in her basket. We have moved from a world where things are sold, to one where things are bought, and that is why the brand has become so incredibly important.

A good brand pre-sells the product. It means that when that housewife stands in front of the serried ranks of detergent in the supermarket and reaches out her hand—and that moment has a name actually, it is called the Zero Moment of Truth (ZMOT)—it is your product that her eager fingers close around. But don't think this is only applicable to consumer goods, this is as important for GE as it is for Coca-Cola. And what it illustrates is that whilst the googly-eyed purple monsters are the tactical tip, there's a whole strategic berg under the water that the public neither sees nor understands. That massive berg is the brand. And the ultimate goal of a brand is to reduce all the complexity of what it is, does and stands for, to one simple and easily understood phrase. And if you're really, really good, just one word.

The biggest brands in the world have spent billions of dollars trying to own words in our heads. Perhaps the greatest brand ad of all time for my money is one created by a Japanese agency for Volvo. It sits on a plain white background and there are no words at all. It is an image of a safety pin bent into the shape of a car. It illustrates beautifully what Volvo has spent decades and billions doing. When it comes to cars Volvo owns the word 'safety' in most people's heads.

But here's the really interesting thing. Volvo doesn't just sell safe cars. It sells all sorts of cars, some of which go extremely quickly, or over rough ground. But it doesn't try to own that real-estate in your head. What the big brands that have been created in the decades until now have done is to concentrate on one simple value and benefit and then leverage that position to sell you anything else they choose.

This is the concept of singularity and relevant differentiation, around which to date great brands have been forged. Your brand has to make people believe that it has a singular and unique benefit, one that's really different. But—and here's the kicker—it also has to be absolutely relevant to your target audience. And that's not all, your company has to have a unique, sustainable competency and avowed strategic intent, to deliver against that benefit. It has to be one that your competitors are not delivering against, and which they will find difficult to in the future. Finally, the benefit must be unique, compelling, motivating, understandable and believable.

If you can do that, so the logic goes, you can sell anything to anyone. And possibly the most pure expression of that paradigm is Virgin. Created by Sir Richard Branson more than 40 years ago Virgin has ruthlessly (he really hates being called ruthless, by the way) exploited the traditional mass broadcast channels like TV. Using both advertising and public relations Branson has leveraged his own personality via memorable stunts, to craft something which is less a proposition and more a corporate personality, based around, and symbolising, both individualistic attributes and quality of service.

Most brands are created to shift product, and Virgin has shifted plenty, from cola to airline seats, but what Virgin has managed to do is to make the brand the product. If there were ever an example of a brand that stood for everything and nothing, Virgin is it. And they know it full well. As Robert Devereux, former Chairman of the Virgin Entertainment division and Richard's brother-in-law told me when we talked about it few years ago, Virgin doesn't really own anything or run anything. What the Virgin Group has become is a huge family office with a portfolio run by professional investment managers. The value of that portfolio is around £5bn with around £120m coming directly from the licensing of the Virgin brand itself.

I know that, and Robert knows that, and now you do too. But the vast majority of people who interact with the Virgin brand each day don't really understand that at all. Ask the guy in the street and he will tell you that Sir Richard Branson is a great entrepreneur running a multifarious business empire. But he isn't. And Virgin doesn't do much to counter that misapprehension.

The truth is that there are some massive inconsistencies between the values the Virgin brand espouses and the reality of its operations, and under the old broadcast paradigm that was manageable. But that was before social technologies started to drive the kind of transparency that was unimaginable in the 1980s.

Back then when Helen Mirren starred in a Virgin Atlantic ad all about legroom in which her legs were the sex-drenched focus of the ad, but belonged to an anonymous 20 year old model, very few people took much notice. Imagine if that happened now? Whereas the Virgin machine could comfortably contain that inconsistency in the late 1980s, it's beginning to struggle with others today. How does it square the social conscience of Branson's brand with the fact that he lives as a tax exile? How does the Carbon War Room sit alongside someone who owns an airline, and wants to send the wealthy elite into space?

These are the difficult questions occupying Virgin now as it begins to realise that the transparency it's being subject to is exposing the flimsiness of its values. One suspects that when shipping folk talk about better branding and PR they have precisely the Virgin model in mind. Something that stands for everything and nothing. A brand we can all leverage across whatever we like, that is strong enough to glide over inconsistencies and is media-savvy and nimble enough to control what people think about the industry.

And I think that's really the key word here. Control. It is what brands, and companies, once had. And it is at the heart of understanding the new order. Because that control has almost completely shifted out of the hands of the organisation and into the hands of the public. The general public used to be something that companies broadcast information to. Now they are individuals who have to be engaged in conversation. Millennials and Gen Z's don't trust brand and company messages they way they used to. They get their information from each other, sharing experiences good and bad and forming opinions on businesses, events and industries without reference to the PR line. In real time. With video. And emojis.

That is why shipping's first, and most grave mistake is to assume that we should either seek, or are in a position to start controlling in any shape or form, what the public thinks about us.

To be fair to the advertising and marketing industry, it gave repeated health warnings about the dangers of assuming brand and PR was a panacea. "Advertising doesn't create a product advantage. It can only convey it," was one of the famous utterances of Bill Bernbach, founder of DDB Worldwide.

And yet companies around the world are at a point where they have carefully crafted mission statements, distilling their key brand benefit, signed off by senior management, and then trotted out religiously by the PR department on media releases directed at traditional media journalists.

But the world is just getting too complex for that. The idea that a brand exists separately from the company, or a reputation can be maintained by high quality public relations on behalf of the industry, via a select pool of friendly print journalists is dangerously outdated. A mission, and a brand that encapsulates it, isn't enough any longer.

So what is? The answer lies in the new fast-growing digital companies we've seen emerge in the past few years, the ones leveraging exponential technologies and new business models to deliver exponential growth. These exponential organisations have something very interesting in common. In this new age of transparent business and new generational mindsets these mega-companies have exchanged mission for purpose, and brand for culture.

In the book 'Exponential Organisations' Salim Ismail and my Futures Agency colleague Yuri Van Geest characterise it as a 'Massive Transformative Purpose'. What it boils down to is, why are we doing this work? And why does this organisation exist? The answers that companies like Uber, Quirky, AirBnB and Google give to those questions don't outline a mission, but an aspiration. "Organise the world's information," is Google's. It's both imaginative and ambitious and it's designed not to state what the organisation does, but what it hopes to accomplish.

These are BHAGs—Big Hairy Audacious Goals—and they are the kind of thing that Millennials and Gen Z's with their keenly developed sense of the relationship between people, profit and planet are drawn to and engaged by. That's why these companies and others like Apple have developed massive tribes around them who buy into the purpose and the culture and take the message out themselves to the world, because they believe it's the right thing to do.

And what does shipping offer by comparison? A desperate, rigid focus on trying to make a profit. Now, in days gone by that might have been enough, but these days not even the bankers can get away with it. Of course the totemic irony is that shipping is failing to make money. And it's failing to do so at the expense of the environment it pollutes, the low-cost labour it exploits, the regulations large parts of it ignores, and the customers it disappoints with monotonous regularity.

Shipping has become decoupled from any purpose, so it's no surprise that it's become rudderless and directionless. Counter cyclical investment in tonnage and lowest-cost, lowest-common-denominator service is not a purpose, it's an excuse. And you will find no sympathy or engagement from the smart Millennials and Gen Z's while it continues.

The industry has recognised that its poor image is impacting everything from investment to recruitment, but what it has spectacularly failed to realise is that shipping doesn't need to get better at PR, marketing and branding. Shipping just needs to get better.

Those outside shipping are utterly mystified as to why the shipping industry cannot see this. From the perspective of the average Millennial, shipping is a pig, and the constant efforts of the interminable list of maritime associations and organisations to pump out good news press releases, is just so much lipstick.

But explaining that to the shipping industry pig is like teaching one to sing. It's fruitless and eventually it irritates the pig. And that's because of all the problems shipping has, its most intractable is its culture.

What a Millennial is interested in is a conversation. But maritime doesn't do those. The culture of PR in our industry is traditional and pre-social. The role of the PR department is a big guard dog that makes a decision about whether it thinks you're worth wasting its valuable time on, and then either tears your throat out, or tries to hump your leg. Here at Futurenautics it's about 80/20—and we've really struggled to get where we are today. If you're a member of the general public, forget it. The message is that PR people are professionals. And they're very, very busy.

But where does that attitude come from? It's part of the cultural myopia that's embedded into shipping and it's driven by a lack of diversity of thought, what I'm calling cognitive diversity, and experience that's rife in the industry. At a recent Futurenautics roundtable on Big Data Capt. Kuba Szymanski, Secretary General of InterManager put the problem in a nutshell.

"If I asked you to give me five examples of a shipping industry, ship management company where someone has not been promoted from within the industry you will struggle," Kuba said. "We don't have the example of a British Airways CEO who is now leading MOL or Maersk because we only train and promote from within. We are so siloed, we expect to hear that someone has 20 or 35 years in shipping, and we value that, and if you can't demonstrate that then we aren't interested in talking to you at all. It would be nice to have someone who came from the outside and got into senior management."

Kuba gets it, and he isn't alone. There are voices of reason popping up all over the place, but they aren't getting any traction. Take the Danish Maritime Forum for example. The avowed intent of this 'unique' event is, and I quote, "to unleash the full potential of the global maritime industry to increase long term economic development and human wellbeing." Wow, good for them. That is one big hairy audacious goal.

And how did they go about achieving it? Here's how. Someone who has spent their entire working life in the shipping and maritime industry personally invited all the people currently working in the shipping and maritime industry whom he considered to be important and influential to talk to each other about the shipping and maritime industry. And who did he get on the stage? The Crown Prince of Denmark, a bunch of shipping ministers and—oh, you're good, you're way ahead of me, say it with me now— Koji Sekimizu.

It will be absolutely no surprise to you whatsoever to hear that there was broad agreement about what the woes of the shipping industry were, and on the need for better PR, but no obvious unleashing of full potential. More a 'coalition of the willing'. Maybe next year.

The tragedy is that this was considered by all concerned to be a massive success. How can that be? It is because the shipping industry is run by white, late middle-aged, middle class men who have got to the top by conforming to the beliefs and prejudices of those layers of similarly white, middle-class late middle-aged senior management who have gone before. Go on. Argue with me. I dare you.

I warned you that you weren't going to like this. No one likes to hear this kind of stuff. And that's the reason that there weren't any dissatisfied customers, or whip-smart Millennials with data in their pockets and a purpose in their hearts who would stand up in front of the pig and call it one to its snout on the bill in Copenhagen. That's why the really interesting, truly disruptive thinkers behind companies and brands like RightShip, Xeneta, ShipServ and even Inmarsat and Rolls-Royce weren't on the stage either. It's why none of the people behind the data-driven shipping technology start-ups that keep getting in contact with me are even on the radar of the Danish Maritime Forum. And it's why the shipping pig is likely to end up as sausages.

Chris Andersen former editor in chief of Wired magazine once said, "The reality is that most of the world's smartest people don't have the right credentials. They don't speak the right language. They didn't grow up in the right country. They didn't go to the right university. They don't know about you and you don't know about them. They're not available, and they already have a job."

That's a warning to industries who are willingly and actively revisiting their long held assumptions, recognising and adjusting for the bias in their organisations whether it's based on gender, race, age or historic industry beliefs. Where leaders are deliberately and desperately seeking out people who will irritate and challenge them.

What our industry needs is some cognitive diversity, and it needs it badly. Farming has recognised it needs it too and it's trying to inject some via an initiative called AgriHive. Founded by an Australian farmer who saw that the damaging cyclical nature of farming was driving more and more people out of it, AgriHive doesn't pull together a bunch of eminent farming experts. Instead it creates summits where it takes a dairy farm case study and puts it in front of a range of business leaders and CEOs from completely different industries. They specifically look for people outside agriculture because what they want is a broad spectrum of other industry knowledge. Because as Einstein said, you can't solve problems with the same thinking that created them. He could have been talking about shipping today.

Shipping never really did brands and PR because it never felt the need, and large swathes of it still doesn't. But we're beyond all that now anyway. Brands are already giving way to purpose and culture, God help us. All this tactical fiddling around the edges making schoolchildren fonder of us is fruitless, and, like the pig, I'm beginning to get irritated by it.

That's because the opportunity to create exponentially successful organisations that use data, prediction, analysis, connectivity and all the rest of it to transform the shipping pig's ear into a silk purse is just so achingly obvious it's almost funny. If you want a BHAG then ending the managed dissatisfaction shipping delivers at the moment and using it instead to transform the way the world moves is about as big, hairy and audacious a goal as you can hope for. And it's the kind of purpose that the people shipping needs to engage might just be interested in helping to pursue.

Like the guy in *Two and A Half Men*, I have to admire shipping for ferociously defending an unwinnable position, but the reality is that, as the great Bernbach said, "No matter how skillful you are, you can't invent a product advantage that doesn't exist. And if you do, and it's just a gimmick, it's going to fall apart anyway."

This industry is reaching the zero moment of truth. In the new world there is nowhere to hide, and no way to control what the general public thinks about us. As transparency scythes through shipping the world is reaching out its hand, and deciding whether to pick us up or leave us on the shelf. The shipping industry pig needs to stop slathering itself in lipstick and singing its own praises and take a long, hard look at itself in the mirror. And it has to accept that what's looking back is unappetising to the majority of people. That's the first, essential step.

Then, and only then, will it have the slightest chance of going the whole hog, and learning to fly.

London, October 2015

6

BOTH BARRELS

People are sometimes a bit nervous about speaking to Futurenautics, but they soon realise that we're believers in the Robustness Principle—the software design guideline—which says you should be conservative in what you send, and liberal in what you accept from others.

Despite my criticisms of the shipping and maritime industry, by and large people's hearts are in the right place. And we all expect maritime charities to be the epitome of that. So when they aren't it needs to be exposed. And that's why the Maritime Foundation needs to be getting nervous right about now.

One area everyone seems to agree on is that shipping has an image problem. Now I believe that in this new era of hyper-connectivity and transparency, the idea that we can try to control shipping's image through better PR and branding is dangerous.

As I outline in the feature article *Pigs Will Sing*, brand and PR is giving way to culture and purpose, and until we improve one and find the other, shipping is going to struggle to cut through to the Millennials and the Gen Z's we need to engage. Reaching out beyond the narrow confines of the maritime and shipping industry was what Futurenautics was designed to do, and we're passionate about it. Which is a good job because if you write about the shipping and maritime industry for either the money or accolades then you're onto a loser.

There are however, a set of awards which seek to give, "recognition to journalists, writers and film-makers whose work deepens public understanding of Britain's dependence on the sea and maritime matters." They are called the Maritime Media Awards and they are run by the Maritime Foundation.

I came across them last year when someone—three separate people in fact—nominated my writing for the Desmond Wettern Award for the best journalistic contribution of 2014. And having nominated me, they decided to let me know they'd done so, and wished me luck. A few weeks later someone from the Maritime Foundation rang us and told us I'd been nominated for the Wettern award and suggested it would be a good idea for us to spend some money advertising in the awards programme too.

So it was somewhat of a surprise when a month or so later I had an email from the Maritime Foundation saying that I'd been nominated for the First Sea Lord's Digital Media Award, which is basically about having a website. I think. Actually, no one's really sure what it's for, not even the Maritime Foundation, nor one suspects, the First Sea Lord. But nothing about a Wettern Award.

So I went back to the Maritime Foundation and thanked them, and asked where the Wettern nomination had gone. And they didn't like that. Because in actual fact I hadn't been nominated for the First Sea Lord's Digital Media Award at all.

What had happened was that the Maritime Foundation had discovered it had a problem. It had introduced the First Sea Lord's Digital Award, whose criteria, by its own subsequent acknowledgment, makes no sense at all, and surprise, surprise, it didn't have any nominations for it. And it had decided that Futurenautics was part of the solution. It had decided that seeing as Futurenautics was a digital first publication, it would ditch the fact that the nominations were for the quality of the journalism, and shunt it into the digital category. Now, as we all know, shipping doesn't raise us to rock the boat.

But you'll be unsurprised to hear that I did. Because I thought that a charity which sought to give out gongs to journalists, really shouldn't be engaging in that kind of shady horse trading behind the scenes. Particularly when it's all to prevent upsetting the First Sea Lord.

Unfortunately for the Maritime Foundation, I couldn't care less about upsetting the First Sea Lord, so I demanded that I be allowed to lose in the category in which I'd be nominated. Because I was never going to win after that, obviously, even if I had a chance in the first place.

So my nomination finally appeared in the Desmond Wettern Award, and I—together with a host of others—duly lost to a cub reporter on a local UK paper. Which was actually fine, because I'm a fairly old-school Brit in many respects, and for me, it wasn't about winning, it was about the fact that people had taken the time to nominate me, and I was proud of that.

But it prompted me to take a closer look at the awards and the people handing them out, because as the only annual gongs in the whole industry dedicated to recognising those of us who are trying to engage the wider public with shipping and maritime, they've got an important role.

As I've written elsewhere in this issue, the public image of shipping is one of the biggest problems we're facing and considering it's front of mind for everyone from the CEOs of shipping companies to InterManager, WISTA, and every organisation in the industry that wants to continue recruiting, the Maritime Media Awards should be a really useful tool.

And even though I really didn't like the arrogance and expediency behind the arbitrary shifting of our nomination to suit its own ends, I assumed that what I'd seen was a temporary aberration. And that having stood up and said it wasn't on, it wasn't ever likely to happen again.

So I thought maybe we at Futurenautics should try and support them a bit. And, as our website stats have gone through the roof, and I felt a bit sorry for blowing off the First Sea Lord, I dropped the Maritime Foundation an email earlier this year and asked if they'd like us to enter ourselves for the award—if that was how it worked.

They told me they'd check if that was allowed, but in the meantime I would be delighted to know that I had been nominated once again for the Wettern Award for the best journalistic contribution.

Once again, I was pleased. And so when they came back and said we couldn't self-nominate to cheer up the First Sea Lord, I thought OK, and left it. Because I'm really, really busy. And frankly, if the First Sea Lord's that bothered then he needs to get out more.

You know what's coming don't you. And you're right. They did it again. When the nominations list for the Wettern award was published I wasn't on it. But mysteriously someone had nominated Futurenautics once again for the First Sea Lord's Bell.

And this time it all got rather more serious. Because it became clear that what had previously appeared to be arrogance and expediency was actually more insidious. This time they told us that the judging committee had collectively decided that what I'd written simply didn't meet the criteria for the Wettern award. It wasn't good enough.

And as the secretary of the Maritime Foundation told our CEO by phone, the judging committee, which includes representatives from the Nautical Institute, Babcock International, and the journalist Rose George, collectively decided that Futurenautics isn't a publication. It is a digital, internal magazine designed for self-promotion. And as the person responsible for writing it, apparently I have therefore made no discernible journalistic contribution to the maritime industry.

Now just in case you think this is sour grapes, you're absolutely bloody right. Because I will match any of the 100+ articles that have appeared in Futurenautics and elsewhere over the past two years against anything that has appeared in any other maritime publication, and indeed anything that Ms George produces. But actually the rot is far deeper than that.

Because even if you agree that Futurenautics is a pile of ordure, and everything that Mr Harvey of the Maritime Foundation says is absolutely correct, it still shouldn't stop me appearing on the Wettern Award nominations list. Because not being a journalist isn't stopping anyone else.

It already includes someone who does the PR for the Royal Yachting Association—although you'll be reassured to hear that they're considering sponsoring the awards next year, so there's a good reason for that—and the News Editor of an advertising website that doesn't have any original content. At all. And it's a website. And someone who's a consultant. And a former First Sea Lord. Talking of which, despite the fact that Futurenautics is a pile of ordure, it's not steaming enough that it doesn't meet the criteria for the First Sea Lord's Digital Award. Again. I think he likes me. Maybe I'm being groomed?

It would be quite funny, except it's really not. Because these people who claim to be 'eminent' in the maritime establishment aren't promoting what's best in maritime. They're promoting what's best for them, and ignoring what they don't know and don't understand. The media landscape has transformed in twenty years, and yet these awards are still stuck in the same mindset they were in 1995. That's why—aside from the book award—the categories and the criteria are hopeless. How can you judge an article by Futurenautics against a retail website selling photographs of ships?

Award sponsors shouldn't really be judges, and judges shouldn't be nominees, but the Maritime Media Awards have got both. And the poor quality of so much of what's been nominated calls into question how fairly the criteria are being applied. A campaign website with a contact page that's still showing placeholder text and an address in the Hague, with a Google map of Canada because they haven't updated the stock content it shipped with is up for the First Sea Lord's Digital Award. Wow. For real? That's proper ordure, and it's being shown off as the best the maritime industry can do.

The secretary of the Maritime Foundation was at pains to point out that this was all being done for free. But that's not an excuse. Facebook is free. And so is Google. And so, coincidentally, is Futurenautics. So there is no justification for being amateur. Particularly not when you're representing the maritime industry. Because there are some highly professional people in shipping and maritime, and you're doing them a huge disservice.

Entries like that just reinforces the idea that maritime is a heritage industry, slightly inept, not very tech-savvy and just a bit amateur.

Mark Twain once said that you should never pick a fight with people who buy ink by the barrel. The Maritime Foundation is still stuck in the mindset and the culture which says that if something isn't printed it doesn't exist. If someone is not a journalist they have no influence. And, most importantly, if they haven't heard of you, you are of absolutely no consequence. But they couldn't be more wrong.

We shift 20,000 downloads of each issue and get thirty thousand hits on the website each month, and although we don't buy ink by the barrel, we get eyeballs. And judging by the comments we get from pretty senior people, we're getting some hearts and minds too.

To be clear, I did tell the Maritime Foundation that I intended to write about what they'd done. I also told them to remove Futurenautics from the First Sea Lord's Digital Award with immediate effect—he knows where I am if he wants me—and that we had no interest in being involved in these awards in the future.

Aside from calling to tell us what rubbish we produced, as I go to press we've heard nothing else. Although they've hired a PR agency recently, they haven't got in touch. But then, we don't make a journalistic contribution. So how could we possibly cause them any PR headaches?

For those of you who don't know, Desmond Wettern was a journalist, who wrote about defence for the Daily Telegraph, and the award for journalism is set up in his name. I never met Desmond Wettern, but I know people who did, because I grew up Royal Navy.

Wettern wasn't afraid to expose bad practice and shortcomings, and the Royal Navy respected him for that. Which is why I was quite proud to be nominated for his award. I'm not any longer. So whilst I really appreciate those people who have nominated me in the past, please don't bother in the future.

If you like what I write then share it with as many people as you can, as often as you can. Use it to start conversations, provoke arguments and challenge entrenched thinking. And maybe have a laugh or two here and there. Because when people say that what I wrote made them think differently about something, that's worth more than any gong ever could be.

I'm not sure what constitutes a journalist any longer, so if the Maritime Foundation say I'm not one, then okay. I'm just going to carry on pointing out to the shipping and maritime establishment when something's rotten, without fear or favour. And that includes the Maritime Media Awards, because they don't smell too good.

And whether Wettern would have appreciated my writing or not, I am absolutely sure that he'd be right behind me on that one.

London, October 2015.

7

LEAN TIMES

I'm writing another thriller at the moment, which involves a night-shift most nights. So it was that I happened to be awake at 2.30am when, for the first time I can remember, I saw a shipping company which had not just lost a vessel, mentioned on the BBC News 24 ticker. The headline was about Maersk and the fact that it had downgraded its full-year outlook for underlying profit by $600m to about $3.4bn, citing deterioration in the container shipping market.

When you're connected with the maritime and shipping industry then news about Maersk is ten-a-penny, as is evidence of the industry's broader financial woes. But it's rare indeed for the massive problems shipping is facing to make it onto the BBC news ticker. Even if it does only stay there for a couple of hours, during which most people in the UK—who aren't currently writing thrillers—are safely tucked up in bed.

With even the mighty Maersk struggling you would have imagined that pretty much every piece of low hanging fruit on the profitability tree would have been identified, plucked and sucked dry by everyone in shipping by now. So what if I told you that there was something your company could do that could potentially improve your profitability in comparison to most of your competitors in shipping by up to 26% over a six year period? And that one thing had no additional cost to your operations than what you're doing now?

According to a six year study by the Credit Suisse Research Institute involving data from 2,360 companies, those with women on their boards outperformed those without by up to 26%. So there you go. If you don't have a woman on your board create a position for one, or preferably two, and go and find one, or preferably two. And if you have a couple of women on your board already, get some more.

Not convinced? Like a few more stats? I know you love the stats. Try these. McKinsey has been tracking and evaluating diversity in the workplace for quite a number of years now and its latest report 'Diversity Matters' examined proprietary data sets for 366 public companies across a range of industries in Canada, Latin America, the UK and the US. The research looked at metrics like financial results and the composition of top management and boards, and here's what they discovered.

Companies in the top quartile for gender diversity are 15 per cent more likely to have financial returns above their respective national industry medians. But it isn't just that they're leading. Because companies in the bottom quartile for gender diversity are statistically less likely to achieve above-average financial returns than the average companies in the data set. Which means those with poor rates of gender diversity are actually lagging.

If you're a UK based company then the figures get really interesting. Here, greater gender diversity on the senior-executive team corresponded to the highest performance uplift in the McKinsey data set with EBIT rising 3.5 % for every 10% increase in gender diversity.

In the past few years there have been a variety of national initiatives to improve the number of women on boards and they've met with some success in the UK and in Scandinavia. But the issue is rising up the agenda as more and more studies begin to point out that behind all the 'soft' talk about equality lies a cold, hard, commercial reality.

Gender diversity is good for business. And, it seems, the global economy. McKinsey have projected that a 'full potential' scenario where women participate in the economy identically to men could add $28 trillion or 26 per cent to annual global GDP by 2025. To get that into perspective, that's an impact roughly equivalent to the combined size of the Chinese and US economies today.

For any company in any industry trying to squeeze out single-digit percentage growth, leaving this kind of value on the table is madness, but for shipping it's particularly so. I've quoted this statistic before, but it bears repeating. Over the past fifteen years the container shipping sector's return on net assets (RONA) has only been around 3 per cent compared to the 9 per cent RONA of the S&P 500 over the same period. Not only is that far lower, it's also nowhere near enough to cover the approximately 7 per cent cost of capital needed to finance the assets deployed, which means value in those companies is actually being destroyed.

McKinsey's research has led it to conclude that 'diversity is probably a competitive differentiator that shifts market share toward more diverse companies over time,' but statistics about how gender diverse shipping and maritime actually is are hard to come by.

Journalist Wendy Laursen cited a report in an article for Maritime Executive a few months back which indicated that Brazil, Russia, India and China had the highest number of female senior managers in the maritime industry at 26 per cent, followed by G7 countries with 18 per cent. But beyond that there doesn't appear to be anywhere near the kind of detail that the industry needs about the percentages of women on boards and in the C-suite, and at every level throughout organisations across the industry.

It's the kind of data that other industries are lousy with, and the fact that shipping isn't is instructive. It's almost as if everyone just accepts the situation is woeful and a bit embarrassing, but no one has actually bothered to quantify what it's costing us. As the old adage goes, you can't manage what you can't measure, but just measuring it in the first place is a way of concentrating minds about the scale of the issue. I'm going to do something now that I never expected to. I'm going to point out a characteristic which the shipping and maritime industry and that hotbed of innovative technology, Silicon Valley, both share. There are hardly any women in either.

If there was any place you might have expected there to be an acknowledgement that diversity was an essential component of success, it's the progressive trailblazers like Google, Yahoo, LinkedIn, et al. But Silicon Valley is increasingly focused on the gender diversity issues that affect technology businesses and venture capital firms, and for good reason. These guys are all about the data, and boy, does it suck. According to a recent Babson College study, only 15 per cent of VC-backed companies have even one single woman serving in an executive role; fewer than 3 per cent have a female CEO; and just 6 per cent of venture capital firm partners are women.

Take Facebook for example. The company recently reported that nearly 70 per cent of its employees are men. That's despite the fact that it serves 1.4 billion users, an awful lot of whom are women. Facebook isn't alone in its poor gender diversity showing, but it's bound to attract comment considering the very public stance taken by Facebook's COO Sheryl Sandberg on the subject. So passionate is she about seeing more women in senior positions she wrote a book giving advice about how other women can go about securing top jobs like hers.

"Lean In: Women, Work, and the Will to Lead," was published in 2013 and with chapters entitled, amongst others, 'The Leadership Ambition Gap: What Would You Do if You Weren't Afraid?', 'Don't Leave before you Leave', It's a Jungle Gym, Not a Corporate Ladder', and 'Sit at the Table', Sandberg created what's now being described as a 'movement'. Together with its associated non-profit LeanIn.org, Sandberg's manifesto has sold in its millions and spawned everything from events to 'Lean In' circles for women around the world. The phrase 'Lean In' has itself now passed into the popular lexicon as shorthand for women taking control of their working lives. Sandberg's core argument is that women can get to the top, and that whether they do or don't has more to do with the way they approach the task. In essence, according to Sandberg it's mostly your attitude that determines your altitude. But as an increasing number of commentators have pointed out, the advice Sandberg is giving is just another way of saying that in order to succeed in male dominated companies you basically need to operate more like a man.

One of my all-time favourite movie scenes is from *Monty Python's Life of Brian* which, for the uninitiated, is a spoof version of the life of Christ. Made in 1979—coincidentally the same year that the UK elected Margaret Thatcher its first, and only, female Prime Minister—the film contains a scene where Brian and his mother are going to a stoning. The problem is that women aren't allowed to attend the stoning, but they go anyway by disguising themselves with ridiculous beards and speaking in very low voices.

Everyone knows they're women, but as long as they look like men and sound like men, then the men are prepared to overlook it. The truth is that for a lot of women in the corporate world, getting anywhere has meant slapping on a fake beard and dropping your voice—literally in the case of Margaret Thatcher. She deliberately adopted a lower register voice because she was advised it made her sound less shrill. Fortunately she drew the line at the beard.

Putting yourself forward for a promotion, a raise or just an interesting project when you're a man is considered assertive and confident. Lots of evidence exists that when a woman does the same she's seen as pushy and arrogant. And let's be clear, that perception doesn't just exist amongst men. The more insidious problem with women adopting the beard and the deep voice is the pressure to accept and often replicate behaviours that undermine the opportunity for further gender diversity, and that includes perpetuating bias.

There are plenty of women in senior positions who aren't doing anywhere near enough to get the pipelines in place to ensure female succession. Which is hardly surprising when getting into the boardroom has meant putting on the beard and conforming as closely as possible to the male stereotype of an executive. Women haven't been adverse to chucking female colleagues under the bus if the need arose, just the same way men do.

There is also evidence that even where policies exist to help women climb the corporate ladder, many don't want to take advantage of them for fear of appearing as though they need help. And that means when they do get somewhere near the top the last thing they want to be seen as is a woman banging on about being a woman, or loudly championing other women.

In every industry you'll find a women's networking group of some description, designed to be a safe place where you can swap tips on the best beard for your face shape and adhesive that won't make your eyes water and look like you've been crying. These groups are always trying to apply collective pressure for better gender diversity, but I know of none which have really moved the needle. The truth—unpalatable as it may be—is that the only way companies are going to do gender diversity is if men decide it's important.

So I think the time has come to shift the focus from creating successful women to harnessing women's potential successfully. And in a corporate world where the higher echelons are dominated by men, logic dictates that's not something women can do on their own. There's been a recognition of this recently in the 'HeforShe' programme. Created by UN Women, the United Nations entity for gender equality and the empowerment of women, HeForShe aims to mobilise one billion men and boys in support of gender equality.

The programme has major corporate involvement worldwide with male figureheads taking their turns to 'lean in', and actively champion gender diversity in their own companies and professional spheres of influence.

And what's becoming clear is that it's this kind of personal commitment and belief that can make a real difference. eBay is a great example of how. It's CEO John Donahoe came into the post in 2008 as a firm believer that in a competitive marketplace for talent eBay needed to create an environment where talented women could thrive. The result was the Women's Initiative Network (WIN) which saw its first global summit in January 2011.

eBay's 200 highest-ranking women met with its senior-executive team for three days of professional development and networking. "At the outset, John went onstage and described, in quite personal and moving terms, why gender diversity matters so much to him. He recalled one of his wife's more challenging career experiences and concluded, "I just remember thinking: my God, she has a tougher row to hoe than me."" recounts Michelle Angier, global leader of eBay's WIN. "He went on to discuss her career experience over 25 years, the issues she has faced as a successful professional woman, and how it felt to observe all this. John finished by explaining his aspirations for WIN and his desire for a more supportive, inclusive environment at eBay. "This is personal," he told us."

Angier is clear that it was the personal conviction of its CEO rather than a conventional business case that was the inspiration for eBay's gender diversity initiative. That isn't because the business case isn't important, but because in itself it can't generate the passion and conviction necessary to sustain gender diversity as a priority.

"Our company's experience thus far suggests that a committed chief executive and C-suite are essential to telegraph the importance of the effort," Angier confirms. "When senior leaders engage with something, others are encouraged to make individual commitments, establish shared goals, and accept collective accountability. Real change can't happen without a commitment from the top, because that's where people take their cues."

There is change coming though, whether companies like it or not. It's coming in the form of the new generation of Millennial women who within 10 years are going to represent 75% of the workforce, and who are bringing a whole new attitude to the party.

"Millennials yearn for acceptance of their thoughts and opinions, but compared to older generations, they feel it's unnecessary to downplay their differences in order to get ahead," says a report on Millennial attitudes to diversity by Deloitte and the Billie Jean King Leadership Initiative. "Millennials are refusing to check their identities at the doors of organizations today, and they strongly believe these characteristics bring value to the business outcomes and impact." In short, Millennial women are refusing to put on the beard. Because their generation has managed to identify that when a company commits to gender diversity, it isn't just the women it employs that makes the difference, it's the commitment itself.

This generation is recognising, as the report says, that a range of different thoughts and opinions within a company actually delivers a value all its own both to the quality of the work, and to the bottom line. That gender diversity is one element contributing to a broader, more powerful, cognitive diversity. And putting on the beard and checking their female attitudes at the door is totally counterproductive, all round.

"The disconnect between the traditional definitions of diversity and inclusion, and the millennial definitions, is already causing business hardship," the report goes on. "These generations view diversity as a representation of fairness and protection to all, regardless of gender, race, religion, ethnicity, or sexual orientation."

In which case shipping and maritime had better brace itself. Speaking to women about gender diversity in this industry, the almost universal reaction has been a rolling of eyes and 'don't get me started' look. Because I think in shipping the beards have had to be denser and bushier than anywhere else—if not a full-set. That facial furniture is a useful thing to hide behind when a couple of naked women covered in body paint drape themselves over your male colleague at an exhibition, in the hope that he'll be more pleasantly disposed to using the ship repair yard the company which hired them to take their clothes off is trying to flog him.

It's a useful screen when you're handed a copy of a maritime magazine that has a woman on the front with a captain's cap and a shirt open to the waist exposing her breasts. Or when you go out with a group after a conference and they decide it'll be great fun to go to a strip club.

Does that make uncomfortable reading? Because it bloodywell should do. But for a large number of people in the industry it won't. They will shrug their shoulders and say, that's just the way shipping is. Just the same as when Brian asks his mother why women aren't allowed to go to the stoning and she replies, "Because it's written."

And if the industry loses out on talented women because of it, then so be it.

It's an attitude beautifully illustrated by the CEO of Roper Industries, which makes engineering products for the water, energy, transportation and medical industries. The company was called out by Bloomberg for not having a single woman on its board and in a telephone interview its CEO Brian Jellison told Bloomberg that although it didn't have an open slot for a director, the company was "more than willing to consider female candidates for the board and would be anxious to find one that would fit in." Fit in. I say again, 'fit in'.

Software engineer Kate Heddlestone put it very well earlier this year, just substitute the word 'shipping' for the word 'tech'. "Women in tech are the canary in the coal mine. Normally when the canary in the coal mine starts dying you know the environment is toxic and you should get the hell out. Instead, the tech industry is looking at the canary, wondering why it can't breathe, saying "Lean in, canary. Lean in!" When one canary dies they get a new one because getting more canaries is how you fix the lack of canaries, right? Except the problem is that there isn't enough oxygen in the coal mine, not that there are too few canaries."

If you are the type of woman who considers it unacceptable to be exposed to female nudity designed to titillate male colleagues in the course of your professional life then the message is that really, shipping and maritime isn't for you. And let's be absolutely clear about this. I am not talking about being the only woman in a crew of 15 men on a container ship and being forced to look at rude posters on the walls. I am talking about walking around one of the biggest global shipping exhibitions in a Scandinavian capital city and having naked women paraded in front of you.

It isn't really about the tits, it's about the fact that if you think having to put up with that isn't acceptable, you aren't going to fit in. So what we have in the shipping industry is quite a few women who have either become so inculcated into the prevailing culture that they honestly don't see anything wrong with that, or they're so convinced there's nothing they can do about it they don't even bother trying. And that's where you get to the heart of the gender diversity problem in shipping. It's part of a far bigger cognitive diversity problem which is getting really quite urgent. And IMO is the worst culprit of all.

For thirty years its relentless focus has been on getting women to go to sea. But the very last thing that this industry needs is another generation of women who have been inculcated into the same culture, beliefs and group-think that their male counterparts have been.

If you put a human being on a ship for ten years then bring them ashore and send them through the same course at a maritime university you are going to get the same cognitive approach whether that's a man or a woman. What we're desperate for in this industry is some fresh, diverse thinking, but what IMO is determined to deliver are a load of women who conveniently think exactly the same as the men do. It doesn't want them in beards. It wants them in Chewbacca suits.

It's the same as the Iranian women's football team which was recently found to have been fielding eight players who were biologically men. This move was defended by the Iranians on the basis that they were all going to have sex changes. The idea that as long as you have a hoo-ha you've ticked the box (if you'll forgive me) is one that's persisted for a while in shipping, but that's to completely miss the point of what gender diversity should be delivering.

The orchestrator of the Nor-Shipping 'Nipplegate' affair, the person who not only hired the semi-naked women, but also defended their use on the basis that the furore generated valuable publicity, for the ship repair yard, and men really liked them, is Christina Ørskov Nettavisen. She is a woman. And a board member. And she has a truly magnificent set of whiskers.

The key challenge we face is convergent thinking, and changing it is a huge undertaking. But whereas in most other industries gender diversity is a pretty guaranteed way to make a dent in that, as Christina so ably demonstrates, in shipping a hoo-ha can be a bit of a red herring.

What we need is not big hairy women like Christina, we need

women with big hairy audacious goals, and men who find the idea of working with them to transform their businesses and the industry together, sexier than the idea of taking their clothes off and painting them with gouache.

These are lean times in shipping, so the business case for gender diversity should be enough. But in an industry where if a woman 'leans in' there's still an above average chance that the man next to her will take the opportunity to look down her blouse, it probably won't be. Because there are still too many men who don't see anything wrong with that, and too many women who think there's no value in disagreeing.

So I'm looking at you, gentlemen, because this has to come from the top. There is money on the table here, but actually there's far more than that. Gender diversity, and the cognitive diversity it brings could be what secures the future of your organisations. But if you want it you're going to have a fight on your hands.

It's time to stop bearding-up our women, and beard shipping in its den instead.

London, October 2015.

8

MEET YOUR MAKER

This time last year I wrote an article called 'Shipping's Next Lightbulb Moment', trying to bring together some of the major technology themes we'd covered in Futurenautics and see if we could extrapolate some hard future predictions.

As part of the article I flagged up the importance of machine learning algorithms, and how sophisticated they're becoming. And how quickly. In 2011 the IBM computer known as Watson went on the US quiz show Jeopardy! and—in a test of similes, jokes and riddles—beat the humans. By 2014 Google's machine learning algorithm mapped the precise location of every household, business and street number in the whole of France, in one hour. Which, as I pointed out at the time, in France isn't even long enough for lunch.

Machine learning and deep learning algorithms are possibly one of the most disruptive of all the exponential technologies today. They sit at the heart of everything from what Amazon tries to sell you next when you've just made a purchase, to the complex high-stakes pattern matching exercise which drives Google's autonomous vehicle.

Machine learning and deep learning research in particular has already achieved breakthroughs in speech, text and image recognition. In essence it's based on endowing an artificial neural network with multiple hidden layers which enables a machine to learn tasks, organize information and find patterns on its own. The speed with which this field is developing is the reason behind Google's director of engineering Ray Kurzweil claiming that by 2029 machines could be conscious.

Whilst the terms machine or deep learning are getting more familiar, the more accurate and technical term 'artificial neural network' isn't so well know. And I'd never heard it used in shipping. So when I heard DNV GL's Tor Svensen introduce the winner of its 'Smarter' 2015 Young Professional Award earlier this year, and the title of her paper 'Predicting Added Resistance in Wind and Waves Employing Artificial Neural Nets', I wasn't sure whether my excitement was justified.

It was. Catching up with Eva Herradón de Grado afterwards and reading her paper it was very clear that, although she wasn't bandying around the term machine learning, that was exactly the technology Eva had leveraged.

As part of her studies towards a master's degree in naval architecture at the Technical University of Madrid (UPM), Eva spent a year at the Danish Technical University as an Erasmus student and participated in the DNV GL summer student project in Hamburg. She won the award for a research paper she prepared for an international conference.

As a female Millennial I was interested in why she was attracted to a Masters in Naval Architecture, and whether she had any prior connection with shipping and maritime. "Before I started my degree actually, I had no connection with the field," Eva told me. "In fact I live in Madrid, right in the middle of Spain as far away from the sea as you can get! However, as I have always been attracted by the ocean, I decided first of all to study marine science." In Spain at least, according to Eva it's tough to find a job in that speciality, so she took her aptitude for maths and physics and, on her father's advice, decided to study Naval and Oceanic Engineering at the

UPM (Technical University of Madrid) instead. "I finally followed his advice and I do not have any regrets about my decision, because I have not only been able to study the ocean with all its amazing phenomena like waves, currents, etc. but also I have been able to understand those giants of the seas."

As those giants have grown relentlessly larger, so has the need to understand how best to design them to withstand the forces they're subject to. Despite the increasingly sophisticated testing processes available, like computational fluid dynamics (CFD), Eva zeroed in on an issue that's still proving difficult and expensive to address.

"Added resistance due to wind and waves is still a difficult issue for the design of a ship because there are not many simple and economical methods to obtain an accurate prediction of this added resistance, and it can have important effects on ship exploitation due to its effect on fuel consumption and the reduction in propulsive efficiency," explains Eva. Considering its importance, Eva found it was a comparatively underdeveloped topic, and one ripe for a disruptive approach.

"In the maritime and shipping industry there are different ways to predict the added resistance, the cheaper one is to consider a sea margin factor—usually 15-30 per cent of the ship's calm water power—based on some literature or from the experience with other similar ships sailing on the same route," she says. "The other way to predict it is through theoretical methods using some empirical formulae. In this option there are different studies providing different formulae obtained from model tests or other calculations. And finally the most accurate ones are using towing tank tests or some numerical computer program, most of them apply potential flow theory as CFDs."

But whilst towing tank tests and CFD are accurate they're also very expensive and time consuming. But the applications for the results extend well beyond ship design, particularly into the new types of ship optimisation software operators are beginning to implement. So finding a way to predict the added resistance more efficiently and cheaply offers a potentially very wide benefit. What Eva recognised was that the problem was particularly well suited to the application of Artificial Neural Networks (ANN). ANN technology can be a good tool when problems depend on several parameters, as is the case with the added resistance.

"There are some studies in which Artificial Neural Network (ANN) technology is applied to ship design and sea-keeping, for example to predict the motions and force of a ship, the ideal propeller to install, etc." says Eva. "I think that ANN is particularly well-suited to this problem because the added resistance is predicted in the early stages of the ship design when the values of the different parameters of the ship are still not completely settled and some modifications could still be made." That means that within the ANN it's not necessary to create any physical or numerical model of the ship, "It only depends on the values of the parameters, so just introducing the new values it could be possible to predict the added resistance in an easy, cheaper and fast way." This is fairly cutting-edge stuff, and if you're interested in how it works then I'd recommend you read Eva's paper which, as the judges of the DNV GL prize commended her, is "particularly clear, complete, and easy to understand."

It takes some concentration but it really does give an insight into the way that machine learning operates, and as it's addressing a real-world maritime problem, does it in a useful context for us in the industry. If you want to download it then you can find it on the Futurenautics website. I guarantee that you will feel cleverer for having done so, and—if you don't already—have a good deal of respect for just how smart Eva is.

What's clear from the paper is that the selection of the input and output parameters for the ANN is absolutely vital to the quality of the predictive result, and here's where Eva encountered an issue.

"I didn't have all the time, or all the data that I would have wanted and needed," says Eva. "To train the ANN technology you need some known input and output parameters, and in the database that I used, there was just values about one ship, so I couldn't consider different length, beam, depth, etc. which I think would have an important influence on the wave added resistance."

To combat that Eva tried different combinations of the parameters she did have, trying to identify which ones might have a greater influence on the added resistance. "I tried different, non-dimensional forms of these parameters until I obtained the best combination. Also, the software that I used had the advantage of being able to tell you if some of the input parameters don't affect the output."

The exercise also threw up some surprises, like the influence of one particular parameter. "Yes, there were surprises!" agrees Eva. "I expected that the draught of the vessel could have some effects on the added resistance but I did not imagine that it could have an influence so important."

The data Eva used was taken from the simulation program GL Rankine, which is an in-house sea-keeping code of DNV-GL, but the work on the ANN was done via a programming language which Eva had pretty much taught herself. As the DNV GL judges noted, her competency in Matlab didn't come through her university curriculum.

Matlab is a programming language with lots of applications, including naval architecture, but although Eva had contact with it superficially in her first year of Naval and Oceanic engineering, it wasn't until she went to the Technical University of Denmark (DTU), she found she needed to get to grips with it, and fast.

"I needed to do all the assignments in Matlab to calculate the RAOs, the spectrums and other parameters and functions related to ships," Eva recalls. "Everyone there knew how to use it really well, so it didn't occur to them to explain it to me. But in the end, after some desperate days and the help of Mr. Google, I learnt how to get by in Matlab."

I think of all the things about Eva's achievement, to me that really stands out. It's the most clear illustration of how and why digital natives like Eva approach the world differently to those digital immigrants currently trying to keep up. Whereas in days past, not being able to use a program would have stopped most people dead in their tracks, that simply isn't the case any more. The Internet is a phenomenal resource and its judicious use by those who want answers is transforming the way that clever people with ideas, but who aren't necessarily trained and expert in something, can make huge contributions.

But it still takes someone to spark their interest, and Eva is absolutely clear where that spark originated. "When it come to the ANN technology I owe everything to DNV GL," Eva says. "Because during the summer I was doing an internship there and it was my supervisor who told me something about neural networks. I realized then the big potential of this technology and I started to investigate more and finally to write my paper."

Of course the idea of bringing ANNs to bear on this problem is interesting, but to be of any use it does have to actually work. And Eva's really does. When considering the errors in the predictive results against the validation data, both the Average Angle Measure (AAM) and the correlation coefficient (R) were accurate to 0.93 and 0.99 respectively. A score of 1 indicates perfect correlation between the predicted and experimental data. So the ANN was amazingly accurate. I asked Eva if that surprised her.

"I had to try different input parameters and non-dimensional form combinations of the parameters until I got these good correlations," points out the self-effacing Eva, "But it didn't take as much as I imagined at the beginning so yes, it was a kind of surprise."

And the results also made Eva think about where other applications of this technology could be lurking in maritime. "The first thing that I realized during the project is the big potential of the ANN technology for the maritime and shipping industry, for example it could be very useful to predict the sea-keeping of the ship under some circumstances, also it could be useful to predict when the lines of a moored ship will break or the fenders will exceed their limits, things like that."

What Eva has demonstrated is that in shipping, just like in a myriad of other industries, platforms and software are enabling faster and faster innovation by building on what's gone before, dropping costs and increasing efficiency as they go.

That's how we're seeing exponential advances as the costs for equivalent functionality in a variety of areas are scaling massively. A drone with the equivalent functionality to one you bought in

2013 for around $700 would have cost $100,000 in 2007. That's 142 times less in 6 years. For 3D printing it's even more impressive, equivalent functionality has come down from $40,000 in 2007 to $100 in 2014—400 times in 7 years. But perhaps the most stunning is in biotech, where DNA sequencing of one whole human DNA profile cost $10 million dollars in 2007, and last year dropped to $1,000. That's a reduction of 10,000 times in 7 years.

What's driving a lot of this is the combinatorial effect of the technologies involved, but also the ability of new iterations of software and computing power to enable people in unlikely places to work on these problems and to start solving them. Biotech is a prime example. A new generation of DIY biologists are setting up labs in their bedrooms that a few years ago you would have had to be a Pfizer or a GSK to afford. Sometimes described as 'maker culture' these biotech entrepreneurs are conducting experiments and uncovering new knowledge in their back kitchens and garages that is changing the world. "To transform bacteria was once a huge deal, a new method," explains one biotech enthusiast. "Today, you can do it with Epsom salt and an over-the-counter brand of laxatives."

What Eva has shown with her ANN project is that maritime is about to have its very own Big Pharma moment. What until now has required huge investment and complex equipment to test and evaluate is now shrinking down, and that's going to put it into the hands of people not just like Eva who work in maritime, but anyone, anywhere in the world.

There is one brake on that of course, and that's the data. The data that Eva used to train her algorithm isn't publically available, but when you see what she's done with it, and understand what others might make with it, you have to wonder how valuable making it available could end up being for DNV GL, either open source or as part of a more structured contest. Hope Remi's reading this. Because I don't think it'll be lost on him.

It isn't lost on Eva either. "I think that the availability of data can be very useful for a faster development of the maritime and shipping industry, it allows people who work on their own without being part of a company to develop programs which could help to improve some aspect of the ship design or maritime industry. For example in my case if I could have access to more data I could continue investigating ANNs."

Everyone's warning about the Big Data tsunami about to engulf the industry, and scrabbling to understand how its relevant. This is a crystal clear example. "In the case of ANN, if there were some daily data available about a merchant ship, for example the motion which the ship experiences under wind or wave forces, maybe it could be investigated and ANN code developed to predict the future sea-keeping of the ship. The availability of data could also be very useful for other programs and to improve ship design."

Last issue I covered Eva's fellow award winner Alexander Iley—who I am delighted to say we've managed to keep in the industry courtesy of a job with V-Ships—and I pointed out that he'd taken a longstanding problem and gone about solving it by applying existing technology which hadn't been considered for the task before. It's a very Millennial trait and you can see that Eva has done precisely the same thing.

"New applications for the technology are constantly being discovered and in the end technology can be applied to every field and improve it, helping to get some parameters or make some prediction faster and easier," she says. "Moreover, technology, such as computer programs are becoming more accessible to everybody with more friendly interfaces and more information about how to use them. Therefore I think that as the "Millennials" increase there will be more applications of the technology to many fields."

And that trend is likely to be accelerated by the fact that Millennials aren't likely to stay in one industry for decades the same way Gen X'ers have. Does Eva favour the idea of a portfolio career which include stints in various different industries?

"Actually yes, I've studied Naval and Oceanic engineering, which is a mix between Naval architecture, mechanics, marine renewable energies, oceanography, etc., and includes the degree and the master together, so at the end I have a general expertise across all those topics, and I like all of them," says Eva. "So I'll try to look for a career related to more than one topic in order to learn about more things. Also, I think that many sectors are very interrelated, therefore if someone has experience in more than one sector, it could be useful to apply some things of one field to another."

For the moment at least we've managed to keep Eva too. She's currently working in the shipping and maritime industry, for the Spanish Siport21, a technical consulting company where she's focused on ship manoeuvring studies and ship behaviour in port areas. And at the moment she's content to stay. Considering we're talking about diversity and brand this issue I wondered how Eva felt about gender diversity in shipping and maritime, and whether we had a good proposition for smart Millennials like her.

"I am not that smart Millennial, I just had the opportunity to get involved in the application of the technology," says the modest Eva. "The way that I discovered the ANN was through a summer internship and after that it was because of my curiosity that I was be able to develop my work. Therefore, I think that the best way to engage young professionals with the industry and the technology is through internships, courses, company visits or other ways to teach them how all the theory learnt as part of their degree can be applied to the real world."

Eva's views on gender are also interesting. "I think that this sector is a good place for a woman," she says. "It is true that historically the shipping and maritime industry has been a place for men, but this is quickly changing and the consequences are quite visible—for example in my degree in Spain we were 60 per cent men and 40 per cent women!"

According to Eva her current company Siport21 employs more women than men, although how senior those women are I didn't ask. But she's well aware of the size of the challenge. "On the other hand, I have been enlisted in some vessels doing internship and most—not saying all of them—of the crew and the captains were men, and the senior positions in this industry are still occupied by men. But I think that women are as valid as men in any sector, the problem is that unfortunately there are still some obstacles and people who do not believe that."

She's absolutely correct of course, but what she's done already is a signal that those mindsets are living on borrowed time. In the same way that the 'maker culture' has disrupted Big Pharma, the age of individuals using new technologies and data from the shipping and maritime industry and starting to solve its problems in their back bedrooms is dawning. And that has the capacity to change everything. As Inmarsat Maritime's COO Trond Leira pointed out during a Futurenautics roundtable recently, the companies that could be dominating maritime in five years time might not even exist yet.

What you've just read should be a big red warning sign to incumbent companies in our space about just how alert they need to be. And far from size being an advantage, that, coupled with the prevailing culture and lack of cognitive diversity in most organisations, could just be the death of you.

There will be shipping and maritime companies who go to meet their maker. And Eva Herradón de Grado could be yours.

London, October 2015.

9

BUNKER MENTALITY

L ast month shipping went—temporarily—viral. The reason it did so was thanks to an article on the UK's Guardian website that was written back in 2008. The article was entitled, "Health risks of shipping pollution have been 'underestimated'," and if I tell you that it contained the sentence, "One giant container ship can emit almost the same amount of cancer and asthma-causing chemicals as 50m cars," then you'll probably get the gist of it.

Unfortunately, whilst those in the shipping industry know about the progress in environmental regulations which has been made since that article was written six years ago, and the reality of our CO_2 emissions per tonne mile in comparison to rail or freight, the same cannot be said for most of the 3,000 members of Joe Public who chose to comment on the article. And you will be unsurprised to hear that they were broadly uncomplimentary.

There were a range of suggestions—perhaps exhortations would be more precise—regarding the methods of propulsion that should be considered as alternatives to HFO in the future. The most interesting part was that virtually all of them have, and are, being considered in minute detail by an industry trying to come to terms with a looming sulphur cap. With the exception of attaching reins to pods of dolphins. Or using the Force. As far as I know.

Yet despite the research going into everything from methanol, glycerine and hydrogen, to batteries, solar, wind, and midi-chlorians—okay, not the midi-chlorians—the environmental lobby still accuses shipping of wanting to continue burning heavy fuel oil.

And actually they've got a point, because a lot of people do. But that's hardly surprising when you consider the advice and forecasts we're being given.

Anyone who works in shipping will tell you that—after rates—fuel is one of their top operational priorities, and not simply in terms of what they're putting in their tanks on a daily basis. The tightening emissions regulations is part of a trend you don't need to be a futurist to recognise, and for operators investing in ships that could easily have a 25-30 year life, decisions about what they should—or could—be able to run on are crucial.

Getting those decisions right is becoming ever more complex, but assistance comes in the shape of Class, academics and consultants. The Lloyd's 'Global Marine Fuel Trends 2030' report uses a powerful model to create a range of scenarios for the expected fuel mix in the future. DNV GL's 'Alternative Fuels for Shipping' and 'The Fuel Trilemma' reports and the Boston Consulting Group's 'Forecasting the Future of Marine Fuel' all offer in-depth assessments and are well worth reading.

But they all come to broadly the same conclusion, which is that despite all the expected pressures exerted by environmental legislation, by 2030 and well beyond, the dominant fuel in the maritime industry is still likely to be bunkers.

That's all the more significant when you reflect that a lot of the analysis is at least in part reliant on an oil price which hadn't yet commenced its precipitous nosedive. At the time of writing there is speculation that IFO380 bunker prices could get close to $200 per metric tonne (pmt) before there is any significant upswing. Bill Baruch, chief market strategist at Chicago-based consulting and advisory services firm iiTrader recently told CNBC, "This market is headed to $40 before we go to $60 again." Goldman Sachs have already predicted crude oil to fall as low as $30 per barrel, or $226 pmt which would push that IFO380 price to $158 pmt.

It's not quite the $40 pmt you could have got it for in Houston in the late 1990s I'm told, but it's not really that far off either. And the impact of that on the maritime fuel mix could be significant.

In its reports DNV GL makes the point that choice of fuel comes down to three things: affordability, sustainability and safety. And it's clear that those are in listed in order of importance. If the price of bunkers continues to slide then the uptake horizon for other fuels and propulsion systems will be impacted.

So if all the forecasts are telling us that bunkers are still going to dominate, is it any wonder that interest in other options remains muted?

You could argue it's a chicken and egg situation, and what's required is a critical mass of operators to move towards another fuel that will then tip everyone else towards it too. But the reason bunkers look like hanging on to the top spot isn't anything to do with shipping at all. The fact is that whatever the maritime industry does, as by-products of the refining process bunkers aren't going anywhere.

"Some in the industry see the current and planned environmental regulations are being unreasonable, or not very well thought out," says Martyn Lasek, Editor of Ship & Bunker and authority on the bunker industry. "Yes operators want to improve emissions, but they don't necessarily want to get rid of oil-based products. They are happy to burn HFO, which irrespective of it being used by the marine industry is a product that's going to be produced anyway as it's a by-product of the refining process, and vessels are designed to use it."

It's an important point. If the oil industry is going to continue producing petroleum and its short-chain, high-value cousins like kerosene and jet fuel, and the world would like to continue its use of plastics, then how can we ban the use of bunkers?

Even reducing the sulphur levels is beginning to get seriously problematic. As a residual, and therefore unrefined product, the lower sulphur requirement is narrowing the pool of useable crudes. If the sulphur cap stops us burning it what do the refiners do with it?

Speaking at the CMA conference oil industry veteran Dr Rudy Kassinger made the point that once the target sulphur level, "hits about 1.5 percent, even residues from low sulphur crudes need to be reduced in sulphur content, and refiners would then probably desulfurise gas oil and blend to the 0.5 per cent spec." But once the level gets below 0.5 per cent things change altogether. Then the only real option is residue conversion. Shell have indicated that disposing of the residue currently used as marine fuel would take an investment of $100 billion.

"I thought that was in fact a lowball estimate," said Kassinger. "But it's a number that you can rationalise because ExxonMobil just published their information about the Antwerp 50,000 barrel per day coker at a cost of $1 billion. You'll only need about 100 of those to get rid of the residue currently used as marine fuel. That's $100 billion."

It's a pretty fundamental issue, and part of the pressure that's led IMO to call a review of the proposed sulphur cap in 2018. It is entirely possible that the oil industry won't be able to meet the demand for bunkers at the sulphur cap specification by 2020. According to Rudy Kassinger it could be 2075 before the infrastructure is fully in place to convert all the bunkers we need.

But even if we accept that bunkers are going to dominate for the next twenty or thirty years—or longer—its continued use doesn't, and can't mean the continued current level of emissions. But mitigating them is a complex business and highly dependent upon both the sector, vessel and nature of operations.

It's extremely important to make the distinction between what can and could power smaller coastal, short-sea and RORO vessels, and what the deep sea fleet can reasonably use. As technologies proliferate it's a growing divide and one which is driving a real diversification in the marine fuel mix.

Vessels that don't stray too far from land can take advantage of technologies which deliver major environmental benefits without compromising security of operation. Deep sea vessels face a greater challenge in order to do so. In many respects it's a similar situation to connectivity. Close to land it's possible to use a wide variety of connectivity options, but deep sea those options are rather more limited, and expensive.

There is bold work going on to develop renewable powered ships and systems which utilise solar and wind. The Vindskip from Lade AS made headlines a couple of years ago with its futuristic, sail shaped hull, whilst B9 shipping and EcoMarine Power are sporting designs which make use of sails and, in the case of EcoMarine, a solar-panel covered retractable sail. But B9 will also need a biogas powered engine—courtesy of Rolls-Royce, whilst the Vindskip makes use of an LNG engine. In short, these are all hybrid vessels, and hybrid is where a lot of the smart money seems to be going.

It may be a surprise to some readers that we are almost 1200 words in, and I've only just mentioned LNG. It's certainly the case that LNG has a reputation for being the future maritime fuel. And it has a jolly good press, particularly compared to other fuels. In fact if you read the maritime media you would be forgiven for assuming that LNG powered vessels were everywhere. But the reality is quite different. There are indeed LNG vessels around, but they are almost exclusively short sea, coastal and offshore. Virtually the only ones operating deep sea are those which are carrying the stuff in the first place, which makes its own sense.

I think this is where we come down to the nitty gritty of the whole future fuels thing, and why LNG probably isn't it. If the chicken and egg situation applies anywhere then it would appear to apply to the adoption of LNG. The infrastructure for bunkering isn't there, so I won't order the ship, but if I don't order the ship the infrastructure is unlikely to be built. But step back and analyse that. 70 per cent of all fuel is bought in ten ports around the world, so in reality it wouldn't be that hard to put the infrastructure in the right places.

But for operators there are other concerns about LNG. Yes, it will get you through the ECAs, but it's a technology which requires a completely different method of operation, new standards and different training and competencies of crew. It will also cost you around 30 per cent more for the ship.

These are real considerations, but of course you have to set them in the context of what you'll save on your fuel bill. But even then the picture is mixed. According to the Society for Gas as a Marine Fuel (SGMF) and it's briefing document, 'Gas as a marine fuel: an introductory guide', depending where you buy your LNG it could cost virtually as much as HFO. In Rotterdam in 2014 you would pay 14-15 US$/mmBTU as opposed to 7-8 for LNG, but go to Tokyo and the HFO will cost you between 16-17, whereas LNG could cost as much as 15-16. And of course those figures are from early 2014, well before the price of oil crashed.

But perhaps what's more important is that LNG is still a hydrocarbon, so when you look at the sustainability index it's not really a great leap forward. Natural gas is promoted due to its CO_2 emission intensity being lower than that of coal or oil, but methane, the prime constituent of natural gas, is 25 times more potent as a GHG than CO_2.

'Methane Slip' is the elevated methane concentrations in exhaust which results from the use of engines operating using the Otto cycle—which apparently includes almost all marine LNG engines. Published data related to this is scarce but according to DNV GL fuel losses of 2-3 per cent is typical. A 3 per cent slip is equivalent to a 24 per cent increase in GHG emissions.

"Methane leakage during production, transportation, and use of natural gas may, in principle, offset the benefits gained from fuel switching," says DNV GL. "Our calculations show that a total methane leakage of 5.5 % (including both production/transportation, and combustion) would bring GHG emissions from LNG to a level equivalent to those from diesel fuel."

So the bottom line is that it won't take very much at all to make LNG as polluting as diesel fuel—at least in terms of GHG.

Of course there are ways to mitigate that, but what may be harder to deal with is dear old Joe Public. LNG is not universally considered to be the future fuel that many in maritime like to paint it. Opposition to fracking, LNG pipelines and LNG bunkering is widespread, with demonstrations in the UK and Europe, Canada—where one local mayor was elected on an anti-LNG platform— to Gibraltar which is mired in an ugly political row over the expansion of its LNG storage, bunkering and regasification facilities with the opposition quoting a Lloyd's Register report which apparently concluded LNG operations in the North Mole and Detached Mole could pose "potentially intolerable risks".

So it's no surprise that LNG has a very good PR machine, and there's absolutely nothing wrong with that. But the future of marine fuel it isn't. And even DNV GL—often seen as a cheerleader for LNG—seem to have come to that conclusion. "It is obvious that fossil-based LNG cannot be classified as a sustainable fuel, but it has the advantage of reducing SOx, NOx, and particulate matter emissions, while offering some reductions in GHG when used properly," it says in its position paper on fuels. "It could act as a bridging fuel towards a future in which air pollution from shipping is significantly reduced."

I'm sure it will, but even on the most ambitious projections LNG still makes up only around 20 per cent of the marine fuel mix by the 2030's. That means the bridge needs to include a lot more mitigation and abatement, and efficiency. Fortunately—or not depending upon your point of view—the bunker industry and the fuel efficiency of ships in general offers incredible scope to do so.

In researching this issue of the magazine I've heard some frankly jaw-dropping stories about the inner workings of the bunker industry. But here's what I'm going with—the bunker industry is slowly seeing an acceleration and acceptance of technology and transparency, but it remains very opaque and volatile. And that may be the greatest understatement I've made this year.

For many reading this none of that will come as a surprise, but for anyone who isn't close to the bunkering industry some of the practices are scarcely believable. I was astonished to learn that there are crew delivering bunkers to ships who aren't paid a salary, but instead make their money on arbitrage. It was almost as surprising as being told that even if you buy 1,000 tonnes of fuel within the

ISO8217 specification it can legitimately contain 5 tonnes of water. That means a supplier can quite lawfully charge you hundreds of dollars a tonne for water. And whilst the water content in fuel from European refineries is typically less than 0.05 per cent—effectively a trace—the industry average water content of marine fuel according to DNVPS testing is 0.26 per cent. Overall the quality of marine fuel has been falling. FOBAS have indicated that between 3-5 per cent of all the samples they test weekly are out of spec and other testers report higher percentages. By some estimates $1.3 billion of fuel purchased in Singapore alone is off-spec. And, of course, up until very recently, it very difficult indeed to know exactly how much you were actually getting pumped into the tank anyway.

"Back in 1999 when buyers were paying as low as $40 per tonne, bunker costs were of a lower concern because they represented a much lower percentage of the overall operating costs. As the price of bunkers has gone up, and their percentage of overall operating costs is now around 60% of overall voyage costs, the cost consequences of bunker related malpractices - such as not receiving the volume of bunkers paid for, or any deliberate lowering of the quality of bunkers - is much higher," explains Martyn Lasek. "One of the unintended consequences of new environmental legislation could be to improve overall bunker quality and even curb some of the quality related malpractice."

Lasek points out that the sulphur cap could see more distillate fuels used in the future, which have historically had fewer quality problems. At the same time it's predicted that those still using HFO will move to using an even higher viscosity product such as 500cSt as opposed to the 380cSt more common today, "and it's harder to mess with those higher viscosity, lower priced bunkers."

It seems that the combination of price rises and forthcoming environmental regulation has already begun to shift things. But on a broader level whereas flow meters are a start, there doesn't appear at the moment to be much evidence of the industry leveraging pretty mainstream technologies like sensors, data and the industrial internet.

Opaque and volatile may in the past have been shorthand for

'too difficult to tackle', but now it's the equivalent of hanging out a big sign saying, 'ripe for disruption'. Particularly when you consider that things are only going to get more complicated.

With the range of fuels broadening and the regulations tightening the days of a vessel running on just one fuel are pretty much behind us. For operators the practicality of using fuels which have different characteristics and aren't always compatible is a growing area of concern.

Fuel switching issues in the past have led to loss of power—distillates are used at ambient temperatures as opposed to bunkers which require heating and those different temperatures can in some cases risk thermal shock. Then you can add LNG into the mix at the other end of the scale—that's cryogenic. New risks are emerging around fuelling a vessel, even as simple as making sure that two separate tanks of two separate fuels don't co-mingle in the lines.

But streamlining the bunkers industry is only one part of the puzzle. According to the New Climate Economy report some operators are paying five times more in bunker costs than their competitors even though they're using vessels of a similar design.

"Ship efficiency varies widely based on design, fuel and power sources, and operations," says the report. "Even ships with similar designs can operate with vastly different efficiencies. The most efficient crude oil tanker is about one-fifth as fuel-intensive as the least efficient."

Operational efficiency is a lot about speed and utilisation rate—the report contends that a 10 per cent reduction in speed equates to a reduction in fuel use of 27 per cent per hour—but that really is the low hanging fruit. In fact the scope for improved operational efficiency is massive for ship operators. The report says that reliable data on operational efficiency is scarce and presents a 'significant challenge' for the industry, but it really doesn't have to.

Outgoing DNV GL CEO Henrik O Madsen recently described ship operators as 'too conservative' and the society unveiled research last month which showed that most ship operators simply aren't ambitious enough with either their targets or their efforts to become more efficient.

The burgeoning opportunities offered by sensors, data and optimisation algorithms and software could cut deeply into the amount of fuel shipping uses, and thereby its overall emissions. The New Climate Economy report has even gone as far as to put a figure on it. They claim improving vessel efficiency could save $200 billion in bunker costs by 2035.

You might think it was great in the good old days when you could burn whatever the heck you liked in your ship and got charged peanuts for it. But we can't go back. And the complexity of fuelling vessels appropriately and profitably, and efficiently has become an area of real competitive advantage. Buying bunkers at the lowest price just isn't enough any longer. Quite aside from the fact that buying old spec or out of spec fuel may mean cat fines screw up your expensive engines, there are wider considerations now.

Already the likes of Rightship are changing the way that Charterers evaluate vessels. From a CSR perspective fuel is likely to become an area where ship operators can add value, or disadvantage themselves in the market, and that kind of transparency of operations is part of a growing trend.

The UK will shortly be bringing in a reporting requirement for British companies to disclose details of their supply chains to expose any connection with slavery or people trafficking. It's the first time that a company will have been made responsible for the actions of its supply chain, and as a key part of so many supply chains it's an example of a trend which will impact shipping significantly in the coming years.

Improving the transparency and efficiency of the bunkering industry and the efficiency of ship operators is undoubtedly overdue and necessary. Together with LNG and hybrid operations it will form the bridge to the cleaner operations that DNV GL talk about.

But there are other potential technologies which could hold opportunities for maritime to mitigate its emissions. And although they've been around some time, they just don't seem to have gained traction.

Fuel emulsification additives and catalysts aren't new, and reading the significant number of case studies available at least some of them do seem to work. And when they do work they are offering on average between 8-16% in fuel savings, together with reduced NOx and SOx, plus reductions in engine wear. For any operators those figures should be of real interest. And it seems astonishing if so, that they aren't more widespread.

One such catalyst, Enerburn from a company called Enerteck, was originally developed by Exxon and Nalco Chemical and claims proven fuel efficiency improvement of 8-12 per cent in various diesel engine applications plus NOx reductions averaging 10-11 per cent and a 50-70 per cent reduction in particulates. Another, H2Oil, has a letter of no objection from Wärtsilä, and a case study on a Yang Ming container ship which shows verified fuel savings of between 8.1 and 12 per cent.

With figures like that I asked Enerteck President Gary Aman why the marine industry wasn't beating a path to his door, and the door of other additive producers. " Too many technologies make claims that just are not true. They are sold and then cannot perform. It really hurts the market."

H2Oil agree that too many claims are being made, but believes the real problem lies in the lack of agreed and approved methodology behind evaluating the additives.

"Fuel saving claims for devices and additives are rampant right now, but these are typically anecdotal or supported by poorly conceived testing protocols," says Technical Director Richard Hicks."It is our opinion that there is no widely accepted testing protocol yet developed which is able to accurately predict average real life fuel savings over a large number of vehicles/ships. Most fuel savings claims are based on a single test on a single vehicle/ship operating under a unique set of conditions."

Which begs the question, why aren't there? When the cost and emissions from bunkers are so incredibly high on the shipping agenda why hasn't this potentially promising area been more thoroughly looked at?

Dimitris Argyros, Lead Consultant, Environment & Sustainability at Lloyd's Register Marine and one of the authors of its GMFT2030 report says whilst additives can potentially deliver benefits in terms of reduced wear/tear and reduced emissions, the scale of NOx emissions reductions required is a significant challenge to achieve using emulsification or additives alone.

"At LR, we have been involved in full scale trials with technology developers and ship operators, but whilst promising in some areas, the emissions reductions achieved to date are simply not sufficient to help comply with the 0.10% limit for SOx or with NOx Tier III unless alternative fuels or emissions abatement devices are used. These techniques, if successful, may provide part of the solution combined with other techniques."

But surely we want any emissions reduction we can get, and fuel saved is emissions saved. And this technology could benefit every vessel in the fleet, with no upfront infrastructure investment or change of operations, tomorrow. If credible testing protocols are required, surely that's a job for Class?

"There have been cases of fuel additives and similar technologies which appear to defy basic laws of chemistry," says Argyros."At LR we try to keep an open mind and offer our support in independently verifying performance claims, however in many cases we are not provided with sufficient information/data to carry out any meaningful analysis or verification."

Which seems to throw the ball back into the additive manufacturer's court. Looking at them in the round they are mostly small companies without well-known maritime brands. If their technology really does work then one wonders if the real problem is that they lack the critical mass, brand power and marketing dollars to make the industry partnerships, and noise that are required. Ben Song, New Business Director of H2Oil takes a different view.

"I think the size of company doesn't matter much. The potential and credential of a technical product are the main factors," he says. "I believe a good product should not have the problem of lacking marketing dollars."

It's a noble but potentially very naive view, particularly for a company trying to sell into a notoriously insular industry like shipping. H2Oil believes it knows exactly why additives have not been embraced or even considered by shipping though. "We should be clear. The oil companies or government agencies will never embrace any technology which is capable of reducing their profitability or tax base," says Richard Hicks. "Always follow the money if you want to know why something apparently strange happens in business. Between them, these powerful groups have many tools to limit the widespread use of fuel saving technologies. Even large corporations can easily be prevented from introducing any new technology which the oil company cartel does not approve. Protectionism is alive and well in the oil industry."

Okay, except according to everyone I've spoken to in the bunkering industry, the plain truth of the matter is that the oil industry really doesn't care very much about marine fuels. According to an ex-oil company executive the marine fuels division had a turnover that would have put it in the FTSE100, but it made absolutely nothing in profit. Plus in the maritime industry it isn't just ship operators who are buying fuel, it's charters too. And I can find no evidence to support the idea that either are being leant on not to use fuel saving additives by oil companies or anyone else.

There's a reason that this is significant, and that's because some of these additives—both fuel and lube oils—are leveraging some really cutting-edge technology. Nanotechnology is already helping the oil and gas industry to both identify and extract previously uneconomic oil and it's that same technology which is now finding its way into additives. So it's important that our industry continues to evaluate these technologies and identify those which could really help us. Because they are changing and improving all the time.

When one considers the research going into technologies which we all know are never going to be a suitable solution for every ship in the fleet, surely there's a strong imperative to direct some research dollars to one which could make a small, but significant difference to absolutely everyone. Particularly if we are looking at bunkers remaining dominant in the near term.

We've talked about a bridge. But what no one can really get their heads around is what's likely to be on the other side. I'm fond of telling the maritime industry that it's unique—just like everybody else. But on this occasion, when it comes to the fuel that ships—and particularly deep sea ships—are going to use in the future, we do have a unique challenge.

Like aeronautical, maritime has to ensure that whatever fuel it uses, it offers a great deal of mobility and security of operation. For other transport industries, and consumers ashore the developments in battery power and solar are going to begin to change the way they operate quite quickly. But for us it doesn't look as though those are really going to be real game-changers.

There is only one really game-changing fuel development on the horizon that could deliver what hydrocarbons currently do. In fact it could do far, far better.

The ITER project is an international scientific project designed to build a demonstration nuclear fusion reactor to deliver power to the consumer grid. There seems little doubt amongst experts that it will manage First Plasma by 2020 and be operating at full fusion by 2030.

But it is in the area of Compact Nuclear Fusion, announced last year by Lockheed Martin, that it seems most likely shipping, and aeronautical's paradigm shift may lie.

Lockheed's notional 100MW compact fusion reactor would measure roughly 10 metres by 7 metres in diameter. It will fit on the back of a truck, and is a similar size to a shipping container. But it could power 80,000 homes, or vessels, or aeroplanes, eliminating the need to refuel and offering unlimited range. According to Lockheed it would burn less than 20 kg of fuel in an entire year of operation.

What's really exciting though, is the timescales. Because of the size of the reactor, instead of taking four years to design, build and test one, the whole cycle can be completed in as little as a year. They are looking at an operational prototype within around four years. Coincidentally, the same sort of timescale as Rolls-Royce's prototype autonomous ship.

Fusion has always been the fuel of the future, but its time is widely believed to be close at hand. Shipping expects its ships to have a 25-30 year lifespan and the implementation horizon for fusion is well within that. For a more in-depth analysis of the technology read this issue's "Sunlit Uplands" article.

Fusion will be a turning point for the energy mix for the globe, but of all the potential fuel technologies around, compact nuclear fusion would have a truly profound effect on ships and aircraft. In combination with autonomous operation, it would usher in a whole new era for shipping that was genuinely sustainable, and profitable too.

So what is the upshot of all this? Well, probably that the real fuel of the future for the maritime industry isn't available yet. That, in short, there is no right answer—no 'silver bullet' as DNV GL describe it. The hard truth is that fuel is becoming ever more complex and requires an entirely different and more strategic approach than it has done in the past. In common with almost every other area of operation the situation is volatile, uncertain, complex and ambiguous. And whilst the advent of nuclear fusion is a genuinely near-term prospect, it isn't going to solve your problems tomorrow.

What can contribute to solving them are other technologies that are around now. Like the relentless gathering and analysis of data from sensors using the industrial internet, the streamlining and transparency of the bunker industry, and the restructuring of shipping organisations to consider fuel not just as a consumable to be purchased as cheaply as possible, but an area of competitive advantage.

When it comes to fuel, and a lot of other things besides, shipping has been considered to have a bunker mentality, in every sense. But there is a generation moving into shipping who take criticism of shipping's environmental performance on the chin. For whom being expected to use sustainable fuels and methods of operation aren't a bloody nuisance, but a morally and ethically necessary cost of doing business.

And to be honest, the real fuel of the future, is them.

London, July 2015.

10

SUNLIT UPLANDS

For millions of sci-fi fans around the world October 21st this year is going to be special. Really special. And it's been a long time coming. It's thirty years since the biggest grossing movie of 1985, '*Back to The Future*', gave the world a time machine made out of a DeLorean, in which a teenage Marty McFly accidentally gets sent thirty years into the past, and then deliberately heads thirty years into the future—arriving on 21st October 2015.

In 1985 our vision of what the world would look like today missed the mark in many respects. The movie failed to spot the impact of mobile phones or the internet, for example, yet assumed flying cars would be routine. But in the same year that the movie was made US President Ronald Reagan—mocked in the movie itself—was busily signing up to make the most game-changing technology of all those it imagined, a reality. Not self-fastening shoes, hoverboards or dehydrated pizza, but nuclear fusion. And thirty years later, we're very nearly there.

The Geneva superpower summit of 1985 was historic because it marked the first time that Reagan and Mikhail Gorbachev had actually met in person and was the precursor to the end of the Cold War. But the summit achieved something else which may prove to have been of far more lasting significance.

Together with Britain's Margaret Thatcher and President Mitterand of France, Gorbachev proposed an international project aimed at developing fusion energy for peaceful purposes.

The result was the ITER project. It's initial signatories, the former Soviet Union, USA, the EU and Japan later joined by Korea and India, now represent over half of the world's population.

ITER, which means, 'the way', in Latin was, and is, one of the largest and most ambitious international science projects ever conducted requiring unparalleled levels of international scientific collaboration. It's success—which is already widely anticipated—will open the way to unlimited clean energy for the world. And yet despite the urgent need for this technology, the majority of people have never heard of it, much less understand what nuclear fusion really is.

In a nutshell up until now the human race has mainly relied upon setting fire to things in order to generate energy. The most successful attempts to do so without the use of matches has been nuclear fission, and although it continues to power everything from cities to ships and submarines, the hazards associated with the technology, and the radioactive waste produced means fission is never going to be a solution. Fusion however, looks like it could be.

In 1985 when the cinema audiences saw the DeLorean arrive back from 2015 it had an important modification—a 'Mr Fusion' about the size of a coffee maker made by the fictional Fusion Industries. Fuelled by any old garbage this little thing produced energy equivalent to the 1.21 gigawatts necessary to propel the time machine across dimensions.

It seems like sci-fi serving up something which is too good to be true, but it isn't. The reality is that fusion has the potential to deliver the same amount of energy as burning 100 tonnes of coal using only a small bath of water and the same amount of lithium you'll find in one laptop battery. It will also do it inherently safely, without any carbon dioxide emissions or significant radioactive waste. Fusion is what keeps the light on down here on earth: it is what keeps the sun shining. The extreme conditions in the sun's core allow protons to fuse together releasing energy in the process and ensuring it continues to burn rather than collapse under the weight of its own gravity.

The objective is to use those same basic physics to generate sustainable and infinite energy here on earth, but there are problems. When protons fuse they generate around a million times more energy than is released in a chemical reaction, but getting them to do so is difficult. It will take a proton in the sun around 5 billion years to fuse.

So we fuse deuterium and tritium, heavy partners to the proton whose extra mass makes fusion easier to achieve. They are also sustainable. Deuterium is found in abundance in seawater and by reacting outgoing neutrons with lithium, tritium could be manufactured indefinitely.

The other issue is gravity—used by the sun to compress the hot fuel mix referred to as plasma, the effect of which we have to replicate by other means. The solution at ITER is to operate the reactor at a temperature 10 times higher than the sun's core and force the plasma inside a doughnut-shaped container using magnets. By doing so it should be possible for ITER to generate energy at a rate of 500m watts, which is equivalent to the level of a small power station.

Construction work on the tokomak reactor at the 180 hectare ITER site in St-Paul-lez-Durance, in Southern France began in 2010 and is expected to finish in 2019. Following a commissioning phase the ITER reactor expects to achieve First Plasma in 2020.

There seems remarkably little doubt about its success, so little in fact that there is already a third phase expected to launch around 2030 with the reactor operating frequently at full fusion power as a 'demonstration power plant'.

There are good reasons for the widespread confidence in ITER. We may be waiting until 2020 for First Plasma in France, but at the Joint European Torus (Jet) in Oxfordshire, UK—a mini-ITER running a similar tokomak design and using the same physics—fusion is described as a 'routine event'. Twenty years of research into plasma behaviour, neutron damage and a variety of other challenges have brought continuous advances in understanding.

Professor Chris Llewellyn Smith, director of energy research at Oxford University is clear that fusion's reputation as a 'future fuel' is no longer deserved. "With enough money we could probably build a fusion reactor now but it would not be economical," he told The Guardian. "The challenge is to make it reliable and competitive."

Fusion's time would appear to have come, but at a cost. Budgets are constantly being updated, but the construction phase of ITER is projected to cost around €13bn. Fortunately that cost is being shared between the seven ITER members for which the bill amounts to a few tens of millions per year. It's still a massive project though, and one which is focussing on grid power generation rather than any kind of mobility application. Elsewhere though, Lockheed Martin is focussing on making fusion not only economical and competitive, but mobile.

ITER's site is the size of 60 football pitches, but the Skunk Works at Lockheed Martin is working on a different scale altogether. Its focus is Compact Nuclear Fusion, using a new magnetic field geometry which offers a 10x reduction in size compared to mainstream tokamak reactors such as the ones in the UK and at ITER.

According to Lockheed Martin a notional 100MW compact fusion reactor would measure roughly 10 metres by 7 metres in diameter with superconducting coils which produce a border magnetic field to contain the hot fusion plasma. Neutral beams injectors ignite a burning plasma and the device then runs in steady-state. Neutrons from fusion reactions deposit their heat in the reactor wall and that heat is carried to turbine generators to generate power or propulsive thrust. Tritium fuel is continually bred in the wall and fed back into the reactor along with deuterium gas to sustain the reactions.

That's the science bit, and it's fascinating. But stop for a moment and think about the size of this thing. It will fit on the back of a truck. It's a similar size to a shipping container. And it would power 80,000 homes and could be aggregated to power large cities. It would be ideal for safely powering naval vessels, providing unlimited range and could be made small and light enough to fit on a large aeroplane eliminating the need to refuel and giving unlimited range.

A 100 MW system would burn less than 20 kg of fuel in an entire year of operation. Small fusion reactors could generate significantly cheaper electricity than current technologies, bringing the cost of desalination down to the point where it could be more widely deployed in water scarce regions. Compact fusion would be an ideal technology to power our future electric-based transportation systems. And, of course, ships.

The other significant part about the Skunk Works' technology is the timescales. The preliminary results are very promising and because of the size of the reactor, instead of taking four years to design, build and test one, the whole cycle can be completed in as little as a year.

They are looking at an operational prototype within around four years. Coincidentally, the same sort of timescale as Rolls-Royce's prototype autonomous ship. And the similarities between the two organisations don't end there.

When Rolls-Royce decided to go public with its autonomous ship development project it faced a hostile reaction in many quarters, but the belief in the company was that a paradigm shift was necessary, and it wasn't something Rolls-Royce could achieve in isolation. By going public with its research and development—and vision—Rolls-Royce aimed to find and bring together the kind of partners it needed to make that vision a reality, and generate an informed debate for the industry and public. From class societies to flag states and ship operators that strategy is already paying off.

Lockheed's approach is very similar. Asked why it has chosen to tell the world about its potential fusion technology now a spokesman says, "As we gain confidence and progress technically with each experiment, we are looking to build our team. We are looking for partners to work on the project and support it. We think it is important for the public and decision makers to understand the real promise that compact fusion has for our nation and the world as a near-term solution to our energy needs."

The phrase 'near-term' is a key one. The Skunk Works team are looking at an operational reactor within ten years. "In ten years we have great military vehicles, in twenty years we have clean power for the world," says Thomas McGuire PhD, Aeronautical and Astronautical Engineer at MIT and the Compact Fusion Project Lead at the Skunk Works. "This isn't online by 2100, this is online by..." McGuire pauses to try and contextualise just how close the technology is. "I can't even retire after we finish this. I still have to find another job after this is done."

As one would expect, the military are expected to be the initial customers for Lockheed's technology, but both aeronautical and maritime are considered to be prime industry targets for early commercial deployment. And it would be entirely fitting to see a merchant ship in the vanguard of what Thomas McGuire calls the 'new atomic age'.

It was as part of US President Eisenhower's 'Atoms for Peace' initiative that the 9,000 dwt nuclear powered NS Savannah was conceived and launched in 1959. Described by him as a 'peace ship', her purpose was to serve as an ambassador for the peaceful use of atomic power. In a statement to the American Congress the administration wrote, "The President seeks no return on this vessel except the goodwill of men everywhere." The operational challenges of nuclear fission saw that goodwill evaporate, but in the new atomic age both goodwill and return are unlikely to be in short supply for ship operators who embrace the technology early.

Game-changing is an overused phrase, but nuclear fusion really is just that. And it is incredibly close. In an industry where ships are expected to have a 25-30 year operational life it is entirely feasible that some sailing today will either be powered themselves, or share the water with sisters running emissionless nuclear fusion reactors. Burning less than 20kg of fuel in a year of operation. It will make shipping genuinely sustainable, both in terms of profitability and environment.

If we truly plan to run the world without burning fossil fuels then it's increasingly clear that with the possible exception of solar power, renewable energy sources are not going to satisfy the demand, or ever be cheap enough to allow us to do so.

For shipping, we are faced with a range of technologies which all have significant limitations, the adoption of which will depend on very specific modes of operation and requirements. Fusion is the only genuinely new energy source we have, and it is not now a case of whether we can do it, but whether we can do it economically.

Considering the investment going into propulsion, LNG, batteries and wind in the maritime space it seems curious that no one is responding to Lockheed Martin's call to arms and calling out fusion as a future solution. This is a technology which is so utterly transformative that we have to be aware of it and preferably supporting its development and application for shipping wherever we can.

And before we categorise it as too expensive, consider the recent IMF estimate regarding the global subsidies being paid to fossil fuel companies. For 2015 it will be approximately $5.3 trillion, equivalent to $10 million every minute of every day. It's greater than the total health spending of all the world's governments, and it makes the cost of ITER or Lockheed Martin's project look like very small change indeed, in return for putting the sun in a box.

During the Allies' dark days of WW2 British Prime Minister Winston Churchill famously promised that victory would mean, "all Europe may be freed and the life of the world may move forward into broad, sunlit uplands." Nuclear technology played a key role in bringing an end to that conflict, and now it looks as though it may do the same for the great global struggle of our generation.

As Lev Artsimovitch, the famous Russian academician and one of the major figures in fusion history, used to say: "Fusion will be ready when society needs it."

Clean, sustainable energy from fusion may seem a utopian prospect, but those broad uplands are in sight. And we aren't going to wait for the sun to shine on them. We're going to take it with us.

London, July 2015.

11

HEART OF THE MATTER

When Germanwings flight 9525 crashed into the Alps on 24th March this year the shock and grief of the loss was immediately followed by speculation as to what could possibly have happened.

In that initial 24-hour period before the events onboard became clear, many press reports chose to focus on the highly automated operation of the Airbus A320, and to what extent it could have played a role in the tragedy. "The A320 is known to be very easy to fly. Actually some pilots even don't like it because it's too easy to fly, it's fully automated and it provides computer assistance to pilots preventing them from overstressing the plane, from slowing down too much. The computer will cut in if you try to make a manoeuvre that might be too extreme," said pilot Marin Medic speaking to one news outlet. "So basically it's kind of a nanny-aircraft. If you make a mistake it will try to catch it and correct it. So as far as basic handling of the aircraft goes it should have been even easier to handle than let's say a classical type like the Boeing."

A plane that goes out of its way to stop you doing something extreme and is very easy to handle is exactly what we all want isn't it? From the original autopilots, to computerised automation that kicked off with the first fly-by-wire aircraft in the 1970s, aviation has been steadily evolving in pursuit of just that aim. But in recent years there have been a growing number of serious questions about the unintended consequences of decades of increasingly sophisticated automation.

Following many experiments and research the evidence is pointing to the fact that our desire to dial down the risk of human pilot error is actually creating a situation where it's becoming more likely.

In recent years the crashes of Air France Flight 447 in the Atlantic, Continental Flight 3407 in Buffalo both in 2009, and Asiana Flight 214 which failed to make a landing in San Francisco in 2013, have all been linked to pilot errors that were related to the automation onboard.

It may sound like a rather simple observation, but what it comes down to is that if you allow the plane to fly itself, pilots get out of practice. Between take-off and touch-down most aircraft these days are flown by the computer and that leads to what Qantas has called 'automation addiction'. Aviation researcher Matthew Ebbatson describes it as 'skill fade', "Flying skills decay quite rapidly towards the fringes of 'tolerable' performance without relatively frequent practice," he says. That becomes a real problem when pilots who are used to sitting back and looking out of the window are suddenly faced with an emergency situation the computer can't cope with.

But the technology that allows planes to fly themselves, cars to drive themselves and will soon allow ships to sail themselves, is not levelling off. Not by a long chalk. The advances in algorithms, connectivity and machine learning means that it is growing at an exponential rate. But it is doing more than automating the work we don't want to do, it is actually altering that work to suit itself.

Take the cars of the 1970's. They broke down. Frequently. Particularly if you had one from British Leyland here in the UK. To set the scene for younger viewers, they also had windows you had to roll by hand, windscreen wipers that sometimes went on a go-slow, and vinyl interiors which adhered themselves like napalm to bare legs on hot summer days.

But these cars differed in a more fundamental way than comfort. These were cars that you could lift the bonnet of, take a look around and actually fix if the need arose. But as computers got better and started to run the car for you, skills like using the choke, double de-clutching and breaking an egg into the radiator to plug up a leak have gone the way of the Dodo. Today the vast majority of cars on the road will simply give you a fault code that it takes another computer to recognise, and some highly skilled technicians to fix. As a result most people stuck at the side of the road will have zero chance of doing anything useful with their car to get it moving again.

Now no one's arguing that the world would be a better place if we still had to break eggs into our car radiators occasionally—there are enough people maintaining classics who are handing down the old ways of the British Leyland Jedi—but there's a wider point here.

The automation we've introduced into our cars, as our aeroplanes, isn't built around supporting the human being. It is designed to supplant the human being wherever possible. The idea that machines are better than humans has been integral in the development of computing and automation from the outset. And the downside of this machine-centred development is beginning to reveal itself in unexpected ways.

In an article for the Wall Street Journal Nicholas Carr describes what happened to the first patient in the US to die during the recent Ebola outbreak. Thomas Eric Duncan presented at the Texas Health Presbyterian Hospital in Dallas but was misdiagnosed, leading to a lack of appropriate treatment which might have saved his life. The misdiagnosis was of course very sad, but the reasons it happened have bigger implications.

According to research published in the journal Diagnosis, the digital templates used by the hospital's clinicians to record patient information may have contributed to a dangerous kind of 'tunnel-vision'. "These highly constrained tools," the researchers write, "are optimised for data capture but at the expense of sacrificing their utility for appropriate triage and diagnosis, leading users to miss the forest for the trees." They conclude that medical software can't be a "replacement for basic history-taking, examination skills, and critical thinking."

The efficiencies that computing has brought to every industry from aviation to healthcare have meant that in most cases the way in which humans work has been altered to make it easier for the machines. And in a double-whammy, by taking away the routine tasks that are often the building blocks of higher cognitive input—taking histories, flying the plane, or plotting courses on a map—we have allowed our skills to atrophy and compromised the very thing that makes us superior to the machine.

When Professor Stephen Hawking made his comments about the inevitable dominance of artificial intelligence over humans they were widely reported. But it isn't the artificial intelligence getting smarter that's the real problem. The real problem is that to date we've voluntarily dumbed down to give it a leg up.

The evidence is showing us that our insistence on building automation around the machine and not the human is not sustainable in the long term. And that's as key for shipping as it is aviation or medicine. Crewless, autonomous ships are on their way, but right now we're entering a highly disruptive interim period when the ships are going to get much smarter, and with relentless speed, and we're still going to have to sail them safely and efficiently.

But in shipping and maritime we have a very different relationship with technology. Airline pilots are well aware that the automated systems on board are there primarily to ensure the safe and efficient operation of the aircraft. As a result they are expected to fully justify any decision to override the automated systems onboard, and can face serious consequences from the airline if they do. Here in shipping, we take a rather more relaxed view. Which quite often takes the form of just switching stuff off.

Ship operators have spent increasing amounts of money on technology solutions both to comply with safety and environment-related mandates and also to improve efficiency and oversight. Privately many are tearing their hair out over the fact that crews just won't use the technology they've been given. Expensive route optimisation software is worthless if the Master decides to head out of port like a scalded cat and sail the ship like it's been stolen until he gets some miles under his belt, then slow down and take it easy.

Admittedly some of this is generational but a lot more of it is about trust. The bottom line is that many crew don't trust the technology they've got on board. In maritime we have a culture of self-reliance which machine-centred automation strategies are having difficulty challenging. And we all know that culture eats strategy for breakfast.

ECDIS is a perfect example of machine-centred automation, perceived by many as something foisted on the industry by the IMO e-maritime agenda, automating the basic functions of the navigator and thereby degrading their historically vital skill set on the bridge.

A brief look at the dozens of different types of ECDIS, each with its own unique interface and logic is instructive. The overwhelming message of ECDIS is that the gubbins inside the box is more important than you are, and if you want to get it out then it's up to you to learn to speak its language.

Humans have accepted that premise in their interactions with technology for some time. It has in part been driven by programmers creating from the machine's perspective, rather than from the human. But there is a new wave of scientists now who are upending the traditional machine-centred model of automation and putting the human at the heart of things instead.

Utilising machines effectively means finding ways to bridge the divide between the physical and tangible and the digital and virtual, allowing us to communicate and work with machines in a way that works for us, first and foremost.

Researchers from Australia's RMIT University have done just that, developing a system that lets drones communicate with air traffic controllers, not via a screen interface, but using a synthesized voice. The system was developed by RMIT in collaboration with Thales Australia's Centre for Advanced Studies in Air Traffic Management (CASIA), and software engineering firm UFA Inc. It utilizes UFA's ATVoice Automated Voice Recognition and Response software, allowing drones to both verbally respond to spoken information requests delivered by radio, and to act on clearances granted by air traffic controllers.

"Our project aimed to develop and demonstrate an autonomous capability that would allow a drone to verbally interact with air traffic controllers," said Dr. Reece Clothier, leader of the RMIT Unmanned Aircraft Systems Research Team.

"Using the system we've developed, an air traffic controller can talk to, and receive responses from a drone just like they would with any other aircraft."

This kind of human-centred automation is not geared to eventually remove humans from the equation, but to optimise the utility of both human and machine. And there are other developments which are going to make that interaction even more human-focussed.

We've written before about SAFFiR, The Shipboard Autonomous Firefighting Robot, a human-sized autonomous robot developed by the US Navy which is capable of finding and suppressing shipboard fires. Whilst it's also designed to work seamlessly with human firefighters, it's not hard to see how—in common with all automation to date—it is also expected at some point and in some circumstances to replace them. But whilst SAFFiR is a remarkable piece of technology, there is another piece of firefighting tech which has been developed not to replace, but to work as an extension of the human.

Called Robot Reins, the small mobile robot—equipped with tactile sensors—will lead the way for firefighters moving through smoke-filled buildings, saving vital seconds by identifying objects and obstacles. Developed by King's College London and Sheffield Hallam University, with funding from the Engineering and Physical Sciences Research Council (EPSRC), the robot not only acts as a pathfinder, but using haptic feedback will send vibrations back through the reins to provide data about the size, shape and even stiffness of any object the robot finds.

This is just one application of haptic technology, the potential of which could be huge in bridging that gap between human and machine. The technology uses an actuator to convert electrical, hydraulic or pneumatic energy into vibrations, which can be managed and controlled by software that determines the duration, frequency, and amplitude. When external forces engage the receptors in our somatosensory system, humans respond to that touch, texture or vibration in a highly-sophisticated way. By translating digital interaction into tactile feedback haptic technology is opening up the possibility of doing away with screens and headgear and making machines touch and speak to us more like we speak to and touch each other.

Consumer products like gaming and even the Apple smartwatch are already making use of this technology, and for us in maritime the potential of haptic feedback for both remote operations and maintenance, and simulation and training could be massive.

Critics of remote operations, autonomy and maintenance often point to the inability of someone on land to feel and experience the swell and movement of a ship at sea. Haptic technology, and in particular a new technique developed by researchers at the University of Bristol using projected ultrasound to directly create floating, 3D shapes that can be seen and felt in mid-air, could change all that.

Building on previous work at the university, the researchers have used an array of ultrasonic transducers to create and focus compound patterns of ultrasound to shape the air at which it was directed.

To make these shapes visible, the manipulated air is directed through a thin curtain of oil and a lamp used to illuminate it. According to the researchers, this results in a system that produces such accurate and identifiable shapes that users can readily match an image of a 3D object to the shape rendered by the prototype ultrasound system.

"Touchable holograms, immersive virtual reality that you can feel and complex touchable controls in free space, are all possible ways of using this system," said Dr Ben Long, Research Assistant from the Bristol Interaction and Graphics (BIG) department at the

University of Bristol. "In the future, people could feel holograms of objects that would not otherwise be touchable, such as feeling the differences between materials in a CT scan or understanding the shapes of artefacts in a museum."

That's pretty clever, but in combination with an algorithm this haptic feedback could be truly revolutionary. Haptic will allow us to feel the digital world, but in combination with an algorithm, it could allow the machine to feel and interpret the physical.

The Robot Reins not only guides the follower and offers tangible feedback, it also senses any hesitation or resistance and adjusts its pace accordingly. This is adaptive automation, using sensors and algorithms to take mental and physical feedback from the human and translate it into a real-time appreciation of the state of the human being that the machine can understand.

Using that knowledge the machine can then decide how much, or how little responsibility to assign to the human, and how much to manage itself—once again in real time. If the system detects that the Master or the pilot is struggling with a difficult procedure it will allocate more tasks to itself to free up the human. But if it senses the human is losing focus or interest it will shift more of the workload back again forcing the human to concentrate their attention on the task and build their skills.

The implications of this adaptive automation are far reaching. It could eventually remove the need for traditional training altogether, allowing crews on flight decks and bridges to be trained and upskilled daily as they go about their tasks.

But perhaps most significantly it would change the machine from being an uncommunicative, inflexible boss, to adding value as part of a team seafarers trust, and in which the machine itself has learnt to trust.

In fact the Robot Reins are already doing just that. Based on the way the human is moving and their previous actions, it is programmed to predict the human's next actions. And using its algorithm, in tests of blindfolded volunteers, it could even successfully detect the human's levels of trust in it.

Of course the Germanwings disaster wasn't the result of error, computer or human, it was something far more wretched.

But it doesn't change the fact that aviation has pushed machine-centred autonomy to a point where it now has to find ways to mitigate the problems that approach has thrown up.

Here in maritime we have a chance to avoid those problems by embracing the potential of human-centred, adaptive autonomy at sea, and building the kind of interdependent trust that is going to characterise successful adoption and management of artificial intelligence in the future.

Machines are getting very smart indeed, but humans must be at the heart of them. They should augment us, not control us. And once we demonstrate that's possible we'll have a chance to build more of the trust amongst seafarers which is badly needed.

And in reality it isn't just a chance, it's a necessity.

London, April 2015.

12

CUTTING THE CORD

If you've never heard of the novel *Nineteen Eighty-Four* by George Orwell, it was written in 1949 and is set in a dystopian world of perpetual war, surveillance and public manipulation overseen by a malevolent presence known as Big Brother. The hero of the book works for the Ministry of Truth which is responsible for propaganda and historical revisionism, and erases all traces of news articles embarrassing to Big Brother by sending them down the 'memory hole' to be incinerated.

The themes of bureaucratic control, surveillance and persecution of individualism and independent thinking mean that the book and its elements are frequently cited today in discussion of how the technology we have so readily adopted, allows others to watch and control us. So it was breathtakingly ironic that in 2009 it should be that very book which suddenly exposed just how radically different the new realities of ownership and control in the digital age had become.

The Amazon Kindle e-reader was still a comparatively new, but reliable product, so Kindle owners who had bought digital copies of *Nineteen Eighty-Four* and another Orwell title *Animal Farm*, were mystified to discover both had suddenly gone missing in the night.

After much consternation and online chatter it rapidly became clear that the same wireless network Amazon used to synchronise books across devices, could also be used to reach into the device and delete the book altogether. Which was precisely what Amazon had done, without reference to the customers who had purchased the titles.

The outrage which followed wasn't lost on Amazon which rapidly realised it had a PR disaster on its hands. "We are changing our systems so that in the future we will not remove books from customers' devices in these circumstances," spokesman Drew Herdner said, but for many it wasn't so much that they promised not to do it again, it was that it was possible in the first place.

From Wikileaks to Edward Snowden recent years have seen a steady stream of stories demonstrating that most of us aren't really aware of the bargain—some might characterise it as a Faustian pact—we're entering into with the companies whose products and platforms we consume. Whether they are monetising our eyeballs or our data, there is a strong movement advocating better understanding amongst consumers about just how these technology companies operate and how the rules of engagement have changed.

The Amazon incident tends to be cited as an example of a greedy monolithic company using the black art of wireless technology to steal goods back from people who had paid for them in full. But that wasn't the whole story.

Amazon had undoubtedly gone about things the wrong way, but the motivation for its actions was sound. Herdner explained that the books had been added to the Kindle store by a company that did not have rights to them, using a self-service function. "When we were notified of this by the rights holder, we removed the illegal copies from our systems and from customers' devices, and refunded customers," he said.

Far from a thief in the night, Amazon's systems were actually allowing it to right a legal wrong it had unwittingly allowed to be perpetrated against the rights owner, in this case the estate of George Orwell. The real criminal here was the vendor which had scanned and digitised copies of the titles without authorisation and then offered them for sale on the Kindle platform.

When those books went AWOL it was the first time that an author's copyright had been enforced by a bookseller in both a retrospective and proactive way. It was a glimpse into the power a corporation had within its own digital ecosystem. It was also a glimpse into the future of regulation which is now coming to fruition.

Post-Snowden there is a lot of pressure from governments and public protection agencies worldwide on the big digital service providers and platforms to help in the fight to keep us all safe. From Facebook using its algorithms to identify potential terrorists on its platform to Twitter proactively closing down accounts which are used to be abusive to others, we are looking to these companies to both police and uphold the law.

It was reported earlier this year that if Facebook was a country it would now be the most populous on earth, so it's no surprise that we're expecting it to enter the family of nations by protecting freedoms and enforcing laws the way our democratically elected governments do.

Where those governments may not have looked far enough ahead though is where devolving that responsibility to democratically unaccountable companies will take them. The bureaucracy which surrounds the creation and maintenance of international and national laws is massive, as is the cost of policing and applying those laws, including the apparatus to levy and collect fines.

What none of that bureaucracy has had the power to do in the past is to stop the laws being broken in the first place. But commercial companies can, and they have already started.

In February of this year a drunken member of US Intelligence was showing off his new drone to a friend when he lost control and crash-landed it onto the White House lawn. Unsurprisingly the White House got a bit windy about the fact that an unauthorised flying vehicle—which could easily have had a payload of explosives, chemical or biological material—had managed to turn up literally on the POTUS doorstep and neither the military, security services nor Bruce Willis in a dirty vest had prevented it.

President Obama went on television to call for greater regulation of drones as America conducted a media autopsy and wrung its hands as to how such a thing could be prevented in the future.

Meanwhile the manufacturer of the drone in question had quietly solved the problem. Within a day or so the company, DJI, revealed that it was to put out an update for its drone operating software system. This update would automatically disable drone flights over Washington D.C. and, for good measure, fence off no-fly zones around more than 10,000 airports across the country.

"We are pushing this out a bit earlier to lead in encouraging responsible flight," said DJI spokesperson Michael Perry. "With the unmanned aerial systems community growing on a daily basis, we feel it is important to provide pilots additional tools to help them fly safely and responsibly."

Unlike Amazon's clumsy attempts back in 2009, DJI's approach is far more evolved. Instead of punishing drone owners by threatening to disable their drones if they don't download the software patch, DJI is bundling it with some new, desirable features. So you don't have to download the software patch now, or tomorrow, but if you choose not to you will miss out on even more new, cool features down the road.

For a fledgling (if you'll excuse the pun) drone industry, in the firing line for closer regulation DJI have taken a sensible step, neutralising potentially damaging PR and demonstrating a responsibility and civic-mindedness that won't do them any harm at all. But what we're witnessing here is just the tip of the iceberg and it could cause a seismic shift in the way shipping, maritime and every other blue industry is regulated.

The pace of technology development and implementation is relentless in maritime and IMO is already showing signs of fatigue. But don't assume that this is an IMO problem; this is a global problem for regulators of all colours.

Most regulators are required to fully examine any areas slated for new legislation, take soundings from industry and other stakeholders and model the impact of new regulations carefully before actually enacting anything. But with the technology that drives the world accelerating in some cases exponentially, the efficacy of this model is failing.

Quite simply, things are now moving so quickly that regulation is rapidly approaching the point where it can no longer do its job—and this point is being referred to as the Bureaucratic Singularity.

"The complexity and ubiquity of technology (and our capacity to hack it) is growing exponentially, while bureaucracy grows arithmetically in response," explains technology pundit Mark Michael Lewis. "In the relationship between these two curves, there reaches a point where technology outpaces bureaucracy. I believe we are at the inflection point in that relationship—we are in the beginnings of The Bureaucratic Singularity."

So what will the impact of the approaching bureaucratic singularity be on maritime? Already several mega-trends are converging to profoundly affect how maritime might be regulated in the future, shifting power, responsibility and opportunity from regulator to platform, service provider and manufacturer.

Connectivity, autonomy and access over ownership models are changing things. Increasingly systems onboard ships are highly integrated and sophisticated to the point where those onboard aren't really qualified to maintain them.

But as connectivity allows manufacturers to monitor, tune and intervene where necessary—remotely and independently—it makes far more sense for both ship operator and supplier if maintenance comes as part of the package. It's mirroring a wider trend for the Millennial and Gen Z'ers, a philosophical desire for access over ownership and a willingness to see the use of products and services as a collaboration rather than a transaction.

For maritime suppliers, moving from a one-off transaction to a service partnership with recurring revenue which allows them to embed deeper customer relationships, is an opportunity. For ship operators there is the chance to eliminate heavy capex and ensure their systems are always running the most up to date software allowing them to operate at maximum efficiency. Over time, and probably less time than we anticipate, the extent to which an asset is really owned will become questionable. We won't so much be talking about owners, as about an ecosystem in which the owner is just one part.

It is this new ownership ecosystem, and it's imminent massive expansion, that may hold the key to how we regulate and enforce in the future. With the internet of things and industrial internet poised to throw billions more physical connected devices online, the ability to effect mass, real-time regulation via the ownership ecosystem will arrive.

If your national laws require you to wear a seatbelt, a software patch from your car manufacturer may prevent the vehicle from starting unless it verified you're wearing one. As part of national infrastructure management, government may decide to mandate thermostat settings or water usage during a drought, which would be instantly enforceable via a home energy platform like Nest or Hive.

For the blue industries the potential of this kind of real-time regulation via prevention holds totally new possibilities. With severe environmental issues facing our oceans sulphur emissions have been identified as a threat which requires regulation. But despite IMO bringing in mandates, not everyone follows them. In fact the problem is so acute that a group of operators has formed the Trident Alliance. According to its members, which include Maersk, Stena, Spliethoff and Hamburger Süd, the threat of weak enforcement of sulphur regulations is escalating fast and the Trident Alliance represents responsible industry taking the initiative to mitigate the threat, on behalf of a healthy environment and a level playing field for operators. It claims that in Europe only one in every 1,000 vessels is tested and of those 50 per cent are found to be in violation.

But in a new ownership ecosystem where connectivity allows us 'perfect knowledge' of who's where on the ocean, and a ship's engines and systems are maintained by several large manufacturers, whose sensors are streaming operational data in real-time, compliance is instant. The required software patch from the appropriate manufacturer will simply prevent the vessel from operating in certain zones unless its emissions are appropriate. Regulation and compliance will be immediate and universal.

Of course there will always be operators who choose not to download the software patch, and who will try and circumvent the rules, but the ownership ecosystem doesn't just include operator and ship's suppliers, it also includes a variety of stakeholders who will be able to see the data coming off the ship in order to monitor its own interests.

From financial institutions checking that the ship isn't breaking any sanctions areas or carrying cargo it shouldn't, to insurers checking that the vessel is being operated in compliance, to flag, class and port state control, the ecosystem around the vessel will grow so integrated that it will end up being far more trouble to try and evade it than to get on with things. In short, if you want the money to buy a vessel and an insurer to cover it, you won't have much choice but to make sure you're being regulated and complying in real-time.

This model could see the costs involved in monitoring compliance and bringing transgressors to book, fall significantly. Which raises another question. If that's the case, then shouldn't IMO be looking at driving the uptake of just this kind of technology? With shipping a huge part of the blue economy what wider benefits could a model which accelerated regulation and compliance have?

But sharp-eyed readers will also have identified another issue here. The manufacturer in the ecosystem may act as a proxy regulator, ensuring compliance with existing mandates, but there's nothing to stop it going far further. Like DJI and its drone software patch, maritime suppliers could take the public temperature on an issue and decide to get ahead of the legislation.

If a major marine accident caused environmental damage the owner ecosystem and its stakeholders may decide not to wait ten years for new regulations from IMO, but update its systems to prevent a recurrence. And perhaps of more concern, if the industry believes the regulation is a bad one, the ownership ecosystem may well choose not to comply.

There's a saying amongst futurists which reminds us that the future isn't somewhere we go, it's something we create. The mega-trends underlying these scenarios are already there, but how maritime decides to capitalise on them is still very much up to us.

Regulation is about to be disrupted by the digital age in shipping and everywhere else, and we should be alert to the dangers of that. IMO, for all its faults, has been a constant for shipping for a long time and for many the idea that regulation and enforcement should devolve to suppliers, and owners and be guided not just by industry experts but by public expectation—essentially the crowd—is scary. But in many respects it's not revolution but evolution.

Regulation has always been characterised by red tape, and so far digital has only really changed that from tape to cable. But we are already seeing the birth of what promises to be a new culture of collaborative regulation where our responsibilities are not to a regulator, but to each other.

The opportunities for maritime are there, if we can find the courage to cut the cord.

London, April 2015.

13

THE COOKIE CRUMBLES

When Apple's new iWatch went on sale recently the consensus from commentators seemed to be that whilst it was very nice, it just wasn't something anyone really needed. But the iWatch is already proving very useful indeed, and not for telling the time.

In early April Manulife Financial Corp.'s John Hancock Life Insurance announced that it would discount premiums by as much as 15 per cent for policy holders who tracked and performed well on metrics such as daily exercise, annual health screenings and flu shots. "We want to make life insurance more immediate and relevant in the daily lives of our policyholders and help them connect their financial well-being to their long-term health," John Hancock President Michael Doughty said in a statement.

But Hancock wasn't going to blithely hand out discounts to customers on the basis of their own activity reporting. The deal came with a Fitbit wearable fitness tracker which monitored every step its customers took. A month down the line with the launch of the Apple watch the insurer has already moved from a mere step tracker to an app which allows customers to use the Apple Watch, iPhone and iPod Touch to meet the health-tracking requirements of the insurance policy.

The app allows policyholders to post and view their points and status, earn points by submitting prevention screenings and athletic events, and log health club workouts. It also integrates with Apple's HealthKit so that participants can complete their health review via the app, which itself gathers data from the Apple Watch—including real-time steps.

The whole idea of your insurance company having intimate, near real-time knowledge of your exercise and activity habits might make you very uncomfortable. But if it does then the chances are you're not a Millennial, or one of the subsequent generational cohort, Gen Z.

For those generations the idea that data—and your own in particular—is a currency you can use to purchase goods and services either discounted or for free, is already deeply embedded. The combination of this digital native mindset, connectivity, and advances in a variety of technologies are colliding to fundamentally reinvent the way that we evaluate and manage risk, and the consequences will be wide-ranging for individuals and businesses, on land and at sea.

In 1960 a movie called *The Apartment* was released. It stars Jack Lemmon as CC Baxter who opens the film by telling us that he works on the 19th floor, Ordinary Policy Department, Premium Accounting Division, Section W, Desk number 861, for an insurance company called Consolidated Life of New York. Baxter's character is obsessed with the kind of statistics which have traditionally allowed actuaries to analyse and understand the cost of risk, and quotes them frequently.

But whilst these statistics have provided the bedrock of the practice of insurance, they have always been broad and often blunt tools. The shortcomings of Baxter's statistics are pointed out to him by the girl he's in love with. She tells him she never catches colds to which Baxter replies that according to figures from the Sickness Accident Claims Division the average New Yorker between the ages of twenty and fifty has two and a half colds a year. "That makes me feel just terrible," she responds. "To make the figures come out even, if I have no colds a year, some poor slob must have five colds a year."

In essence everyone who's ever been insured to date has been paying for the poor slob. But in the past 10 to 15 years advances in computing power and the proliferation of new digital data sources means that insurers are moving beyond the core actuarial disciplines of advanced maths and financial theory and opening up a new paradigm.

The core data for insurers used to be internal—claims histories for example. But third-party data sources have expanded massively, with previously inaccessible public-sector data now available and both the EU, UK and US governments launching open data websites containing huge datasets of statistics around health, education, safety, energy usage and much more. Add to that the constant streams of 'exhaust data' from social media, multimedia, smartphones, computers and other consumer and industrial devices, and the landscape of behavioural insight alters completely.

But as Hancock's policy shows, advances in our technological ability to monitor and visualise in real-time may disrupt the way we approach risk the most. Hancock is in health, but in car insurance the trend towards Usage Based Insurance (UBI) and telematics has been steadily growing. Using increasingly small and sophisticated devices inside the car insurers are monitoring the real-time driving habits of their policyholders. That means that instead of you paying for what the poor slob might do, you're saving money based on what you're actually doing.

It is a fundamental shift both in the way risk is evaluated and also of the relationship between us and those who insure us. And what's particularly interesting is the influence of this new, real-time relationship on driving habits. According to McKinsey one UK insurer offering telematics-based policies has demonstrated that monitoring leads to better driving which has led directly to a 30 per cent reduction in the number of claims. Another reports having used telematics to enable a large client to reduce accident-causing risky manoeuvres by a stunning 53 per cent.

The underlying mega-trend here is what's been called 'perfect knowledge'. Connectivity, the Internet of Everything, advances in computing power, machine learning, algorithms, the falling cost of microprocessors and the ability of technology like GE's Direct Write to ink sensors on the parts other technology cannot reach, means we are creating a world where in future we can know everything about anything immediately and accurately. At least, that's the idea.

As the sci-fi writer William Gibson pointed out, the future is here, it's just not very evenly distributed. And one place where that future is particularly patchy is the blue domain.

"Man marks the earth with ruin; his control stops with the shore," wrote Lord Byron in his poem *The Ocean* in the early nineteenth century. And despite the advent of deep sea satellite communications in the twentieth century, that control—and crucially knowledge—to a large extent still stopped at the shore until comparatively recently.

I've written in depth before about how profound and fundamental an enabler connectivity at sea has become. (Read our connectivity issue of July 2014). The proliferation of communications technologies from HTS systems like Intelsat's EPIC and Inmarsat's GX to nanosats from companies like Google, Spire and Space X are seeing the future distributed far more evenly across the oceans than ever before.

The lesson is that digital operation and connectivity breeds transparency and that's exactly what's happening in maritime right now. The flows of what I describe as Blue Data are vast and increasing, and they are offering the opportunity of unprecedented insight, knowledge and advantage. The future is spreading fast.

The early-adopters seizing the opportunity however, aren't shipping and maritime companies per se. Those leveraging the insight this data can give them are different stakeholders. But when it comes to transparency they've got considerable skin in the game.

Following the financial crash banks and other institutions have been subject to an increased level of scrutiny, and not just around their financial health and viability. Focus has also fallen on other risk, including corruption, money-laundering and compliance with global sanctions. Considering it transports 90 per cent of world trade the shipping industry has remained stubbornly opaque, using its complex ownership and operation structure to defy the kind of transparency commonplace in other industries.

But perfect knowledge breeds a new kind of expectation and the new availability of maritime data and insight means that those who make money from the sea aren't going to be able to use ignorance as a defence in the future.

Earlier this year speaking at an anti-money laundering conference Adam Szubin, director of the U.S. Treasury Department's Office of Foreign Assets Control said that big potential sanctions risks may lurk within the business operations of securities firms and reinsurers. Omnibus accounts, he went on to tell his audience, which combine the transactions of multiple parties, pose a risk for securities firms if they don't know whose assets they are holding. "We often speak to companies who are reinsuring ships where they don't know who the operators are and they certainly don't know what cargo is being carried," said Szubin.

Pointing out that opaque lines of business have proven to be a big compliance challenge for companies, he had this warning, "I urge you all to think carefully: what in your business lines do you see as those black boxes? That's typically where the threat is going to come from."

And the threat to institutions from regulators is also growing as post-financial crisis there has been a new toughness of approach. Under Benjamin Lawsky the relatively obscure New York Department of Financial Services suddenly showed its teeth in 2012 by threatening Standard Chartered Bank—accused of laundering money for countries including Iran—with revocation of its New York banking license without which it could not operate.

With that kind of repercussion on the horizon it's little wonder that financial institutions, traders and insurers would be first in line to sign up for platforms which leverage blue data flows to deliver transparency and knowledge. And they're funding them too. As we went to press it was reported that Israeli company Windward had secured $10.8m in investment from Horizons Ventures amongst others in order to, "accelerate Windward's ability to build the largest, most comprehensive maritime data and analytics platform in history."

That's a big claim from a company you might well never have heard of, but Windward's intelligence solution, MARINT, is apparently already in wide use by security, intelligence and law enforcement agencies worldwide, who use its data and insights to pre-emptively identify threats before they reach their shores.

Windward has taken datasets including 'port agent reports and ship bookings' together with either the past two, or four years worth—depending on which report you read—of AIS data for more than 200,000 ships, plus cargo reports, ownership data and twenty five years of 'ship economics research' according to Ami Daniel, Founder and CEO, mashed it up and allowed its algorithm to go to work. The result is individual ship profiles which allow Windward to identify which vessels may warrant further investigation by the authorities.

Windward has also been aggressively denouncing the unreliability of AIS data, putting out a report claiming that ships on average report their final destination only 41 per cent of the time, 55 per cent of ships misrepresent their port of call or nearby port, for most of their voyage, and that over the past two years GPS manipulation has risen sharply by 59 per cent.

Its platform addresses this by, "checking every transmission on the bit and byte level and cross checking identities, geographical movements and economic profiles globally and historically," Michal Chafets, its Director of Communications is quoted as saying. "Together, this creates a PayPal-like fraud entity resolution and fraud detection technology that vets the AIS data."

If accurate Windward's estimate that around one per cent of all global shipping is up to no good and deliberately trying to throw everyone off the scent means it's little wonder that since launch five years ago Windward has secured government and security services as customers. But as ever stricter IMO mandates begin to bite and stakeholders including banks and cargo owners increase their CSR scrutiny, top tier operators themselves are beginning to demand greater transparency to address their own risk.

Take the Trident Alliance for example, a coalition of owners and operators collaborating to bring about more robust enforcement of sulphur regulations which are raising costs for them and providing those who don't comply with a cost-advantage. According to the alliance only one of every 1,000 vessels in Europe currently gets tested and of those around half are in violation of the sulphur regulations. The Maritime Anti-Corruption Network (MACN) is another example where operators, cargo owners and suppliers are working together towards the vision of a maritime industry free of corruption that enables fair trade for the benefit of society at large.

Both organisations are focussed on transparency that can provide a level operational playing field. New initiatives like the $12.5m EfficienSea2 project—which aims to develop a range of new digital services including automatic ship emission reporting and monitoring—are an example of how this transparency might be delivered in the future, but that's part of a far wider ecosystem developing at sea.

Pioneering connectivity suppliers like KVH are creating new platforms enabling products and services to be delivered and structured in new ways, and data transmitted and accessed far more widely. At the same time there is a revolution in how some of the most humble products are being approached. It is almost incomprehensible to many outside the industry that until recently the Voyage Data Recorder (VDR) onboard was subject to twelve hour overwrites, but the new standard has formed a jumping-off point for innovative manufacturers like Danelec. Its next-generation product includes features such as playback software for real-time monitoring and replay of recorded data, together with data capture and analysis.

We are rapidly approaching a situation where the availability of maritime domain and ship specific data will be available in real-time to a wide variety of stakeholders, and whilst that should enhance security, safety and efficiency it will also expose operators to a potentially disturbing new reality. Like those policyholders checking their Apple iWatches and desperately jogging their way to a fifteen per cent discount on their life insurance premium, ship operators may discover that the availability and quality of their operational data becomes pivotal.

In the same way that car insurers are taking real-time data from their drivers, marine insurers could sometime soon have access to a rich set of data streams that will allow them—if they're given access—to know exactly where a ship is and where it's headed, what it's carrying, who's on board, how healthy they are, how much fuel the ship is burning, whether the engines are being operated in compliance with the manufacturers recommendations, whether the systems on board have been appropriately maintained, whether the ship is transmitting the correct identification data, whether its network and systems are secured, whether its emissions are appropriate, whether its charts and software is up to date, whether the crew hold the appropriate tickets and training, whether the spares it's carrying are authentic and exactly how much that ship is worth on that particular day in any currency they choose.

For those operators for whom operating beyond compliance is the norm, policies based on a transparent usage model could well prove highly attractive, but they could do something else too. By demanding transparency they would not just level the playing field, they could actually tip the balance in favour of responsible operators. The ones everyone wants at sea.

If the experience of this kind of data-led insurance ashore is replicated on vessels then the impact could be significant. In short the opportunity would exist to actually incentivise and reward positive behaviour by ship operators with reduced premiums whilst starting to raise the barriers to entry into the industry for those who currently operate non-compliant or otherwise unsafe ships.

The likelihood is that we would quickly see a two-tier industry develop, with those able to demonstrate a positive dynamic risk profile and those who can't or won't. Ultimately your ability to insure your vessel at all might well depend upon the real-time data you're able to produce.

In fact we've already started down that kind of road. A recent survey by the Carbon War Room found that vessel efficiency rankings such as the A to G GHG Emission Rating developed by vetting company RightShip now form an important part of assessing risk and return in several banks, with inefficient vessels now representing a higher-risk investment.

Energy efficiency data is also being used in credit-approval processes for vessel purchases, loan assessments for retrofit projects and re-sell of scrapping decisions, with banks citing efficiency as a key indicator for a vessel's profitability.

"Banks are now publically stating that they use energy efficiency data in deciding which vessels will receive financing and which ones won't," says José Maria Figueres, Chair of the Board for Carbon War Room and Rocky Mountain Institute. "As this trend continues, inefficient ships will become increasingly unmarketable."

"As a consequence of the correlation of energy efficiency and loan risk we have analysed our shipping portfolio based on the methodology of the EEDI and implemented design efficiency criteria in our credit approval process," confirms Carsten Wiebers, Global Head of Maritime Industries at KfW IPEX-Bank. "In view of the beneficial risk profile and environmental benefits we favour eco-ships over ships with poorer energy efficiency."

This incorporation of efficiency data into financing decisions is seen by the CWR at least as an indication of a dramatic market shift in recent years with banks saying they've seen the formation of a two-tier market comprising high and low efficiency vessels. Eco efficient vessels demand a premium price at new build stage, are more likely to be chartered, maintain asset value over time and have a longer lifespan. "We see a clear trend towards a two-tier market of high and low efficiency vessels—more energy efficient vessels have an enhanced marketability as well as a higher revenue potential for the ship owner and thus a more favourable risk profile for financiers," says Figueres.

The two-tier market in efficiency is beginning to be positively reinforced too. In 2014 three ports— Port Metro Vancouver, Port of Prince Rupert and Port of Barbados—began to use the A to G rating to offer financial incentives to the owners of more efficient vessels entering their ports, and now twenty five per cent of the non-container charter market vet potential vessels for efficiency before charter. But that's just one metric. Where the insurance market could go involves not just the value of the asset but the way it's operated, day after day.

Simply having an efficient vessel by design is as blunt a risk measure as being of one gender or another. When it comes to your risk you're still paying for the poor slobs with five colds per year, even if they're more sustainable colds that burn fewer bunkers.

That data on its own is a start but it only scratches the surface of the rich insight that the vast datasets we'll soon be able to access about ships and shipping could give us. RightShip has been at the leading edge of just this kind of insight for some time and so it's no surprise that it's also leading on potentially the greatest disruptor—prediction.

Speaking recently at a conference in Australia RightShip chief Warwick Norman described how the company is beginning to move from reactionary to predictive vetting and using IBM predictive analytics to help them. In the process it's turning up some counterintuitive insights, particularly with regard to age versus incidence. Tankers are likely to be far safer than other vessel types, but newer vessels aren't necessarily the ones with the lowest risk profile.

It's insights like these that could rewrite the way we insure ships. And that has massive implications for the P&I Clubs. If it's correct, as one source tells me, that the maritime insurance industry hasn't made a profit in the last seventeen years, then it isn't coming a day too soon. Certainly there's at least one P&I Club actively working on a predictive risk model and rumours of many more similar projects in different stakeholders around that same predictive analytics theme.

I stuck my neck out back in October and identified prediction and autonomy as the two trends which were likely to have the most profound impact on the blue industries, but even I've been surprised at how fast that's happening.

Windward's current business may be in maritime domain security but its new funding is designed to support its expansion into different territory, enabling it to expand its deep learning capabilities via its data platform called 'the Windward Mind' and to operationalise FORESEA, its finance solution. Currently in beta testing FORESEA is the first significant vertical extension of the Windward Mind and according to the company is providing traders, investors and analysts with access to unprecedented amounts of unstructured data, critical insights and untapped market opportunities.

"The Windward Mind, the world's first maritime data platform, brings cross-vertical and industry visibility into ship activity worldwide that is critical given the economics at stake," said Ami Daniel, co-Founder and CEO of Windward. Tom Glocer, the former CEO of Thomson Reuters, who will also be joining Windward's Advisory Board took up the same theme. "Windward is a game changer because it is bringing a data sciences perspective to today's maritime data and making it accessible and relevant for the entire ecosystem," Glocer said in a press release. "Financial institutions, the next market for Windward's unique data platform, are hungry for advanced data solutions that can provide valuable trading opportunities by extracting faint trading signals from noisy datasets such as maritime information."

But Windward has some stiff competition when it comes to bringing data science to bear in the blue domain. Warwick Norman at RightShip is leveraging predictive analytics for insurers. This issue's Futurenaut Richard Rivlin's company VesselsValue can now predict the long term value of a vessel. Former Futurenaut Paul Østergaard has developed the Shipserv Match engine that predicts which suppliers are the best fit for your procurement needs based on fifteen years of transaction data on the platform. And what about Xeneta, busily disrupting the $200bn sea-freight industry?

"Predictive is such a huge topic but we are talking to data scientists about how to pull in external sources," says Xeneta CEO and founder Patrik Ølstad Berglund. "We have a German based investor and in their portfolio is Risk Methods who have a dataset we could potentially match with ours which is collecting loads of different data streams to notify you about risks in your supply chain." And whereas Windward may be building a platform, it doesn't appear on the surface to have the proprietary and extremely valuable datasets the likes of VesselsValue, ShipServ and Xeneta have been growing, on which predictive algorithms can be let loose to generate really game-changing insights.

"Predictive opens up hedging and derivatives," says Berglund. "I want to get to the point where we don't report averages any more but that we show the spread—the high and low of a particular carrier—and project what can we expect of its development into the future. Then you can also project/predict that carriers' revenues, and give that intelligence to banks handing out loans to carriers. Who is the most solid? Who has most contracts moving into the future at the highest average price? All kinds of analytics we can leverage the data for to give access to other stakeholders ultimately aside than those mostly focussed on how it can benefit the buying and selling side of the industry."

There are a lot of people who really don't like the idea of an industry exposed to this level of scrutiny, but one suspects that often stems from a real fear about where monitoring, analysis and insight is taking us and what it means for the opaque, murky world some operators thrive in. The reality is though that we need this new transparency and collaboration in order to manage entirely new kinds of risk.

It's been cited often that autonomous, crewless vessels will be impossible because no one will insure them. But the rise of autonomous systems, whether there are crew on board or not, are already creating new areas of risk and responsibility we have to manage. When software and systems are effectively running the ship where do the lines of responsibility of manufacturer, crew, operator and owner get drawn? Shall we see manufacturers having to cover the risk of collateral damage should their own machinery or software fail on board? As cyber-security becomes ever more pivotal could connectivity suppliers find themselves with more responsibility to end-users of the network?

Crucially, how will the responsibilities of the humans on board ships change as more autonomous systems are introduced? It can't be long before the operation of the complex systems on board will be beyond the ultimate control of the Master. Is it reasonable then to assign him or her ultimate responsibility?

These questions will need to be answered, and the insight we require in order to do so adequately resides in the massive data flows we're on the brink of harnessing. And if connectivity is the key to making usage based insurance work then in the same way that car insurers are providing low cost telematics boxes, it may well be that marine insurers realise it's time they did the same.

The insights they stand to gain could cover everything from crew health and welfare via quantifiable health monitoring, to cyber hygiene, competence, machinery health and the comparative safety of autonomous systems and the human element.

That level of deep insight would enable hitherto unimaginable analysis of real-time dynamic risk, and a correspondingly smart insurance industry that reinforced the positive, sustainable operations we're all calling for. And if the data demonstrated that autonomous, crewless ships were a better risk we could even find insurers taking evidence-based decisions to be in the vanguard of moves to cover them, in preference to ones with crew onboard.

But these huge datasets and the predictive analytics we could bring to bear on them aren't just important for risk. They could also lead to entirely new sources of competitive advantage for operators. Not only could insights enable shipping companies to identify potential customers far more accurately, in the future they might just allow us to read the market well enough that we can put ships where our customers need them, before they know themselves.

I put the idea to Xeneta's Berglund, "If you had enough transactional data, you could actually do that. If you had all the booking and all the cargo movements in the world, and we're collecting contract data, AIS data, so if you knew where cargoes moved you could see patterns in that for certain periods—more cargo from India to NW Europe at certain times of the year—and you could start doing predictive analysis on that. You could predict that in two months time there's going to be more volume coming out of Vietnam or Thailand and you could get vessels in the right place. I think it's a fascinating idea."

We're living through the last days of the old risk paradigm, the fortune cookie era when the insight we needed was locked away and all too frequently we only understood the risk in retrospect when things got broken. The technologies delivering perfect knowledge and the power of prediction are already causing seismic shifts to the extent that they are disrupting risk itself. They will change, and probably make, fortunes for many in maritime.

But no matter how powerful the stochastic capabilities of our algorithms, we shouldn't forget that the future isn't somewhere we go, it's something we create, and nothing is going to change that anytime soon.

As CC Baxter would say, that's just the way it crumbles. Cookiewise.

London, April 2015.

14

NERVOUS SYSTEM

I recently gave the keynote address at a conference in London. My keynotes generally don't pull any punches and, with an audience closely involved in implementing a key item on the maritime technology-agenda, this one didn't either.

Having covered the mega-trends and emerging technologies that were going to shape the industry—from AI and 3D printing to the expectations of Millennial Gen Y and the upcoming Gen Z crew and employees—I put the argument that autonomous ships with few or no crew were inevitable in certain sectors. And that as part of a hyper-connected, collaborative industry approach, they provided a real chance to finally reduce the rate of accidents and fatalities in shipping that has remained stubbornly high for decades.

The job of a keynote should be to get people energised and challenged and to be a little bit provocative. So I was expecting some tougher questions and more entrenched views than I got.

It was clear that there were a small but significant number of attendees who were really keen to hear these arguments being made, and they said so. And when you're given the premise that shipping has fatality rates ten times OECD best practice, and 85 per cent of accidents are caused by human factors which smart technology could mitigate, it's hard to argue.

But I wish those silent dissenters had argued. Instead, over the course of the day as speakers came and went and the audience debated what had been said, one by one attendees cited warnings about the dire potential for danger and disaster at sea driven by technology adoption. They expressed a subtle but confident belief that the technology mega-trends that were going to affect humanity weren't going to change seafarers, ships or regulators in maritime. And one by one, their colleagues reinforced those prejudices.

The result was that by the end of the day the premise with which the conference opened, namely that the intelligent deployment of technology offered a once in a generation opportunity to make shipping safer, had been entirely overturned.

The day closed with a solid consensus that shipping had spent a very long time creating the safe environment it currently enjoyed and that technology was eroding the skills and knowledge which was essential to keeping seafarers, ships and the environment, safe.

It was in many respects a fascinating thing to witness. This roomful of experienced and intelligent maritime professionals, despite being provided with statistical evidence that shipping was incredibly unsafe, that human factors were responsible for that, and that technology could and should be used to mitigate it, managed to persuade themselves and each other, that it was the technology which was dangerous. The consensus they reached was irrational, but very human. Understanding why they reached it, and how we can help to prevent it on an industry-wide basis is one of the most urgent issues shipping faces.

A few years ago the results of a study by researchers at the Karolinska Institute in Stockholm, Sweden was published in the British Journal of Cancer. It was one of those stories which the media—and particularly the British media—loves. The researchers reported that the daily consumption of that great British staple, a fry-up, increased your risk of pancreatic cancer by 20 per cent. Naturally, most people listened to this news over breakfast, whilst nose to nose with the smoked bacon and oozing snagger on its way to establish an intestinal beach-head from where it was destined ultimately to wreak a horrible revenge on their soft, innocent, pink underbelly.

Headlines warned us that even a bacon sandwich a day was going to get us that 20 per cent closer to a cancer which is not only almost symptomless in the early stages, but also very difficult to treat, and therefore has one of the higher mortality rates. Little wonder then that the reports made a big impact and even now, three years on, the idea that sausages or a bacon sandwich will increase your risk of cancer is still widely accepted and referenced.

But what did that report really tell us? According to official figures approximately five in every 400 people develop pancreatic cancer, so if all 400 ate a fry up every day the number of people developing cancer would increase by 20 per cent—from five people to six people. But the absolute risk of contracting pancreatic cancer has only risen from five in 400 to six in 400—a risk of 0.25 per cent. Or here's the way it could have been reported but would never have been; that the number of people who do not get pancreatic cancer has gone from 395 to 394.

The other thing that the reports didn't tell you was that if the stress of deciding whether or not to chow down on a bacon sarnie or hot dog makes you light up a fag, then your risk of all cancers, including pancreatic, goes through the roof.

In an increasingly complex world we human beings have little choice but to rely on the data and statistics from researchers, regulators and governments, and follow the advice and policy derived from them. Despite these statistics being carefully researched and mathematically unassailable however, they still don't always help us understand the world and what's risky in it.

The statistician Hans Rosling is famous for having pointed out that the average Swede doesn't have two legs. Thanks to those with one, or none, the population as a whole has an average of 1.9999999 legs. There are other things that are statistically correct but which you may not know, like that the safest year of your life is when you're seven. Or that the radiation a CT scan exposes you to is as dangerous as being a mile from the Hiroshima bomb.

Now you may not have been aware of the risk attached to a CT scan, but most people will mitigate that new knowledge with the confidence that your treating physician will. Your physician is therefore going to make that risk evaluation for you, balancing the medical advantage that scan will provide against its potential dangers.

But now you do know, you might well decide to just mention it if you're referred for a CT scan, even though the risk of that exposure causing you health problems is statistically extremely low. Which demonstrates another real problem with risk—even accurate statistics won't persuade human beings of the real level of risk if they've persuaded themselves otherwise, and conversely, will sometimes encourage them to expose themselves to even greater risk.

Proof of this comes in the study which followed the aftermath of the 9/11 terrorist attacks in the US. People didn't want to travel by plane, which led to a leap in the number of road miles driven of around 5 per cent. According to estimates the increase in car travel and therefore road traffic accidents meant that 1,600 people died on America's roads as a result of the 'understandable' bias against flying. That's six times more people than died on the hijacked planes themselves.

That 'understandable' bias is also responsible for the fact that many of us with teenage sons, and particularly daughters, have a second job as a taxi service, ferrying our offspring to and from parties, cinemas etc. Statistically the likelihood of your daughter being attacked or abducted are vanishingly small, but it's a risk most of us aren't prepared to take, even though actually putting her in a car and driving on public roads is comparatively far riskier to her life and limb.

David Spiegelhalter is the Winton Professor of the Public Understanding of Risk at Cambridge University and he spoke to the Daily Telegraph about why. "You're troubled by what we call the asymmetry of regret," he said. Statistically, the chances of your child being harmed are minuscule but because you value her so much, you're haunted by the potential nightmare of being the unlucky one.

If you know the data, but still feel justified in ignoring it – perhaps because it's a risk to what you hold most dear – then who's to say you're wrong?"

When asymmetry of regret results in a few extra quid in petrol and some late-night excursions in the car, in the grand scheme of things maybe it's no biggie. In fact that visceral, gut reaction to evaluating risk serves a very specific and useful purpose for human beings.

We generally use rules of thumb called heuristics, to enable us to take quick and instinctive decisions. When you catch a ball you don't use mathematical equations to calculate the trajectory of the falling ball, you use intuition and heuristics. If you tried then life would become impossibly complex.

Unfortunately impossibly complex is exactly what technology is making the world, and whereas heuristics are great for catching balls, and a whole host of other things, when it comes to evaluating risk we need a far more comprehensive approach to analysing the probabilities and outcomes of a given situation.

When that situation involves something which we have an instinctive reaction to, it becomes extremely hard. Artificial Intelligence is exactly that. The idea of a driverless car, or bus, or ship challenges us at an emotional level, and how that impacts our decision making and estimates of risk is an important issue, yet one which has rarely been considered among those who manage risk professionally.

Take the British Royal Navy's nuclear submarines for example. One of the most complex engineering achievements known to man it has a unique combination of potential hazards in a relatively small space. These include structural and environmental issues common to all large ships, underwater stability plus nuclear propulsion, explosives and, in the case of the deterrent submarine, nuclear weapons.

The Royal Navy undertakes a rigorous risk assessment of these submarines evaluating the risk of a sailor falling into the sea alongside nuclear accident. The 'As Low As Reasonably Practicable' (ALARP) principle is deployed to continually reduce risk from each potential hazard, until the cost of further effort would be grossly disproportionate to the extra safety achieved.

But in practice, despite the comparative risk of nuclear accident being far lower, it attracts a disproportionate response.

"Far greater resources are devoted to managing nuclear safety than for other potential submarine hazards with the same risk assessment," confirms Admiral Nigel Guild.

"This is required by a public expectation of far greater risk reduction for a potential nuclear hazard, because it is not generally understood and it is held in significant dread." Admiral Guild goes on,

"To take a non-nuclear example, the risk of a seamanship accident, such as falling into the sea while working on the casing when the submarine is on the surface, is assessed in a similar way to any workplace potential hazard. In contrast to this, a potential nuclear event requires risk mitigation to achieve two orders of magnitude smaller risk assessment than would be sought for conventional risks.

Another way of expressing this is by applying the ALARP principle: the effort required before it would be considered grossly disproportionate to the extra nuclear safety achieved is about 100 times more than for other risks."

Thanks to a lack of public understanding and the 'dread risk' nature of the technology, asymmetry of regret leads the Royal Navy to invest 100 times more effort in mitigating the risk of nuclear accident than any other. So this isn't really about safety, it's about perception.

In a classic study, George Loewenstein developed the 'risks as feeling' hypothesis, identifying that there are numerous emotionally-driven factors that help to explain how human beings react to risky situations. One of them is the vividness with which these outcomes can be described or represented mentally.

Stop for a moment and consider the images which come immediately to mind when you read the word nuclear. If that list doesn't include mushroom clouds, burning winds, birth deformities, and an invisible deadly radiation threat then you're in a very small minority.

Now see what comes to mind when you read the words robo-ship, droneship, crewless or cyberthreat. Chances are that those images will be mostly negative too and largely drawn from everything from the Terminator movies to legends like the Marie Celeste. But almost none of you will actually be reacting based on any experience of the technology involved.

"We feel more threatened by certain kinds of risks – ones that are unfamiliar or little understood, that we have no control over – and because we rely heavily on our own experiences and trusted recommendations, we tend to stick with decisions that make no numerical sense," says David Spiegelhalter.

And that lack of control is where autonomy is really pushing our buttons. Nuclear is bad enough because if we get it wrong the consequences could be terrible. But autonomous technology can get it wrong all by itself—by definition we aren't in control—or at least not in the sense that we are evolutionarily accustomed to. But despite our visceral reaction to it, autonomy is far less likely to fail than humans, and that's happening with fatal results at sea every single day.

The speed with which shipping and maritime embraces the technology opportunity is frequently cited as being down to one thing—policy and regulation. The delegates in London comforted themselves and each other that COLREGs would put the kibosh on autonomous ships, and sorting that out on its own would take IMO years to deal with.

In fact having launched the e-nautic agenda with e-navigation and mandatory carriage of ECDIS, a catalyst for technology-adoption within shipping, IMO has now taken its foot off the gas completely. With no new policy or working groups underway the IMO e-navigation drive—a necessary precursor to more sophisticated technologies including autonomy—has fizzled out.

The autonomous ship, like the truck and car is going to be one of the greatest changes for humankind but by not engaging with it in shipping yet IMO is storing up trouble for itself. When interviewed by Bloomberg on the subject of unmanned ships in 2013 an

IMO spokesperson said that IMO hadn't received any proposals on unmanned, remote-controlled ships, and yet we know categorically that they are in development, and that flag states and class societies are involved.

The fact that IMO apparently isn't could be an indication that they are dangerously out of touch with how fast technology is moving in shipping, or perhaps worse, that the innovators involved—from manufacturers to class and flag—believe that IMO involvement could be prejudicial to the adoption of the technology in the industry.

But although flag, class and manufacturer will play a huge part in technology development and adoption there is still a need for authority, policy and importantly, clarity around the implementation of this technology. That role is one which should absolutely be filled by IMO, but if it isn't already grasping the mettle then on current performance we could be looking at 15 years before any useful clarity or policy emerges. And that is just going to be too late.

In that time the vacuum could be filled by the development of a multi-tier shipping industry where one tier adheres to basic IMO compliance and the top tier begins to use technology to develop structures where it effectively regulates itself (see our *Cutting the Cord* article for more detail).

As DNV GL's Tor Svensen told us in his interview last issue, we have developed a system where a ship can be certified to travel all over the world. Disrupting that without a real plan for what replaces it could have far-reaching consequences not just for shipping but for global trade itself.

There are those who privately wonder whether that might not be a good thing, and that IMO has had its day. But IMO is in a unique position to make a powerful contribution to the way we approach technology and risk perception in the industry, if it can establish between us and it what researchers describe as 'critical trust'.

We need to be able to rely on IMO as an institution to manage risk, whilst retaining a critical attitude to its effectiveness, motivations and independence. But IMO must earn that critical trust. Its bedrock has to be a deep understanding of the issues and the technology it seeks to regulate.

Nothing has come out of IMO in recent years which gives any indication that there is a broad grasp of the pace, sophistication or complexity of the technology being developed, and far less how its implications will impact maritime stakeholders. The longer that situation—or perception—goes uncorrected, the more our trust in IMO to successfully regulate will be eroded.

Deep knowledge of the technology landscape is only one part though. The other is in how IMO communicates and influences the narrative on technology. Part of the reason that Futurenautics was born was to counter the accepted standard of technology reporting in the maritime sphere. Real investigative reporting of technology is almost non-existent, and too often shaped by the insular prejudices of the industry. As a result many shipping folk responded to Rolls-Royce's intervention on autonomous ships as merely a publicity stunt to improve its profile.

It shouldn't take a manufacturer—even one as innovative as Rolls-Royce—to drive the technology agenda in maritime. That's the job of policymakers, but with no steer from IMO there is nothing to report, other than prejudice and emotional response.

With media not providing that investigative objectivity that holds industry prejudice to account, technology and prejudice are on a collision course. But IMO could avoid that if it chooses to. The introduction of autonomous technology on London's Docklands Light Railway shows how.

Opened in 1987, the DLR was the first mass transit system in London to use driverless trains, and faced an understandably nervous public. But with the benefits of the system overwhelming the DLR embarked on a proactive communications programme. This included explaining the system, and the extensive and thorough nature of the safety trials taking place.

Exhibitions and literature put forward both the positives of the DLR and the negatives of traditional surface level transport, while the press was thoroughly briefed on the potential for the human operator on board to drive the train if required, and the oversight of humans in the control centre.

Perhaps most significantly, according to Mike Esbester of the University of Portsmouth, the novelty of the technology was downplayed. Instead, the DLR's proponents acknowledged the debts owed to existing automatic technologies that the public might be familiar with, in a bid to demonstrate the tried and tested nature of such systems.

Autonomous ships and the technologies supporting them could bring massive and widespread safety benefits to maritime, but lack of policy, clarity and communication at the top of the industry could impede that.

What is certain is that balancing risk and innovation is entering new territory and regulating and managing it is going to require bold vision, knowledge and real leadership.

The lesson of the DLR is that people can be persuaded to evaluate the risks rationally when it comes to technology, but it takes them having critical trust in the regulators—the humans—to do so.

Defining the statistical risk isn't enough, we need a human response that takes into account the social, cultural and emotional context for the fear. If the system itself makes us nervous, the likelihood is we'll find another. If IMO can grasp that now, it still has a lot of running to do, but it might just change maritime for the better.

I imagine that 'nervous' doesn't begin to describe how the passengers felt boarding Germanwings flights the morning after the tragedy of its Barcelona-Düsseldorf flight. What happened to one group was recorded on Facebook by passenger Britta Englisch.

"Yesterday morning at 8:40am, I got onto a Germanwings flight from Hamburg to Cologne with mixed feelings," she describes. "But then the captain not only welcomed each passenger separately, he also made a short speech before take-off. Not from the cockpit, he was standing in the cabin.

"He spoke about how the accident touched him and the whole crew. About how queasy the crew feels, but that everybody from the crew is voluntarily here. And about his family, and that the crew have a family, and that he is going to do everything to be with his family again tonight. It was completely silent. And then everybody applauded. I want to thank this pilot. He understood what everybody was thinking. And he managed to give me, at least, a good feeling for this flight."

The pilot was Frank Woiton, an experienced Captain who had previously flown with Andreas Lubitz, the architect of the Germanwings disaster. He spoke to Germany's *Bild* newspaper recounting how he hugged passengers as they boarded the hushed jet. Asked why he said, "People should see that in the cockpit there is also another human being."

If maritime is to really benefit from the technology on the horizon then it needs IMO to come out of the cockpit, and start showing it understands that too.

London, April 2015.

15

SAUCE FOR THE GOOSE

Some people get a bit apprehensive about talking to the media. And although we aren't quite the same as most media, that often extends to Futurenautics too. But those who do speak to us quickly find out that while we do ask difficult questions, we're not in search of splashy headlines. In fact we're known to offer interviewees the chance to check over what we plan to print. Because in order to produce a magazine like Futurenautics the ability to have open conversations in an atmosphere of trust with senior industry people is essential.

It's a policy that works well, but I'll admit to a slight concern when I called up Xeneta Founder and CEO Patrik Ølstad Berglund for our video interview, and discovered that following knee surgery he was full of heavy-duty painkillers. Hence I did wonder if a newly-sober Patrik would read the resulting draft and declare everything he said completely un-publishable.

He hasn't, which is good news because as we identified when we asked him to be our inaugural Futurenaut in the January 2014 issue, Xeneta is a truly disruptive force, and its trajectory since serves to confirm that.

Xeneta's offering—for those who haven't come across it be-fore—is pretty straightforward. The Norwegian company offers a crowdsourced price comparison service for sea freight allowing companies to share the prices they are given on its platform and compare them to the market average and 'best of class' for thousands of routes and lanes. That enables cargo owners to make more informed and therefore better decisions around how freight is shipped.

That's Xeneta's offering, but its purpose is bigger. Much bigger. What Xeneta intends to do is to use cutting edge big data analytics and crowdsourcing to re-write the playbook on how logistics decisions are made, and in so doing drag the $200bn sea freight industry into the new century.

"We came from the industry and we understood the volatility and opacity of the market, but what we wanted to do was to help the buyers in the industry get a better grasp of how the market moved," explains Berglund. "In this kind of market the buyers pay a wide range of prices and they aren't certain whether what they have is competitive."

Which in today's world is somewhat of an anomaly, when you consider that a container is just a commodity the same as an air ticket from London to New York. But whereas you can go online and get an immediate and comprehensive view of all your routes, options, carriers and prices for a trip to New York, if you want to send a container from Egypt to Mexico you won't find any online service that can help you.

"That means you have to go through a time consuming process to try and map out the market, but if you do that today then, in a week the market maybe will look quite different," explains Berglund. "So it's impossible to stay on top of all the routes moving around the world and the price at any given time."

But Berglund and fellow founders Vilhelm K. Vardøy and Thomas Sørbø realised that bringing together anonymised data from freight buyers onto a platform where powerful software turned it into actionable intelligence, could solve the problem.

"With crowdsourcing you ask everyone to chip into a network

with their data, and from that we can tell them what the market looks like, and how they compare to the market. If you are a buyer with 50,000 containers and 3,000 routes and all these routes have different volatility at a different point in time we can tell you every single day how well you are performing and on which routes you should focus to get some cost saving potential. And of course which routes you can leave be because you are competitive there."

The network effect is really powerful. With every company that joins the platform gets better and better as its reach and accuracy improves. But Xeneta requires a certain critical amount of data for a combination before it can really say anything about that route. "It's very simple, we start with four companies that have prices on the same route for the same container type on the same period of time," explains Berglund. "Then you have four overlapping prices and you are legally allowed to say something about the average."

But as Berglund is the first to admit, the average of four contracts isn't a great one, which is why the density of data in the Xeneta platform is so important. Put simply the more data you have the better the system works. To demonstrate just how dense Xeneta's data is Berglund takes me into the back end of the system to show me one particular route which over the past six months has had over 1400 contracts uploaded. "The data density is growing nicely and giving us a lot of traction. Customers can see this and that gives them confidence in how much data is generating the insights."

Judging by Xeneta's growth the confidence is not misplaced. The company recently completed a $5.3 million Series A round of funding with investment coming from previous backers Creandum, Point Nine Capital, and Alden, together with new investor Alliance Venture. It brings the total raised by Xeneta to $8.5 million since it was founded in 2012.

With such a radical idea though, the worry in the back of everyone's mind must have been engaging the crowd that was essential to making the platform work in the first place. However Berglund found encouragement from an unusual source.

"I showed an early version of Xeneta to a c-level executive at a big shipping line and he said, 'if you bring my customers this platform then they will kiss your hand, but someone is going to kill you.' So I thought that was pretty decent proof of concept."

In fact that executive was one of the more polite. "When we tried to approach the supplier side they literally told us to 'F-off'," recounts Berglund. Which may not have been a bad thing. Freed from the distraction of working with the carriers and freight forwarders, the team concentrated on developing a robust and valuable platform for buyers. The resulting growth has been remarkable.

The average annual sea-freight spend of a company joining the platform in 2013 was $3.7m; by 2014 it had leapt to $19m, and it's still climbing. As a result Xeneta's crowdsourced database of prices now represents over $3bn in freight spend and the market intelligence it offers has grown from 1,000 routes to 50,000 port-to-port combinations.

And it's caused the supplier side—carriers and freight forwarders—to wake up. "We started building up so many buyers, so many importers and exporters who were the important customers of the freight forwarders and the shipping lines, and they started bringing Xeneta intelligence into the negotiations with the carriers and freight forwarders," says Berglund. "Which led to a situation where the customers knew more about the market than the one selling the product did. That's when the supply side started reaching out to us."

Berglund shows no sign of smugness, although if he was you couldn't blame him. But bringing the supplier side to heel is not how he and the team sees it. It's just a natural evolution in the development of the platform. Where it was always destined to go.

"Our hypothesis has always been that if we start with the customer side of the industry the seller side will eventually budge and join the platform and that's what we're working on now, how to bring them on board, how to give them an attractive platform that's both beneficial for the buying and the supplying side."

Xeneta has positioned itself in a spot where it provides price transparency globally and the pace of development of the database has allowed it to cover more and more routes around the globe, but what Berglund eventually wants to achieve is a platform where buyers and sellers in the industry connect.

"The vessels are state of the art very often, but the whole transaction between buyer and seller is very old fashioned," says Berglund, adding for emphasis, "We still see faxes." Not only faxes but emails, phone calls and numerous in-person meetings. Typically today a freight owner will issue an RFQ and then run a tender process which can take six or sometimes twelve months, and which, when completed, will lock in a price for a further six to twelve months. But in a highly opaque and volatile market tying into a price for that amount of time comes with a lot of risk, and wasting perhaps a year to do it seems, in Berglund's eyes, "crazy."

"To get prices a buyer can either go to the freight forwarder, who would then go to the shipping line, or they can go directly to the shipping line. The process will depend to an extent on the size of the buyer—whether you have a thousand containers per year, or 200,000 or 300,000—but it's still cumbersome."

What Xeneta want to see is that time-consuming, wasteful collection of emails, phone calls, faxes and meetings replaced by a real-time dynamic interaction on its platform. "It would eliminate so much waste," says Berglund. He goes onto describe a fairly normal process where a buyer releases a tender and invites a mixture of thirty freight forwarders and shipping lines, lasting six months and out of which perhaps five shipping lines get more business.

"At the end of that process though, there are twenty-five companies which have wasted half a year's work. I want to enable them to answer not 500 tenders a year but 5,000 tenders a year, without lifting a finger."

Berglund sees benefit for his core customers, the freight buyers, too, "If we have all the data and we know everything about which supplier they should connect to they should also avoid that six month process, and immediately have their new suppliers available to them through our platform."

Xeneta's key focus is still on the freight buyers as it believes they are the ones who will allow it to truly change the industry, but discussions opened with the first suppliers nine months ago and Berglund estimates there are around ten to fifteen companies with which the team are working to tighten and tweak the platform this year so that it has real value for them.

It has to be a balancing act though, because in shipping circles it's an article of faith that whatever benefits its customers will automatically disadvantage the shipping line. But Xeneta is confident that it can identify non-conflict areas where it can build the relationship with the supplier side too.

"It's quite complex of course because we are under strict NDAs with both the buyers and the carriers so we have to be exceptionally careful how we treat the data, but what we do is very sophisticated," counters Berglund. "We can't build a platform that gives transparency and benefits to the buyer side and then discriminate against the supplier side, so in theory I want to have a platform that offers market intelligence to both parties and then I want to leverage that to utilise the data and develop into a platform that allows them to interact and engage in contracting."

That balancing act becomes increasingly delicate as Xeneta develops richer, more qualitative features. Building on the standard price metric detailing market average, highs and lows, the platform is now offering a quality metric too.

Berglund picks on one route, Hong Kong to Hamburg for a forty-foot container in order to demonstrate. In addition to the price metric buyers can also see all the schedules on the route mapped out. Looking at the various options I notice that you can go with Hyundai, or CMA CGM with 3 stops over 30 days, or Evergreen which, despite it using the same vessel, apparently only takes 29 days. It's a fine example of the problem of vessel sharing, but that isn't what Berglund wants to show me. We're looking at the other information on the screen which tells me that if I decide to use Evergreen and its apparently faster ship I am buying 71% reliability, whereas if I choose Hyundai I'm buying 82% reliability.

For a freight buyer that difference in reliability is very significant. Expanding this kind of quality metric requires Xeneta to create a comprehensively matching dataset including tracking all the container vessels out there, but for its buy-side users it's a powerful feature, and one imagines they're going to keep coming.

"We have the technical ability to do a lot and it's just a matter of time. We also have a rating system where everyone can rate their suppliers and we aggregate the data and give intelligence back, but like everything we are developing all the time, it's always work in progress."

It's one of the hallmarks of these exponentially growing, lean technology businesses. When I spoke to Berglund in 2013 there were only five or six of them but that's growing all the time with fifteen now working for the Oslo-based company, and new hires set to grow that total to twenty-two by the end of May. With the platform entirely developed and built in-house, together with the analytics capability I wonder if Xeneta has got one of those elusive data scientists on board?

"I think that's one of those roles. Everyone talks about them but no one really has any," laughs Berglund. "That's because they love the idea of one but they're really difficult to find." I tell him that this month's Futurenaut Richard Rivlin of VesselsValue found one of his data scientists working in his local newsagent having just finished his degree. Berglund isn't surprised, "It's not really my field but I believe that we're in dialogue with one guy pretty much straight out of university, and we have the inside track on a few more."

With the kind of data Xeneta has, the potential for new services based on new analytics, including predictive ones should be huge. Berglund acknowledges that pulling in external sources and utilising the information that the platform has about future contracts could be an area for development, but his focus for now is on fact-based historical data. "We can leverage all kinds of analytics on this data which could be of interest to other stakeholders, but our prime focus is how it can benefit the buying and selling side of the industry."

Similarly, despite being asked frequently to broaden its scope Xeneta is staying focussed on the container shipping industry. "Container is 70 per cent of the industry and it is truly old-fashioned, so changing it is a massive play on its own," Berglund reminds me. "I am cautious to make sure that we really get it right in the container market, but we could do the same in other segments, in air and road freight, and because our customer base of freight buyers are also buying road and air, when we do expand it's likely to be that much faster."

It's clear talking to Berglund that there's a huge amount that Xeneta knows is possible, and it's really itching to do it. Because underpinning all the technology and cutting-edge analytics is a simple and abiding love for the industry. "I love container shipping, it's fascinating and such an important part of the global world we live in, and yet very few people really relate to it. Besides us in the industry."

And that's where Xeneta has a real advantage, because I'm not sure Berglund's obvious love and enthusiasm for shipping is really mirrored amongst the carriers whose customers are joining his platform in their droves. And that they reacted so violently to the idea of the crowdsourced Xeneta platform in the first place tells us much about the adversarial approach carriers have towards the freight buyers who pay the bills.

I've written before about the need for that adversarial relationship to alter radically if the industry is going to function properly and be profitable in the future. And according to a report by the Boston Consulting Group container shipping has reached a point where it isn't just unprofitable, it's actually destroyed value over a significant period.

Over the past fifteen years the sector's return on net assets (RONA) has only been around 3 per cent compared to the 9 per cent RONA of the S&P 500 over the same period. Not only is that far lower, it's also nowhere near enough to cover the approximately 7 per cent cost of capital needed to finance the assets deployed. That's value disappearing before our eyes.

Things don't just need to change, they need to transform, and making death threats towards those with a vision for how the industry can leverage digital opportunities to innovate, isn't the way forward.

How the power of networks and the crowd can work to the advantage of freight buyers has been ably demonstrated by Berglund and co. But now they have to do something far more profound. They have to show that this technology and the philosophy underlying it—which is of real value and benefit to our customers—can also provide the same to shipping. In short that, as the old saying goes, what is sauce for the goose is also sauce for the gander.

And if Berglund can pull that off, then Xeneta really will have laid the golden egg.

London, April 2015.

16

HOPE AND PREY

There's an old joke involving a couple of wildlife documentary film crew, hunkered down in the African savanna filming lions. Suddenly a big male lion spots the two men and roars threateningly. As the soundman slowly starts to pull on a pair of Nikes the cameraman whispers to his friend that he'll never outrun a lion. To which the soundman replies that he doesn't need to outrun the lion, just the cameraman.

When it comes to cyber security, up until comparatively recently, the objective of the exercise has been to outrun the cameraman. For most organisations the risk of finding themselves exposed on the savanna in the first place is considered pretty low. That their digital assets would constitute anything juicy enough to interest an aggressive predator has been judged highly unlikely. So strapping on some Nike firewalls and antivirus and locking down the perimeter of the organisation seemed the sensible thing to do. Because there will always be some other slower, easier target for the hackers.

It is difficult to overstate just how dramatically that paradigm has changed. But it's dramatic enough that at the recent World Economic Forum in Davos fears were raised—both publicly and privately—that concerns about corporate cyber vulnerability are beginning to act as a brake on technology investment, and failing to address it could cost the global economy US$3 trillion.

The cyber security threat landscape has metamorphosed into something entirely different, and outrunning the cameraman is a woefully inadequate response. Now the internet is that savanna, and anyone on it is exposed. In addition the lion is able to maul an un-limited number of wildlife documentary film crew in one go with such stealth and savagery that they may not even realise they've been mauled until they attempt to make use of an internal organ and discover it's no longer in situ. And with the biggest vulnerabil-ity now your own people, the sound guy is just as likely to get eaten by the cameraman.

When writing about cyber security it's easy to get sucked in by the numbers. They're big. Really big. And they're getting bigger all the time. Try this one—last October JP Morgan suffered a data breach which affected 76 million customers. Or what about mobile payments provider CHARGE Anywhere which in December re-vealed a malware attack on its electronic payment gateway systems which had lasted five years. The statistics are jaw-dropping and you can read a judicious collection of some of the most noteworthy in our infographic. But there's only one statistic I'd really like you to take away from all of this.

It comes from Cisco, and more specifically its Global Securi-ty Network which handles 100 terabytes of data and inspects 16 billion web requests per day, has 100 million globally deployed endpoints, 1.6 million globally deployed devices and handles 35 per cent of all the email traffic in the world. The figure I want you to remember is 100 per cent. That represents the proportion of business networks analysed by Cisco which have traffic going to websites that host malware. Suspicious traffic is emanating from these company networks and attempting to connect to malicious malware hosts, which means that every company has shown evi-dence of internal compromise. Every single one.

So let's start by stamping on any lingering hopes—should you be harbouring them—that cyber security isn't really an issue for you. Everyone is vulnerable and everyone is a target. But perhaps even more salient is the fact that you, as senior leaders or board members of an organisation are also something else, and that is responsible.

As the tone in Davos indicated the severity of the threat and the ability of companies to meet it is beginning to jeopardise the significant economic gains that technology can offer the world. The response from the USA and UK is the formation of joint 'cyber-cells' to test resilience and share knowledge and intelligence between the two countries, but while there are moves to help organisations fight back, there is also a regulatory tightening underway. Both the USA and Europe are introducing compulsory reporting legislation and companies who breach data laws, however unintentionally, are being handed significant fines. In short, ignorance is no longer a defence, and nor is unpreparedness.

That has serious implications for the shipping and maritime industry, because there's a good chance that we are massively—some would claim recklessly—unprepared for the new cyber threats we are facing. Wary of generalisation as I am, after the discussions I've had with a whole range of people around the industry on the subject, it does appear likely that on the whole we are neither secure nor resilient when it comes to cyber.

According to recently released 2015 security reports by both PwC and Cisco the volume of cyber attacks has mushroomed year on year, and continues to do so. Cisco Systems CEO John Chambers told a meeting in Davos that "security was bad last year" and unfortunately "this year is going to be much worse." The good news is that the profile of cyber security within our industry is on the rise. The International Maritime Bureau and BIMCO have already issued warnings, and Canada's submission to IMO on the subject was also widely reported.

In the last year we've also begun to see more reports surfacing of successful attacks in the maritime domain. From drilling rigs having their control systems infected and Korean shipbuilders being infected with the 'Icefog' virus, to the Port of Antwerp and Australian customs being compromised by smugglers, evidence is emerging about the scale of attacks and potential vulnerabilities.

Thanks to a previously secret report from the US Senate's Armed Services Committee, we now know that there have been multiple cyber attacks on ship operators and ships themselves contracted by the US Transportation Command (Transcom).

But the problem is that most of these reports are years old—the Transcom attacks happened in 2012/13—and considering the speed with which the threats are evolving, and the sheer scale of attacks that simply isn't good enough.

Despite all the statistics and the reports it is hard to really comprehend that scale. In order to get your head around it though I suggest that you visit the Norse website. Norse claims to have the world's largest up-to-the-second database of live threat intelligence, and you can watch live online, as literally thousands of attacks ping their way across the world. Actually what you're seeing is only part of the activity, but it's enough. If you haven't seen it yet then the advice from Dan Solomon—Consulting Lead for Cisco's Cyber Security Centre of Excellence and head of the Cyber Risk and Security Services division at Optimal Risk—to delegates at the recent Transport Security Expo's maritime conference that they need to go onto a 'war footing', may seem theatrical. It won't afterwards.

Experts divide the threat into four main groups—hacktivists, organised crime, company insiders (either intentional or unintentional) and state-sponsored entities—all of which is true. But that misses the fundamental point—the real essence of the cyber threat, and that is dependence. The only reason that we are vulnerable to these groups is because of our dependence upon the technologies we are implementing, and that's why the dangers are growing and the paradigm is shifting so fast.

Pre-digital organisations used to have solid perimeters, originally the walls of the office building. The advent of email and company laptops bulged them out, but the response was to beef up the firewalls and antivirus. This approach has been described as "M&M" security—a hard shell with a soft centre, where everything outside the network is untrusted and everything inside is trusted. But the explosion in social networking, the BYOD and ATAWAD trends and cloud collaboration platforms has sent it into meltdown.

According to John Kindervag, principal analyst at Forrester Research, that attitude to network security has become a fundamental problem. "The world has changed and we cannot carry on doing things the way we did in the 70s and 80s," says Kindervag.

That's exactly what shipping and maritime are still doing in lots of areas, and with good reason. The huge advances in connectivity which has forced land-based companies to evolve along with the new security landscape have been missing from the maritime domain. Now that high speed IP connectivity is not only affordable, but clearly the key to unlocking significant operational efficiencies, cost savings and service improvements, maritime is taking massive leaps forwards, but without an appreciation of the risks.

"Connectivity offers huge benefits and it's really important to understand that, but people have had quite a rosy picture of what those benefits are or could be and they haven't really considered the potential downsides," says Wil Rockall a director in KPMG's cyber security team. "Vessel cyber security is reasonably immature as the vast majority have paid more attention to physical security, which is only to be expected given the last ten years and where the attacks have come from."

So most ship operators are still dishing out M&M security, relying on the same firewalls and anti-virus, but even the people developing those products are warning they don't work. According to Symantec its firewall and anti-virus products will stop at most 45 per cent of threats getting through and Symantec's SVP Brian Dye went as far as to tell the Wall Street Journal that 'antivirus is dead'.

Actually saying that antivirus is dead is like claiming that an aspirin doesn't cure cancer. Antivirus may not be a panacea, but it is still useful as part of a suite of defences. There are a new generation of products like free software Comodo which provides a virtualised sandbox for users isolating them from the threat of viruses online, but in reality very few people actually come into contact with viruses these days. The far bigger threat is from malware, and that's usually just a user's click away.

For shipping and maritime the key is a shift in mindset, an

appreciation of how the threat landscape has altered and why a 'Zero Trust' model of security is now necessary. That also requires an acceptance that no matter how good your security is, there is a very good chance that at some point you will be breached. So cyber security is only one part of a bigger requirement, and that is cyber resilience. The ability to identify the breach and recover is as crucial as mitigating the threat in the first place. Once we move from security to resilience it's easier to see that trying to protect everything, as we have in the past, is no longer the best option. In short the focus should no longer be on the network, but the data. We have to identify our key dependencies, our 'crown jewel' data. Then we have to work out how to deliver the right data to the right person on the right device in a secure way.

That's why what may once have been an IT problem isn't any longer. This is a c-suite and board level issue, and what it comes down to in the end is risk. But while companies have elaborate models to measure financial and health and safety risks, and insurance products to help cover them, the same doesn't apply to cyber. By and large we don't have the ability to measure cyber risk and even less grasp of how we mitigate it.

It's safe to say that this is a pretty major issue. And yet when you ask those actually running shipping and maritime companies what they're doing about it the response is total silence—both about the scale of cyber attacks in shipping and maritime, and the work that is required and underway to mitigate them.

"Maritime is way behind the curve in standards on cyber-security," says Alex Soukhanov, vice president of international shipping and maritime operations at the United States Maritime Resource Center, a non profit consultancy specialising in navigation safety and maritime risk mitigation. "Traditional risk approaches are leading to common wisdom saying, 'where's the threat?' when the low level of reporting means we don't recognise the threat. But we have to remember that as mariners we're only as good as our last manoeuvre."

There's an argument which says that this could be 'Digital Darwinism' at work. Those who have failed to evolve solutions to the new threats technological changes sweeping shipping and maritime, and the rest of the world, are creating, will just go the way of the other dinosaurs. But the issue is far more complex than that. I imagine a lot of shipping and maritime companies will look at the Sony attack or that on the US Command Center's social media accounts, or Apple, or JP Morgan and conclude that any high-profile organisation with sensitive or valuable digital assets is going to be a target, which is precisely why the largely invisible shipping industry doesn't have too much to worry about.

Unfortunately that couldn't be further from the truth. The reality is that a big organisation's weakest link, after its own employees, is its suppliers. Cyber criminals are far from stupid and they will take the path of least resistance. Why try and breach a well-resourced, alert organisation with a lot to lose, when a smaller, less security-focussed supplier could provide an open door?

The problem is so acute that in other industries large suppliers have sometimes met the cost of upskilling and uprating the cyber security and resilience of smaller suppliers in order to mitigate the risk. But the evidence is that the problem is increasing. The recent PwC survey found that losses from cyber attacks jumped by 53 per cent year on year for large firms, but in small firms it decreased 37 per cent. The suggestion is that smaller firms simply aren't identifying when they've been breached, and when they are breached very often they aren't the ultimate target. Smaller firms are bridging the defences of their larger customers, letting the criminals inside, and they don't even realise.

Considering that shipping and maritime sits at the heart of countless supply chains worldwide and its infrastructure includes support for everything from ports to oil platforms, the potential ramifications of that scenario in our industry is chilling indeed. This was demonstrated by a 'Red Team' exercise—a real-world approach to testing security, protocols, and awareness—conducted on a large port. (We cover Red Teaming in detail in our *The Devil You Know* article this issue)

Tasked with breaking into the port and taking control of the network and systems the attackers found their way in by targeting the portal of a shipping company run from an underdeveloped country. I can't identify either the port or the large ship operator involved, but I can assure you that you will be very familiar with both.

If I'm doing my job properly then at this point you will be mentally running through the suppliers and customers you interact with on a regular basis, whose networks or devices your personnel might use when they visit, or allow to use your network when they visit you. And if you're doing your job properly you will be wondering the extent to which your organisation has vetted, and continues to vet, those companies' cyber security policies and procedures. The extent to which your organisation is exposed.

If the answer to your question is that you don't vet suppliers or customers, then you aren't alone. Despite the growing expectation for businesses to check their supply chains aren't engaged in bribery, corruption or employee exploitation, actually checking that they aren't going to compromise your cyber security barely registers. When one considers the extent to which every business deals online now that's an astonishing situation.

It may seem counterintuitive, but the safest place for shipping and maritime to trade online now might very well be a dedicated e-procurement platform. As a closely integrated EDI trading platform ShipServ is a de facto extension of its customer's systems and is seen as an additional layer of their data. Protecting that data, according to Founder and CEO Paul Østergaard, is a responsibility they take extremely seriously.

"We are dedicated to preventing, detecting, and responding to any threats that may target our infrastructure, and we are constantly working to protect our customers and their data," says Østergaard. "By continuously monitoring all activity, immediately responding to emerging threats and having an in-house security team and external security experts to test and improve our protection measures we are striving to provide the safest environment for maritime trade."

There's no doubt that ShipServ knows what it's talking about when it comes to data, and it operates a continuous cycle of evaluation and implementation of further encryption and data partitioning to prevent potential damage by cyber intruders. So for maritime companies without that security competence using the ShipServ platform could offer major risk mitigation. "This could be seen as a natural continuation of the de-perimeterisation of individual customers' systems," agrees Østergaard. "We work with many thousands of customers and while some companies provide adequate protection for their systems and data, ShipServ remains a more secure option for the majority."

But while there are companies in maritime capable of meeting the challenges of the new cyber security paradigm, there don't seem to be enough, and we're rapidly approaching a crunch point. Increased connectivity is pulling every shipboard system possible online, converging and integrating functions and software and control systems.

Engines can be fixed remotely, images and video can be streamed and within a very few years we will have prototype ships that will sail themselves. Already our dependence upon these systems is heavy—the e-navigation agenda has made sure of that—but in future the safe and efficient operation of the ship at sea will depend upon them utterly. Your vessel has always had to be seaworthy, but now it has to be e-worthy too.

"Seaworthiness is very important concept in English Maritime Law, and is often central to disputes over marine Insurance and the carriage of goods by sea," says Christopher Dunn, managing partner at Waltons & Morse LLP and member of the British Maritime Law Association. "As vessels become more reliant on computer systems, cyber security vulnerabilities which are exploited by hackers, and which lead to physical loss of cargo or other damage, could form the basis of an unseaworthiness claim."

So if you put to sea with malware screwing up your ECDIS there's a very good chance your vessel could be considered unseaworthy. And that's not all. Most marine insurance policies Waltons & Morse see contain the Institute Cyber Attack Exclusion Clause (CL 380) which excludes all losses caused by or contributed to by a cyber attack. According to Christopher Dunn it's something that the industry is waking up to. "We are also seeing an increasing awareness that inadequately defended technical systems present huge risks and there is widespread unease that criminals, pirates and terrorists will gain access to these systems."

Unease is good, but perhaps outright fear would be more appropriate, particularly when you consider the evidence. NCC Group reported early last year on the vulnerabilities they found in an ECDIS from a major manufacturer. They were able to penetrate the system, read, download, replace or delete any file stored in it.

Access to the ECDIS could come from a virus on a USB stick, or an unpatched vulnerability via the IP connection, either directly, or through one of the other systems integrated with the ECDIS. In essence, once they were inside the ECDIS, they were inside the network and everything else connected to it.

NCC Group recommended that manufacturers adopt Security Development Lifecycles for ECDIS products, but it's rather alarming that a mandatory piece of shipboard kit wouldn't routinely have one. "Manufacturers are currently relying on the fact that access to ECDIS systems on vessels is somewhat restricted as their major method of risk mitigation," says the report. "This is inadvisable."

But if the ECDIS research is scary consider the study security company IO Active undertook in 2013 directed at satcom terminals. Maritime terminals including Iridium, VSAT and Inmarsat FleetBroadband were reported as having critical security issues.

These were serious enough to be reported to the CERT Co-ordination centre, and yet according to IO Active, with the exception of Iridium, "the vendors did not engage in addressing this situation. They did not respond to a series of requests sent by the CERT Co-ordination Center and/or its partners." In a climate where everyone is becoming aware of how serious a cyber attack on a vessel, or a company could be, it seems puzzling to say the least that satcom terminal vendors and ECDIS manufacturers could have such vulnerabilities apparently present in their products, and it go virtually unreported.

As one of the major network operators, we asked James Collett, Director of Mobility Services at Intelsat what his network is doing to keep maritime users secure.

"We break the general security model into how we are protecting the perimeter and how we manage access to the network and for the elements of the system that are responsible for transport that we own, we maintain security measures on those," Collett explains. "Integrity of the network carrying customers' transmissions is of primary concern, and Intelsat is the only satellite operator that has gone through independent auditing firm KPMG and completed a Service Organization Control 3 (SOC3) review of security controls. The successful review process provides commercially accepted validation that our products are offered in an appropriately secure environment."

Intelsat spoke to us at length about this—and you can read the rest of what they had to tell us about security on our website—but in doing so they were in a very small minority. We also asked Inmarsat—responsible for the connectivity of the vast majority of vessels at sea and the only one anointed to provide GMDSS services—to tell us how they approached cyber security in the maritime domain.

Unfortunately Inmarsat doesn't discuss security. And they aren't alone. In shipping and maritime, no one wants to talk about cyber security. And I really do mean no one. For the purposes of this article we contacted more than fifteen large ship operators and numerous suppliers. None were prepared to talk about it on the record.

Now we're used to people not wanting to answer the kind of difficult questions we ask—on a variety of subjects—but this is in a different league altogether. And it's a real problem, because the only way we're going to get on top of this is by sharing the information we have. In November 2013 the Bank of England held the 'Waking Shark II' exercise, designed to test the cyber security of the UK financial industry. It's something the maritime industry ought to consider and not just because of the vulnerabilities it could uncover.

Following Waking Shark Andrew Miller, chief operating officer at Corero Network Security, said one of the biggest benefits from the exercise will not necessarily be about banks learning to defend against cyber attacks, but learning to co-operate. "There needs to be more information-sharing within financial organisations on the latest threats and attacks they are facing, so they can develop a knowledge pool on how to protect against them," he said.

Essentially those organisations that work together to develop comprehensive defences are far more likely to remain secure than those that decide to try and do it alone. The bottom line is that maintaining cyber security and resilience in the maritime industry isn't something that should form the basis of a competitive advantage.

"Keeping people safe, operating vessels safely should not be a competitive advantage for anybody, so there shouldn't be an incentive for any owner operator or manufacturer to keep that information to themselves," says KPMG's Rockall. "But at the moment we have two problems: one is that no one wants to be the first to admit they have a problem, come out and say they've been hacked and people were at risk, because the first person to put their head above the parapet is likely to get it shot off. Equally though, nobody wants to do the opposite and say we are perfectly safe and we've spent huge time and effort and we're confident we're secure, because that's painting a huge target on your back."

Whether or not ship operators and maritime suppliers talk to Futurenautics about cyber is of no consequence, but it is absolutely essential that they begin talking to each other. I think the real need here is for a co-ordinated response to the cyber threat, one which allows organisations to come together and share the intelligence they have, understand the problems that others are seeing and how they've overcome them. In that way we can protect and support each other and have a fighting chance of getting ahead of those sods on the other end of the IP.

If that sounds familiar it should: it's exactly what we did with physical piracy, and look at the results.

Someone said to me that when it comes to cyber and technology threats boards just glaze over. When you have seven year old girls hacking into public WiFi networks in under ten minutes you can understand why. In fact it reminded me of Douglas Adams' set of rules that describe our reactions to technology.

The first is that anything that is in the world when you're born is normal and ordinary and is just a natural part of the way the world works. The second is that anything that's invented between when you're fifteen and thirty-five is new and exciting and revolutionary and you can probably get a career in it. The third is that anything invented after you're thirty-five is against the natural order of things.

We don't need scaremongering, but that's inevitable when cyber is shrouded in such secrecy by everyone. What we do need is for those of you who lead our companies and boards to understand that cyber is not about IT, it is about dependence, and that dependence leads to risk. And like every other business risk, it has to be managed. That is your job, and you are perfectly capable of doing it successfully. But it's going to be a lot easier together.

So, unusually, I'm going to give the last word to someone else. In this case James Collett of Intelsat who told me, "When security is working correctly, it's a partnership."

Yes. What he said.

London, January 2015.

17

EXIT WOUND

A mongst the rash of Christmas lists of the best and worst and 'top 10's' of 2014 doing the rounds in December was the 5th annual Lloyd's List *'100 Most Influential People in Shipping'* report.

When drawing conclusions about our diverse industry there is a constant risk of generalisation, but although some sectors have undoubtedly fared better than others, I think it's safe to say that shipping hasn't had a stellar 2014. The florid editorial introduction to the Lloyd's List 100 therefore makes for a rather confusing read.

Far from continuing to over-order and gamble other people's money on increasingly unreliable gut-feelings, apparently those loveable, buccaneering rogues at the top of shipping have outwitted the bad guy, got the girl, grabbed the best lines, the last laugh and are now charging on to fight another day. Roll credits.

"Another message from the shipping world that's hard to ignore: if you're feeling over-extended, just extend some more," says Lloyd's List."You'll always find the money. With private equity backing, main-street investors and banks can always be encouraged to pony up."

The fact that credit has continued to roll in shipping at all has been in no small part thanks to the dramatic, last-minute entrance of PE. And yet despite having filled the funding gap left by the exit—stage left, at a run—of all those shipping banks and literally saving the day for many ship owners and operators, it remains shipping's bad guy.

There is an audible booing and hissing from most of the industry at the mention of PE, and yet plenty were prepared to climb between the balance sheets with them. According to Tufton Oceanic, this time last year PE financed 22 per cent or US$278 billion of the global vessel order book. But things are changing. With Marine Money reporting only 15 PE transactions in 2014 compared with 30 the previous year, it's pretty clear that the PE boom has peaked. And the reasons why are important.

"Many private equity firms were waiting for the freight markets to really come back, the values to go up and then be able to exit their investments at a profit," says Svein Engh of CIT Maritime Finance. "This hasn't happened and has led to many private equity firms opting out of investing in new projects. In addition, we have seen a lot of hedge funds acquire shipping loans in the secondary market with the same expectations...If they are not willing to hold these positions and they want out now, they could be looking at potential losses."

PE is getting nervy, and with good reason. The expectation is that a significant number will find it difficult to get out with the profits they anticipated and so are switching focus from longer-term earning potential to a short-term asset game where the prime consideration is to find a buyer willing to take over increasingly risky positions. There are already reports of heightened activity in PE firms selling to each other.

But while some PE certainly swoops on distressed debt and weak asset values to make a quick buck, it also prides itself on taking failing businesses in difficult markets and accelerating growth and profitability. The PE firms we've consulted for looking to get into the shipping industry aren't flat-eyed money men, and neither are they overconfident traders. Generally speaking they don't rely on assurances and past performance either—they rely on data and models.

But in shipping they've really come unstuck, because the type of data and rigour they usually demand simply hasn't been available.

With warnings that the shipping industry was too complex for them to understand ringing in their ears many PE firms have relied upon the wisdom of the experienced management with whom they have committed to JVs or invested into. The result is that the shipping market—fragmented and highly cyclical, plagued by overcapacity and over-optimism—has failed to recover in the way ship owners and operators privately assured investors it had to. So let's be clear here: PE didn't get it wrong, everyone got it wrong.

The fact that PE firms who entered the sector looking for 15 to 20 per cent return and a 3-5 year exit are going to find it tough to realise either, is very bad news. And yet we are being treated to the unedifying spectacle of a shipping industry rubbing its hands in glee.

"Many of those [private equity] guys who thought it was going to be so easy to understand this industry didn't," Randee Day, of Day & Partners recently told the South China Morning Post. Basil Karatzas, of Karatzas Marine Advisors is even plainer, "There is subdued optimism that there will be better days to get PE funds still interested in shipping, disappointment that the best days of PE investing in shipping are behind us, and outright happiness that PE funds got their investments wrong, and that they will be the next wave of players in shipping who will be realizing big losses (after the shipowners buying ships in 2007 and banks lending 120% of peak phase of cycle)."

That any industry in the 21st century can find reasons to be cheerful that a slew of investors are about to make significant losses is breathtaking. Talk about biting the hand that feeds you. Now go back and read that quote from Lloyd's List, and consider who'll be 'ponying up' when PE has decided it's been backing the wrong horse. But Lloyd's List goes further. "Shipping is one of the last arenas in global business in which an individual can launch a Grand Plan and find the funding avenues to keep on going," it crows.

Well that may not be the case much longer. In the last twelve months the industry saw seven IPOs and five OTC listings mostly in the US and Europe, and none of them have been greatly successful. We reported last issue on the woes of Scorpio Bulkers whose share price was trading this time last year at US$10.44 and on 5th Jan this year stands at US$1.86. Investors aren't impressed and that lack of enthusiasm has consequences. Already several listings have been postponed including Wilbur Ross-backed Diamond S Shipping Group, and the implications for PE, whose favoured exit option is often via the capital markets, are major.

But the colour of the sky in shipping's world is rather different. Here's the Lloyd's List verdict on Scorpio's year. "Scorpio's Emanuele Lauro has moved on to dry bulk and most recently into the largest of the ultra large containerships. It's a bid that would have made Onassis proud."

One doubts the Scorpio share price nosedive would have made Aristotle Onassis anything other than apoplectic, had he been an investor. Of course Onassis died forty years ago this year, but Lloyd's List and the industry it serves still seem to be stuck in that 1970's mindset. It's beginning to sound like the last days of Rome. "Geopolitical events create risk and opportunity and the canniest shipowners always survive, somehow. It is these survivors, from China to Greece to Wall Street, that colour the industry's identity. Long may they prosper."

If this is prospering then it really is time for a wake-up call. Making debt repayment deadlines by the skin of your teeth, over-ordering and then destroying the prospect of anyone getting a successful IPO away until second quarter 2015-16 at the earliest, attracts no censure. It guarantees induction into the shipping hall of fame. As my teenage daughter would say, 'WTF?'

According to shipbroker Gibsons, Wilbur Ross estimated that PE pumped $16 billion into shipping between 2008 and 2013, which is two and a half times the amount generated through IPOs. And the combined portfolios of these outfits is truly impressive. Golden Tree Asset Management (which has a 4.81% stake in Euronav) is managing $21 billion while Oaktree Capital Management has close to $80 billion under its control, so Gibson's report.

So while PE's exit from shipping is likely to be painful, it'll be no more than a flesh wound, and what it has learnt will be of significant value. That's why shipping's smugness is deeply misplaced. Because what PE has learnt is that shipping isn't somewhere they can do business. And that isn't PE's problem. It's ours. We didn't prove PE wrong, PE exposed just what a mess our industry is in.

What it also exposed is that there are structural changes driven by new technologies which are already impacting trade flows and business priorities and realities. Shipping has utterly failed to anticipate them, and continues to do so.

PE may be slightly bloodied but the real victim is shipping, and it's a totally self-inflicted wound.

Telling PE we told you so isn't just shooting ourselves in the foot. It could turn out to be suicide.

London, January 2015.

18

THE NUT THAT HOLDS THE WHEEL

You may be the type of free spirit who drives something cool, vintage and groovy from the 1960's—a VW bus perhaps, an old Caddy, or maybe an original Mini. For those of us who don't divide our time equally between the side of the road and a home inspection pit, and have intact marriages however, our cars now have more computing power than the systems that guided Apollo astronauts to the moon. Yet despite the bewildering array of computers, sensors and other gizmos packed into them, we still manage to crash with monotonous predictability.

There is a well-worn adage about cars which warns the most dangerous part of one is the nut that holds the steering wheel. The inexorable move towards autonomous vehicles offers the hope that this one, overriding vulnerability of modern automobiles could one day be eradicated once and for all. But the weakness of sophisticated systems being compromised by human factors is already echoing across industries including maritime, and nowhere is it more acute than in managing the risk of cyber attack.

One would be forgiven for assuming that the difference between an organisation vulnerable to cyber attack, and one which isn't lies in better computers and software or better connectivity. According to Symantec that is almost never the case. Whilst it may be necessary to have the very best technology available to secure your organisation, it's still going to be insufficient. The weakest link in cyber security is invariably your people.

Cyber threats are usually considered to come from outsiders writing malicious code designed to steal corporate intelligence, confidential customer information or access financial systems. To an extent that's absolutely correct, but they are only one part of the threat. The majority of the time the way these bad guys get a foothold is because the ignorance or negligence of your employees opens the door for them.

According to PwC's Global State of Information Security Survey 2015—whether intentionally or not—employees have become the most-cited culprits of information security incidents. The number of companies citing current employees as the cause of cyber incidents has risen 10 per cent since 2013. Worse still, 32 per cent of respondents to the 2014 US State of Cybercrime survey say insider crimes are more costly and damaging than those committed by outsiders.

Cyber criminals are primarily targeting employees and using sophisticated techniques to manipulate their behaviour in ways that technical security controls organisations apply to their networks simply can't combat. The behaviour of those responsible for data is linked to awareness of the risks, and that's something which for many organisations is a big weakness, and a potential ticking time bomb.

A report from Ponemon Institute revealed that 71 per cent of employees have access to data they shouldn't see. 54 per cent of the end users surveyed said they access such data frequently or very frequently, while 80 per cent of the IT professionals surveyed said their organisation doesn't enforce a strict least-privilege data model.

The impact of insecure human factors is being exacerbated by another growing trend though. Unlike in the old days, digital doors to your organisation are proliferating at an alarming rate, and they're no longer all in the IT department. Traditionally at the heart of modern organisational processes, the IT department was the natural place for cyber security responsibility to reside. Not any longer. Recent research by Gartner has shown that the movement of IT budget away from IT towards other departments and individuals is accelerating. 14 per cent of cloud storage, 13 per cent of social media and 11 per cent of office productivity software is purchased without the IT department even knowing about it. In fact IT is no longer the lead purchaser of technology. According to Gartner the marketing department is the new frontrunner and will outspend the IT department on technology by 2017.

The human element of weak cyber security is already way beyond the realm of the IT department, but for most organisations it's still in an office or at a location somewhere on dry land. More pertinently, that human element will have experience of IT systems and the technology processes of the modern office environment, and often be subject to physical, real-time oversight. Shipping and maritime's challenge is that a good proportion of our human element aren't.

Until comparatively recently our ships and crews were effectively quarantined from the outside world by the prohibitive expense of deep sea satellite connectivity. The rise of IP systems like Inmarsat FleetBroadband and VSAT has seen technology deployment across the fleet rocket. Whereas not that long ago you would have been hard pressed to get a 3MB email attachment out to a vessel without eyebrows being raised, today data is being streamed back and forth in hitherto unimaginable volume. And it's only going to get worse—or better—depending upon your point of view.

Then there are those proliferating doors to your organisation. The Bring Your Own Device (BYOD) trend is gaining momentum with Gartner reporting that BYOD Tablet policies offer better opportunities than those of enterprise-owned laptops or smartphones. "IT leaders can spend half a million dollars to buy and support 1,000 enterprise-owned tablets, while they can support 2,745 user-owned tablets with that same budget," Federica Troni, research director at Gartner, said in a statement. "Without a stipend, direct costs of user-owned tablets are 64 per cent lower. When organizations have several users who want a tablet as a device of convenience, offering a BYOD option is the best alternative to limit cost and broaden access." Between now and 2017, Gartner says 90 per cent of organisations will support some aspect of BYOD and predict that by 2018 there will be twice as many employee-owned devices used for work than enterprise-owned devices.

The annual Crew Communications Survey *(undertaken by Futurenautics Research and free to download on the Futurenautics website)* tracks the adoption of connectivity solutions and devices aboard every type of merchant shipping, and the 2014 report demonstrates these technology and device trends are mirrored in shipping.

75 per cent of crew currently take a laptop PC onboard with that figure rising to 81 per cent amongst officers. And in the coming twelve months over 40 per cent of crew intend to purchase a tablet PC for use onboard. In 2014 the smartphone also overtook the cellphone as the most popular device carried onboard ships with 68 per cent of crew in possession of one when aboard. To compound matters a massive 40 per cent of crew are now routinely offered internet access by operators, with an astonishing 50 per cent of those providing it free of charge. That's a lot of internet-connected wheels, and plenty of nuts holding them. In short, a big target.

The gap between ship and shore is often cited as an issue in maritime IT security, but the truth is the attitude of organisations is a far more pertinent problem. Speaking at the SingTel maritime roundtable just over twelve months ago a variety of senior ship operators indicated that operational data—which they unanimously consider to be of limited interest and value—does not require protection.

As a result, aside from traditional, ethics-based and confidentiality policies, most ship operators don't appear to have any dedicated ship board data security measures in place. One participant even made the suggestion that, as the office is able to see from the logs who has accessed what and when, the technology effectively polices itself.

It is precisely that kind of relaxed naivety which is ringing alarm bells across the industry. No technology can police itself, but the lack of reported incidents in the maritime industry may be lending weight to the view that it is. Having said that there has been a significant increase in reported cyber attacks in the industry in the past twelve months.

"The only cyber attack I have ever witnessed was caused by an officer who had downloaded infested files and folders carried over from previous vessel and caused contamination of ship's computers and as a result all communications ceased, archives lost, ECDIS and digital publications had to be downloaded again after re-formatting computers."

That's just one anonymous example of how serious an employee unintentionally compromising a ship's system can be. But whereas it is possible to lock down office and shipboard computers to prevent USB's even being read, most attacks are far more sophisticated.

Social engineering via phishing emails are one of the most common ways attackers attempt to exploit employees, and not even those in IT who should know better are immune. When Georgia Tech first piloted phishing awareness training using the 300-member Office of Information Technology (OIT), one out of every four people clicked on the link in the phishing e-mail message and could have had their system compromised.

The experiment showed that not only is social engineering common, but extremely effective. "That scared me," says Jason Belford, associate director of cyber security for Georgia Tech's OIT. "One out of every four people responded, and they were all technical. These are the people that had the keys to the kingdom."

Georgia Tech's experience is typical. The click-through rate on phishing e-mail messages typically starts at 20 percent or higher in most organisations, according to training companies. Training can help reduce that to single digits but only very infrequently to zero, which means that combining training with exploit-mitigation technologies is necessary to keep out attackers.

But while employees sitting in an office environment in front of a company PC might be more aware of security threats, that awareness is likely to drop significantly when they're on their own time—or in their cabin. Smartphones are regularly used for business purposes, and are now all-pervasive on ships, but few of us seem aware that they represent a growing attack vector.

"Five or six years ago, everything was targeting the laptop, but smartphones have more data, more features, and more capabilities," says Yeongjin Jang, a Ph.D. candidate in Georgia Tech's College of Computing. "So the attackers are trying to get access to these devices through various means." The response of Apple and Android respectively has been very different and produced correspondingly very different outcomes.

Google opened its Android platform to spur fast adoption and keep access to the app store as simple as possible, whilst Apple has kept iOS closed source and rigorously controls what's allowed in its store. The result of these two policies has been dramatic in security terms. 99 per cent of mobile malware targets Android devices, trying to infect systems via the Google Play app store or persuading users to download and install applications from third-party stores and untrusted sites.

The Apple iOS is still vulnerable though: the well-publicised attack on iCloud allowed cyber thieves to steal intimate photos of celebrities taken on their iPhones and uploaded to the cloud.

Contributing to the problem is the application developers who are focussed on monetising their user bases and not on securing their software. Many, and possibly the majority of, apps have vulnerabilities which can be exploited. In 2014, 91 percent of the top 200 iOS apps and 83 percent of the top 200 Android apps had some risky behaviour, according to data collected by mobile app reputation service Appthority. As the trend towards mobile payments gathers pace the likelihood is that focus on smartphones will only intensify.

Whilst employees are undoubtedly being targeted by cyber criminals, there is a subset who are by no means unwitting victims. A study by Symantec and Ponemon found that 53 per cent of employees think it's fine to take corporate data because 'it doesn't harm the company'. Unfortunately though, there are those employees whose objective is to do just that.

Malpractice accounts for 35 per cent of all data breaches, which also spike around the time employees prepare to exit companies. So whilst the outside threat is very real, the insider threat is actually the most costly. Companies require more time to detect and respond to insider attacks, nearly 260 days, compared to 170 days for other attacks, according to data from the Ponemon Institute's 2014 Cost of Cybercrime survey. Incidents involving malicious insiders also cost, on average, more than $210,000 to resolve.

And it seems that it is this type of threat which really resonates with ship operators. For those at the SingTel roundtable the overwhelming belief was that the security threat was more likely to come from disgruntled employees wanting to disrupt commercial operations, rather than any external individuals or groups.

Captain Tey You Huat of Altus Shipping warned that crew sabotage of a network could have far-reaching operational implications for owners and managers and it would take some time to re-establish many day-to-day automated functions, "Internally if the crew sabotaged, your network is down so most of your day to day functions that depend on downloading data is all gone. It will take some time before you can restore it."

Combating the insider threat is a growing area of concern. A potential solution could be Anomaly Detection Systems—modelling user behaviour and raising a red flag when people begin to act outside expectations. By determining behavioural profiles for employees organisations are then able to identify unusual activity—such as increased sickness absence, reduced productivity or excessive spending—which might signal an employee is about to go rogue. One such research project being run by Georgia Tech is called Layered Ensemble Anomaly Detection (LEAD). "We don't want to catch insiders at the moment they do something bad," says Erica Briscoe, senior research scientist at the Georgia Tech Research Institute. "We want to catch them before they do it."

But Anomaly Detection continues to be difficult, because defining "normal" behaviour is difficult. The reality is that addressing the problem requires a variety of complementary approaches, combining technology, training and access control processes like enforceable two-person security. As rogue insiders often act alone, companies can defend against unapproved actions by requiring another person to sign off on risky activities. Researchers are already developing drivers for popular operating systems which will require two or more operators to sign off on actions like updating the operating system or copying data to removable media. It's the same principle as the two keys necessary to launch a nuclear missile.

But when it comes to insider attacks there is an upside—we know where they are. And that offers us additional, useful tools like deterrence and punishment. "In most computer security areas, we have no ability to deter the attackers—the person who is breaking into your network is on the other side of the planet, and you are never going to find them," says Tom Cross, director of research at security firm Lancope. "Even if you do, they are likely in a country from which they cannot be extradited. But you know the insider who creates the insider threat, you have a personal relationship with them, and you have access to them, so you can manage the problem in a different way."

It's an oft-repeated mantra in maritime that our people are our greatest asset. But in our new hyper-connected industry they're fast becoming a liability. It doesn't have to be that way though. It's worth remembering that when a company gets breached it isn't just commercial information that gets into the wild.

As the recent Sony hack amply demonstrated data and information that employees themselves categorically do not want made public—from personal records to internal, uncomplimentary emails—are as likely to be leaked. So properly informed, trained, engaged and supported our people could become a formidable weapon—a bulwark against the cyber-hordes at the gate.

The nut that holds the wheel will always remain a point of failure. But we're all a lot safer if he's got his head screwed on.

London, January 2015.

19

WRAPPED IN THE FLAG

This year the bitter war between publishers and the mighty Amazon spilled out of the trade papers and onto the world stage.

Amazon and global publishing giant Hachette, never the easiest of bedfellows, have been locked in a six-month long dispute about the pricing of e-books. Failure to reach agreement means the world's largest online bookshop has been refusing pre-orders for Hachette titles, with the result that some authors report sales of their books falling by between 50 and 90 per cent. The whole thing could have been avoided if—back in the mid-2000s, while Amazon was busy developing its Kindle and the digital ecosystem which would lead it to such bookselling dominance—someone had shown that kind of technology and vision to Hachette.

Back then before publishing had the stuffing torn out of it by digital disruption, if only someone had put into the hands of those responsible for Hachette's digital development, a working e-reader from a company with a technology pedigree and a readiness to collaborate on developing just the kind of direct-to-consumer digital book ecosystem which now has them over a barrel.

Somebody did. Before Amazon had even launched an international version of the Kindle, Hachette was handed the iRex DR1000SW, a touchscreen, WiFi-enabled e-reader you could write on. It had the same form factor as the world-beating iPad and was produced by an outfit which had spun out of the Dutch electronics giant Philips. Hachette had in front of it the technology that could have given Amazon a run for its money in the digital ebook space, and they turned it down. Hachette did give a reason for closing the door to its own iPad sized e-reader: they doubted that people would like anything that odd size, because it just didn't fit into its Editors' handbags.

There's a reason this story is important. Because it demonstrates clearly that publishing's woes don't stem from an aggressive competitor with proprietary technology, lots of money and a killer digital idea. Hachette had all that too, at about the same time and yet they failed to appreciate either the opportunity they had, or the threat implicit in any failure to pursue it.

When industries and companies look back on periods of great disruption there's a tendency to assume that they were doomed from the start, and the narrative develops to support that. But the truth is that what determines the outcome is not necessarily the situation but the mindset.

Publishing saw a comfortable business model with happy customers, supportive booksellers and an inexhaustible supply of new authors who all loved paper books and disliked the thought of reading on screens much as they did. By contrast Amazon saw an inefficient model in which 90 per cent of authors fail to earn out their advances, expensive infrastructure and overheads, big margins and a massive, untapped pool of Millennial readers who were also writers, desperate to create and share content.

What everyone always wants is a crystal ball, in fact according to a recent Lloyd's List article it's one of the top five things every shipping CEO needs to have to survive in the business. In reality though change and particularly digital change actually gives industries a reasonable run-up.

And therein often lies the problem. Exponential trends like

machine learning and autonomy—the two in particular which are likely in my opinion to impact shipping—are moving very fast under the radar, but their stealth is allowing many in shipping and maritime to persuade themselves they aren't relevant.

The danger for us is exactly the same as it was for publishing, allowing a comfortable group-think to delude us that digital won't change things. We are a business which is inefficient, polluting and unacceptably dangerous, with frustrated and unhappy customers, and we are ripe for disruption. And falling back on arguments about regulation and public safety to try and fend off the inevitable won't work.

The response by the horse and carriage trade in the 1860s to the dawn of the age of the automobile in the UK was to lobby MPs to restrict their use and protect the trade's livelihood. The result was the 1865 Red Flag Act which required all automobiles to travel at a maximum of 4mph and a man carrying a red flag to walk in front.

This absurdity has gone down in history, but the desire of those threatened by new technology to wrap themselves in the same red flag continues. This week the general secretary of the British Airline Pilots Association, Jim McAuslan told BBC Radio 4's Today programme that when commercial airliners were able to fly themselves in ten years time everyone on the ground responsible for them should have the same equivalent training as a fully qualified commercial pilot. According to McAuslan the general public expects anyone responsible for controlling autonomous airliners not to be, "some whizz-kid trained in Microsoft flight trainer."

Quite aside from demonstrating a fundamental lack of understanding about what autonomy actually means, the language is revealing. Technology in commercial aviation has reduced the number of crew in the cockpit of commercial airliners from five to two in a generation and, like seafarers, pilots are threatened by the prospect that machine learning algorithms within a decade will be demonstrably safer than humans at flying aeroplanes or sailing ships.

Characterising this new technology as the preserve of inexperienced whizz-kids speaks to a generational fear, and in many respects it's well founded. The millennial generation is building a new technology-enabled world which a lot of digital immigrants really aren't comfortable in.

If you're a digital immigrant leading a company there's a way to address that though. Reverse mentoring programmes which pair up young Millennials with senior leaders can allow companies to foster knowledge and understanding which exponentially benefits the organisation as a whole. Understanding the motivations of the Millennials brings the opportunities for new digital models, and customer expectations into sharper relief.

But it isn't enough to understand where we are now, it's essential to know where we're going. In one word that's prediction, and it's powerful enough to be threatening the behemoth Google itself.

You may have heard of Pinterest, you equally might not. Pinterest is a young visual social network company which allows users to create and share image collections of anything from recipes to hairstyles to furniture. Less than five years old it's already more popular than Twitter, which you will have heard of.

There are more than 750 million boards made up of more than 30 billion individual pins, with 54 million new ones added each day on Pinterest, and only Facebook with its 1.3 billion users, drives more traffic to Web publishers. Already analysts are predicting that Pinterest is shortly going to leave Facebook, Twitter and the rest of its social stablemates dead in the water and start bringing in billions of dollars.

The reason for that is that Pinterest is something completely new. Facebook is about your connections, past events and memories, and users volunteer a staggering amount of retrospective information about themselves which Facebook uses to power its highly targeted advertising offerings. But Facebook can only indicate your past performance and preferences and offer your eyes to advertisers on that basis. Twitter has an even harder time: it can only offer advertisers a presence in real-time conversations. But where Facebook is selling the past and Twitter is selling the present, Pinterest can actually predict the future.

"It's about what you aspire to do, what you want to do down

the line," says Pinterest founder and CEO Ben Silbermann. When a user pins a picture of a pair of shoes or a model of car, it's akin to someone tearing a page out of a magazine. It shows intent, and for the first time allows a social network to get into the business of prediction.

Of course there is already an incumbent in the business of prediction, and that's Google. But whereas Google is just about search, Pinterest is talking about 'discovery', which according to its product head Tim Kendall, "is the biggest business opportunity in the last 10 to 20 years for an online business."

Silbermann's mission and its consequences are clear, "How do we do for discovery what Google did for search? How do we show you the things you're going to love even if you didn't know what you were looking for? We think if we answer that question, all the other parts of the business will follow."

Discovery is where the world is going, and it's where shipping will go too. From algorithms which put ships where they're needed before customers realise they want them, to algorithms which identify stresses on overloaded hulls like those which sank the MOL Comfort, in real-time. At its heart though, it is about understanding your customer and your situation in minute, grinding detail, and operationalising those precious insights before the next guy.

I know that Hachette were given that opportunity and that technology when they were because I was the someone who took it to them. And I can guarantee you that right now, somewhere in shipping someone else is schlepping a truly transformative digital technology opportunity around and being told that it's a nice idea, but it just doesn't fit in their eco-ships.

Just make sure that isn't you. Or the rest will be history.

London, January 2015.

20

SHIPPING'S NEXT LIGHTBULB MOMENT

Back in the late 1990s a story made the rounds which has found its way into legend. At the time V-chips—the technology which allows parents to censor TV programmes where bad language appears—were becoming standard in all US television sets. It's limitations were exposed however when in combination with the TV's closed-captioning system the V-chip chose to sanitise the actor Dick van Dyke's name to 'Jerk van Gay'.

The story became infamous because it's funny, but also because it reinforced the comforting and widely held belief that no matter how fast they added things up, computers could never replace the piece of work that is a man. Nuance, language and context would always be beyond them.

Just over ten years later in 2011, the IBM computer known as Watson went on the US quiz show *Jeopardy!* and—in a test of similes, jokes and riddles—beat the humans. This year Google's machine learning algorithm mapped the precise location of every household, business and street number in the whole of France, in one hour. Ray Kurzweil, Google's director of engineering, says that by 2029 machines could become conscious.

To say that we are living through a period of massive techno-logical change really is an understatement. The acronym VUCA, has been coined to capture the characteristics of the world we're currently expected to navigate, which PwC describes as a 'world in beta'. Volatility, Uncertainty, Complexity and Ambiguity are no longer short-term issues to overcome but a new status quo.

Across industries, geographies and societies massive change is underway, and yet a significant portion of the shipping and mar-itime industry is still comfortably laughing at the Jerk van Gay story. There is a mass delusion going on that somehow shipping is going to be immune from all of this. That—to paraphrase Robert C Gallagher—change is inevitable, except from a vending machine, and the shipping industry.

Not only is this myopic and dangerous, it's also illogical. Listen to anyone in our industry and they'll tell you that shipping's for-tunes are intimately connected to those of the world economy, the whims of governments and a host of other external, global, unpre-dictable factors no one in shipping can influence.

Well, the digital trends we're talking about are going to change all those things, and therefore, by extension, shipping. The oppor-tunity lies in not simply allowing ourselves to be passively buffeted by these trends, but harnessing them now to empower, energise and improve our industry almost beyond our current comprehension. We've already proved that's possible.

In the early 1830s a fully laden sailing ship leaving from Great Britain would take approximately five weeks to cross the Atlantic. Then in 1838 Isambard Kingdom Brunel's new steamship the *Great Western* made the voyage in just fifteen days. The *Great Western's* voyage was the first of a new era. Shipping 1.0, the age of sail, last-ed over two thousand years, shipping 2.0 has lasted less than two hundred.

Built on fossil fuels, economies of scale, mass consumerism, globalisation, and improved communications it has been defined by the advent of steam, radio, and containerisation. In shipping 2.0 the experience of building, sailing and operating ships was profoundly different from that which had gone before, but the change to shipping 3.0 will be even greater. Shipping 1.0 was sail, shipping 2.0 was steam, and shipping 3.0 is digital.

This year DNV GL unveiled the ReVolt concept ship, unmanned and battery powered; by 2018 Rolls-Royce anticipate they will have their first fully autonomous prototype ship capable of unmanned operation; by 2025 fully automated ships will be entering the market; ten years later many types of ship will be delivered with autonomous operation capabilities, and by 2050 segments like container shipping could be fully automated and unmanned. It's also entirely possible that all of this is far too pessimistic.

But to focus solely upon the change to our ships—iconic though that will be—is too narrow. Shipping 3.0 represents a far greater set of challenges than a move to autonomous ships and unmanned operations.

"There is no silver bullet in this world of innovation," says Heather Cox, Citi's chief client-experience, digital and marketing officer for global consumer banking. "We don't know where the digital world is heading."

It's a statement which in previous years may have been considered ill-advised for a company in a highly competitive market to make. But it's a reflection of the shift in approach to managing and leading organisations that's happening everywhere.

The more data and information we're getting the less organisations and individuals are realising we know. The traditional leaders, with big personalities and a preference for gut feel at the top of companies are declining in influence. In fact the whole notion that any organisation has all the intelligence and innovation it needs within its confines is being thrown out.

In many respects it almost feels as though there's a humbling of business going on. The digital revolution is forcing transparency, exposing the less savoury bits of organisations that no one ever used to see—like margins—and then broadcasting them to customers across massive, uncensored communications channels. But it's not all bad news, because the communications channels work both ways, allowing businesses to listen and learn and collaborate with absolutely anyone anywhere on the planet, tapping the global brain to solve their most intractable problems.

The mantra of this new normal is 'simplify, standardise, share'. But shipping and maritime isn't adapting quickly enough. Humility is in very short supply and as for simplicity, the industry has always believed itself to be highly complex and used that to justify conservatism, insularity and poor customer service. In the age of machine-learning though, where Google can map every street number in France in an hour, complexity isn't an excuse for not delivering.

In fact we aren't even going into this new era with the most basic requirements in place. Any business must have an attractive value proposition for customers, make money from that value proposition, and adequately organise or access the resources needed to deliver it. Large sectors of the shipping industry haven't even got that right yet.

The upside of that—and something which many outside the industry are recognising—is that shipping is ripe for disruption, improvement and holds huge opportunity. Surviving in shipping 2.0 was tough but success in shipping 3.0 is going to involve a wholesale reappraisal by incumbent companies of just how they are going to be affected by, and capitalise upon new technologies.

Gartner recently grouped the key technology trends for 2015 into three main areas; the merging of the real and virtual worlds; intelligence everywhere, and the emergence of a new IT reality. For shipping you can add to that the massive improvements in deep sea connectivity.

Whilst shipping comes in for a good deal of criticism from other industries about how technologically backward it is, one has to appreciate the gulf between the type of shore-side connectivity they've been enjoying and what was available at a reasonable price to shipping for decades.

The advent of new HTS networks like Inmarsat GlobalXpress and Intelsat's EPIC is a genuine game changer for our industry. But even now, without either network fully on-line, high-grade connectivity is affordable for ship operators, and yet they are not investing in it, or leveraging it at anywhere approaching the scale they should.

There is a cost involved, but actually it's about more than that. Investing in communications infrastructure on board a ship isn't as straightforward as it might appear.

Ship managers frequently know all too well the kind of efficiencies they can drive with better communications, how much better they can fulfil charterers requirements. But with ships on rolling management contracts there's no guarantee the vessel they spend good money fitting an IP satellite system to will actually be theirs to manage a few months down the line.

Trying to persuade owners to make any additional investments over and above the cost of the tonnage is difficult. Ship owning is increasingly just speculation. With customers dissatisfied at one end and owners only interested in maximising returns at the other, it's one symptom of how increasingly dysfunctional the industry has become. Put bluntly though, connectivity is the bedrock of our world in beta, and shipping 3.0. Without it shipping can't exploit and defend against the new digital reality.

We have to improve interactions with customers, employees, suppliers and stakeholders. We must connect with our ships, machinery and other assets and stream that big data home where algorithms can crunch it and provide support for evidence based management decisions. We must also focus on how that connectivity can form the basis of innovative new business models, operations, products, and customer services.

As we identified in our January 2014 Cloud issue, the shipping industry is already seeing digital technology drive transparency. Young companies like Xeneta, Freightos and Vessels Value are opening up opaque business practices and putting pressure on margins and prices.

Vessels Value spun out of a ship broker, but as the 'plug and play' digital business models proliferate and traditional barriers of entry to a global business like shipping are undermined, new competitors from outside shipping and maritime will appear. Digital delivery platforms and marketplaces like KVH's IP MobileCast and Inmarsat's GX Service Enablement Platform will grow and access to the shipping and maritime market will democratise with transaction costs falling and value chains disaggregating.

Maritime software companies used to having the industry to themselves will face new aggressive and globally resourced competitors and lightning-fast start-ups in equal measure. Travel, recruitment, and intermediary services like broking and insurance are all particularly vulnerable to small competitors plugging into cheap infrastructure and undercutting both price and reach, packaging and pricing services in real-time.

Any preconceptions the industry has that seafarers are the only ones whose jobs are threatened in shipping 3.0 won't last long. It's estimated that up to 70 per cent of all white-collar information gathering jobs in the US are vulnerable to being taken by machines in the coming decade. Known as 'knowledge automation', more and more frontline and middle-management jobs focussed on synthesising information used by senior management will be automated.

But as those positions disappear, the bigger headache will be recruiting the kind of highly-skilled Millennials shipping and maritime businesses will desperately need. Creative problem-solvers with an aptitude for maths, science and digital business opportunities will command high salaries and demand the kind of flexible working environments shipping doesn't routinely offer.

Shipping's leaders have to respond to these broad digital business trends, but for an industry which is so closely dependent upon current global trade flows, we also have to start appreciating how our customers are going to react to them.

Delivering our customers improvements in price, speed, reliability and security is necessary, but the reality is that the impact of trends like 3D printing, next-shoring and nearshoring, the circular economy, collaborative consumption, hyper-connectivity and crowdsourcing might mean there just aren't the customers to be had in some sectors in the future.

Speaking at the TOC Americas conference Dr Jean-Paul Rodrigue, of the department of global studies and geography, Hofstra University said, "The shipping market has changed, the core principles have changed and the drivers are changing. We used to talk about economies of scale; now we need to talk about the diseconomies of scale." In the same month that China Shipping Lines prepares to launch the largest container ship ever built, Dr Rodrigue hammered his point home. "Containerisation is entering a phase of maturity and at this point in time we are having a very difficult time finding the drivers for the next wave of containerisation. China is dying; all the drivers pushing for transpacific trade have reached maturity. The offshoring and outsourcing cycle that has benefited the industry so much is now pretty much done. The next driver is going to result in less growth for containers because of nearsourcing."

It seems that our industry just isn't appreciating how the world is changing. It's a position which hasn't improved since the Lloyd's Global Marine Trends 2030 report in 2013 failed to even identify autonomous, unmanned ships as a potential development for commercial shipping between now and 2030. Technology, it claimed, was just too disruptive to model. But that's not good enough. It's crucial that we have an industry-wide awareness of where these technology trends are taking the world.

In short, shipping 3.0 is going to be as much a mindset as an activity. There is no doubt that business models are going to change repeatedly, and the pace of that change, and of business itself, is going to become relentless. In light of that, the lack of diversity on shipping and maritime company management and boards is a handicap.

Hiring people just like us means we're constantly reinforcing our own beliefs and prejudices. That can have a major impact on companies facing digital disruption. The overwhelmingly white, Scandinavian, male board of Nokia just didn't see the threat from Apple coming. The same accusation has been levelled at the all-Japanese, male, family dominated boards in Japan which many believe bear some responsibility for its long recession.

We have to find people who challenge us, and we have to be prepared to fail harder and faster and make iterative improvements based upon what we've learnt. To start with every shipping leader should institute a reverse mentoring programme without delay. Pair up tech-savvy Millennials in your business with senior management and start diluting the corporate-think, then see where those new ideas take you. I can guarantee you will be surprised, because the new world these Millennials are shaping is almost inconceivable to most of us aged 40+.

There are organisations and individuals in the shipping industry who get it already. Even now shipping just doesn't give the returns that other industries do, and that's before shipping 3.0 really starts to bite.

AP Moller–Maersk chief Nils S Andersen recently urged his audience at the Danish Maritime Forum to order a little less and look a little further into the future, focus more on market needs.

"Prices of everything are coming down, and you have technology risk, so why on earth don't we believe that owning ships is a minus game?" said Andersen. "The chance of making money speculating in ships is limited. I don't know many people who get the idea of speculating on the price of trucks or Volkswagen Golfs."

On the supplier side, by driving the autonomy and unmanned operation agenda, incumbents like Rolls-Royce—aiming to be shipping 3.0's number one systems integrator—have already stepped onto the exponential growth track. For those still on a linear path the opportunity to catch them is already diminishing.

Making predictions is a mug's game, but I'm going to stick my neck out here and make one. It is my belief that of all the powerful technology trends shaping the world, the two most important for shipping will be autonomy and the AI which offers predictive analytics.

The introduction of autonomous vehicles is probably the single most disruptive thing which will happen to the world in the next few decades. Add to that the ability of machine learning algorithms to predict the future and I think you can have a stab at extrapolating how at least some of shipping 3.0 might go. You can read our vision in the boxes above and overleaf.

I listened to the maritime economist Martin Stopford at a conference recently saying that shipping was a bit old-fashioned and plenty of people, including him, rather liked it that way. He also said that what the industry needed was a Steve Jobs. I don't disagree that shipping is conservative, and yet we have to remember that it has had lightbulb moments. Literally.

It's largely forgotten now, but the first commercial use of the lightbulb outside Thomas Edison's Menlo Park was on the passenger steamer *SS Columbia*. Having seen Edison's first demonstration of the technology, president of the Oregon Railroad and Navigation Company Henry Villard decided he wanted it installed on his new ship.

Insurers were extremely reluctant to provide cover, and even Edison was hesitant. But when she sailed on May 2nd 1880 with her electric lights blazing in the saloon, *Columbia* made history. Seventy years later Malcom McLean's ingenuity led to the age of containerisation, which revolutionised world trade.

Both those pioneering men however, weren't from shipping. Villard was in railroads, and McLean in trucks. So when Stopford says we need a Steve Jobs, perhaps what he means is not just a visionary, but a visionary from outside the industry.

"Sometimes it's easier to innovate when you don't know the rules," says Mary Monahan EVP and research director at Javelin Research & Strategy. "Once you know all the problems, it's harder to go outside the box."

Going outside the box is something we're going to have to learn to do a lot more of. Google's prediction that we're only fifteen years away from machines becoming self-aware sounds pretty scary. But what's really frightening is that shipping still isn't.

Let's hope we wake up before they do.

London, October 2014.

21

PEAK HUMAN

A horse walks into a bar and the robot barman says, "
01110111 01101000 01111001 00100000 01110100
01101000 01100101 00100000 01101100 01101111
01101110 01100111 00100000 01100110 01100001 01100011
01100101."

Up until now the premise of that joke was ridiculous, and not because of the horse. For generations the one place you've always been guaranteed human company, maybe a sympathetic ear, the odd piece of timely advice, and an alcoholic beverage of your choice, was a bar.

But when Royal Caribbean's new Quantum of the Seas debuts in Southampton, UK in April 2015, it won't just be the guests in the new Bionic Bar that are well-oiled. RCCL's robot bartenders will be behind the bar mixing cocktails ordered via the tablet screens at each table.

The US Navy's ships are notorious for being dry, so you won't find bartenders, robotic or otherwise, mixing anything on those. But the navy is heavily exploiting the possibilities of robots.

Last month it released video showing how autonomous drone

boats could 'swarm' around potentially hostile craft to protect cutters or larger Navy vessels, sparing the ship's company the danger of a boarding party.

Earlier this year the Naval Research Laboratory unveiled a firefighting robot. SAFFiR—the Shipboard Autonomous Firefighting Robot—is designed to move autonomously throughout the ship, interact with people, and fight fires, handling many of the dangerous firefighting tasks that are normally performed by humans.

It isn't just cruise companies and navies embracing this kind of technology. A few of the biggest commercial shipyards are reported to have more than 50 per cent automation in their processes already. As part of its Vision 2020 strategy Daewoo has produced the 'Iron Man' industrial exoskeleton robot, developed using Human-Robot Interaction (HRI) technology, which allows workers wearing them to lift objects of up to 30kg while walking normally. Research is underway to increase that to 100kg and the robots are already being rolled out.

These innovations and the robotics, computing power, algorithms and other technology driving them offer the possibility of significantly increased safety and protection for crew and maritime workers ashore. So one would be forgiven for assuming that the maritime industry would be delighted. Not so. In fact the general attitude is neatly summed up by the tweet from one big maritime charity on the US Navy story, "Another nail in the coffin for seafarers."

Set this alongside comments reported by SeaTrade attributed to Michael Grey of Bimco, who explained to an audience in Greece recently "his conviction that much of the glamour, adventure and resourcefulness once associated with seafaring has been lost as technology and regulations have not only replaced human endeavour and the joy of sailing around the world, but resulted in complacency, and this is not good for safety nor the environment, nor the economics of the industry."

The industry backlash to comments made by Rolls-Royce's Oskar Levander regarding the future benefits of automated/unmanned ships was as blunt as it was predictable. Considering the paradigm shift unmanned ships present, perhaps that's understandable. But for Bimco to claim that technology isn't good for seafarers, safety, the industry or the environment, presumably they must have some evidence.

It's true that as technology advances rapidly we are only slowly understanding some of the hidden effects it's having on the humans who use it—crew included. ECDIS is the clearest example of the digital revolution happening on the bridge, getting rid of the paper charts and switching to a digital screen instead.

However, neuroscience has already revealed that we use different parts of our brains to read from a sheet of paper, than we do to read on a screen. The result is that the more we read on screens, the more we shift towards "non-linear reading", characterised by skimming a screen or having your eyes dart around a web page.

"They call it a "bi-literate" brain," says Manoush Zomorodi, managing editor and host of WNYC's New Tech City. "The problem is that many of us have adapted to reading online just too well. And if you don't use the deep reading part of your brain, you lose the deep reading part of your brain."

Deep reading is the concentrated type of reading we use to "immerse ourselves in a novel or read a mortgage document," Zoromodi says. It uses the type of long-established linear reading one doesn't usually do on a computer. "Dense text that we really want to understand requires deep reading, and on the internet we don't do that."

Maryanne Wolf, Director of the Center for Reading and Language Research at Tufts University, recommends keeping the deep reading part of the brain alive by setting sometime aside each day to read on paper. "I don't worry that we'll become dumb because of the Internet," Wolf says, "but I worry we will not use our most preciously acquired deep reading processes because we're just given too much stimulation. That's, I think, the nub of the problem. I think the evidence someday will be able to show us that what we're after is a discerning 'bi-literate' brain."

Too much stimulation is an issue for most people—adults and children—in the developed world. But in a fast-moving environment, or a challenging situation like a bridge multiple inputs on various devices and screens allow us to process far more information far more quickly and effectively. Or does it?

According to research by Stanford University multitasking is actually less productive than doing a single thing at a time. Researchers discovered that those who are regularly faced with several streams of electronic information cannot pay attention, recall information or switch from one job to another as well as those who are only faced with completing one task at a time. Frequent multi-taskers have been observed to struggle more to organise their thoughts and to filter out irrelevant information and are slower to switch from one task to another.

But perhaps of most concern are the results of a University of London study which appears to show that multi-tasking doesn't just slow you down, it actually lowers your IQ. Those taking part in the study who multi-tasked during cognitive tasks experienced IQ declines similar to those which would be seen in people who had smoked marijuana or been up all night. To put that into context, multi-tasking men lowered their IQ scores to the average range of an 8 year old child.

Worse than that, the cognitive impairment might not be temporary. Researchers at the University of Sussex MRI-scanned people who spent a high proportion of their time on multiple devices and discovered these high multi-taskers had less brain density in the anterior cingulate cortex, a region responsible for empathy as well as cognitive and emotional control.

"I feel that it is important to create an awareness that the way we are interacting with the devices might be changing the way we think and these changes might be occurring at the level of brain structure," says neuroscientist Kep Kee Loh, the study's lead author.

It seems that our brains simply weren't designed to do two things at once, therefore multi-tasking reduces focus, efficiency and performance. So perhaps Bimco has a point.

Technology's onward march does appear to be changing us, but even if the implications—both commercial and safety related—are significant, there seems little prospect that we'll be able to eradicate the necessity of multi-tasking, whether on board ship or ashore. The real fear though, is that technology won't just change us, it's going to leave large numbers of us behind completely.

As the world becomes ever more complex we need to process increasingly vast amounts of data, from multiple sources, reliably and accurately and then make intelligent decisions about how to act on it. Humans appear to be approaching the limits of their abilities in this regard. Peak Oil is considered to be the point in time when the maximum rate of petroleum extraction is reached, leading to terminal decline. Is the same about to happen to the human race? Are we shortly going to hit Peak Human?

The private worry that technology will change the maritime industry we love and take away the jobs we need is a deep-rooted one amongst the older generation. It's an unspoken and unarticulated fear which often underlies a lot of the opposition to new technologies one comes across in maritime. But there's a reason this fear exists—because in maritime we've already seen technology do exactly that before.

Containerisation was the trigger for major struggles between shipping industry managers and workers. Studies demonstrated that its efficiencies in comparison to breakbulk made nineteen in every twenty dock workers redundant. Such changes inevitably led to unhappiness amongst dockworkers and their unions which lasted well into the 1980s. In fact a 2012 strike at the US's largest port complex in Southern California which affected approximately $1billion in trade per day could be traced back to a pact between unions and employers agreed post-containerisation.

Despite all the efforts of unions and others, the results of containerisation was a major reduction in the number of seafarers onboard ships and even more huge drops in the number of dock workers. The number of registered longshoremen on the U.S. East Coast fell by over two-thirds from 1952 to 1972, while the number of dock workers in the United Kingdom fell from over 70,000 to under 10,000 between the early 1960s and the late 1980s. They joined thousands of former UK shipyard workers made redundant because of the shipyards' and the unions' inability to adjust to new technology. These job losses happened in spite of worldwide ship-ping increasing more than 600 per cent between 1950 and 1973.

As the International Longshoremen's and Warehouseman's Union which struck the landmark Mechanisation and Moderniza-tion Agreement in 1960 to protect workers post-containerisation discovered, the technology didn't just affect dock workers, it led to job losses across the port infrastructure. And our industry is about to face a re-run, but far worse. The scale of the changes which tech-nology has brought to shipping have been substantial in the past, but what we are now facing is unprecedented and seismic.

According to data scientist Jeremy Howard the exact moment at which a computer out-performed a human in a human task was in 2011, when an algorithm was designed which could recognise streets signs. Even when these were blurred or it was dark the algorithm was correct 99.4 per cent of the time as opposed to the human's 98.5 per cent. This may sound fairly inconsequential, but it isn't. It is conservatively estimated that up to 70 per cent of all white-collar jobs involved in information processing in the US are vulnerable to being taken by computers, and the implications for our seafarers and shore-based personnel are equally serious.

"I think people are massively underestimating the impact, on both their organizations and on society, of the combination of data plus modern analytical techniques," says Howard. "The reason for that is very clear: these techniques are growing exponentially in capability, and the human brain just can't conceive of that."

It is this combination of data, analysis and algorithms which will create the unmanned ship, but that really is just the tip of the iceberg. Yes, seafaring jobs will be under threat, but the threat to the wider industry apparently hasn't yet sunk in.

Whereas previous technology waves have unseated blue-collar, lower-skilled workers, this one threatens us all. The ability of com-puters to do precisely what the human brain struggles to do, means that their skills are now in the ascendant.

Sometimes called 'knowledge automation', we are already in a situation where computers are able displace professionals working in everything from medicine to the law. Rolls-Royce estimate that removing crew from ships, even taking into account the new autonomy infrastructures, could save an operator 40% of his costs. The industry is burdened with high costs for fuel, emissions compliance and massively costly assets. Seafarers are expensive, fragile and require constant training and assessment, plus a whole host of kit onboard a ship that gets in the way of cargo. Do we really think this isn't going to happen?

Apparently IMO has got no idea what's coming down the track. Writing on his blog following the Danish Maritime Forum where the potential of the shipping industry to 2030 and beyond was discussed, IMO Secretary-General Koji Sekimizu says the following: " If the current fleet were to increase in size by 70 per cent between now and 2030, as was predicted by many participants based on the growth trend of the last five decades, the current number of 500,000 officers needs to be increased to 850,000. If we assume that half the existing officers will retire by 2030, that means 600,000 officers would need to be recruited and trained from now, with an annual requirement for officers in the order of some 40,000. This is a real challenge and further effort must be made to bring new generations into seafaring as a profession."

This kind of comfortable thinking—basing growth predictions on what has gone before—isn't going to be sustainable for much longer. DNV GL predict that the first prototype autonomous ships could appear as early as next year, by 2035 they'll be routine, and by 2050 the entire Container sector could be unmanned. We aren't going to need 600,000 more officers. Eventually we might not need any at all.

Tuck Yew Lui, Singapore's minister of transport also focussed on the "global challenge" of attracting the next generation of seafarers, but made a far more significant point. Shortages of seafarers he believes will be a trigger for more automated vessels. "Will robots work alongside the crew to relieve some of the work and stress?" he said. "I think it is important we must discuss this."

That sentiment is to be welcomed because the issue is becoming an urgent one for industries and governments, and we need to start preparing to respond. We are facing a scenario where those with the data and the algorithms provide and add value, whilst the rest of the workforce adds little or none. A cursory glance back at the confrontations and unrest which followed containerisation are instructional. This time major social disruption could stem from a larger group of people who can't add economic value any longer, but still need to earn a wage.

"I think it's the most important problem facing the world today," says Nobel-prize winning Economist Robert Shiller. "Since we tend to define ourselves by our intellectual talents, it's also a question of personal identity. Who am I? Intellectual talents are being replaced by computers. That's a frightening thing for most people. It's an issue with deep philosophical implications."

The warning is that this problem is going to be upon the maritime industry before we really know it. Those worthy organisations, unions, charities, chambers and associations, whose purpose is the protection of the people who work in the maritime industry, aren't talking about what other industries have already recognised as inevitable. Whether that is because, as Jeremy Howard suggests, they aren't capable of conceiving the sheer scale of what we're facing, or perhaps because our industry is just so insular, they don't know, doesn't really matter. What matters is that the situation changes, rapidly.

The traditional positions are no longer viable for these organisations, as containerisation demonstrated so ably. Resisting the new technology, striking, extracting agreements from employers and then watching men and women lose their jobs while charities pick up the pieces didn't work then, and it won't work for the thousands of seafarers and managers affected this time.

So what can we do? The first thing is to recognise the problem and understand the potential implications for the industry. Maritime is lousy with research into all sorts of things, but no one yet has a clear idea exactly who will be vulnerable in the coming "Second Machine Age." From the unmanned ship to algorithms, those who represent the workforce in all its forms need to get to grips with who and where the biggest impacts will hit.

That information will allow us then to start exploring ways

to mitigate the damage. One promising avenue has already been experimented with by the US Government—Wage or Livelihood insurance.

"Wage insurance is not exactly the right name for this. I call it livelihood insurance," says Shiller. "By using that name we're not talking just about wage earners, we're talking about the earning potential an individual has. It may or may not be wage income."

Livelihood insurance acknowledges that individuals train for a particular occupation and very rarely retrain later for another. As a result their fortunes rise and fall with that occupation. According to Shiller and others, industries could develop measures of occupational risk and use them to write insurance policies against risks to particular occupations.

Such policies would differ from traditional welfare and unemployment benefits in that the insurance was against risk to the occupation rather than the job, avoiding the danger of disincentivisation.

It's never been done before, but if only half of the jobs potentially under threat turn out to be so, it could protect thousands within the maritime industry.

Engineers will still be needed, but probably not in their current numbers, and working at central port maintenance facilities. Shipyard workers are already facing 50 per cent automation: if new ships are built to a standard design as looks possible, the impact on them could be massive. Seafarers will be needed in ever decreasing numbers, and will require increasing amounts of interaction with computers. Livelihood insurance which helped those affected to survive, train or retrain to stay in the industry or transition out of it could be a Godsend.

The future is a scary place, and technology is profoundly unsettling. But that doesn't mean we can't be far better prepared for its impacts. All those involved in the welfare of seafarers and workers in the maritime industry need to start thinking creatively about how we cope.

Focussing on quantifying the potential size of the problem is a first step and needs to happen fast. Working with national governments, industry leaders and insurers to perhaps develop some kind of livelihood insurance for the maritime industry is the next.

There is no point in fighting the technology. Getting ahead of the changes it will bring and identifying the risk areas now is the way to avoid the damage to people containerisation brought, only on a far greater scale.

Whether we are reaching Peak Human or not, the robots will continue to take our jobs, the way they did in the past. Their strength lies in the ability to learn from their mistakes.

Now it's our turn.

London, October 2014.

22

FAILSAFE

A young British Royal Navy officer in the late 1970s was taking a course—so the story goes. When he sat the final exam and got 98 per cent he was annoyed enough to go and ask the instructor where he'd lost the marks. Following a considerable amount of bluster—in which the Royal Navy specialised at that time, without the need for courses—the instructor was finally forced to admit that no errors had been made. But the mark stood because, as the young officer was informed, "no-one gets 100 per cent."

Those of you familiar with the *Star Trek* franchise may draw parallels with the fictional "*Kobayashi Maru*" exercise which all Starfleet officer-cadets must complete. The computer simulation is famous for presenting the officer-cadet with an unwinnable scenario.

No matter what the candidate does, the eventual result is the same: either his ship and crew and/or the refugees in peril die, in addition to which—for good measure—the cadet might also be responsible for violating a peace treaty and starting a cataclysmic inter-galactic war. Then they have pudding.

The *Kobayashi Maru* computer simulation is designed to be unwinnable, the objective being to give every officer-cadet an experience of failure. This piece of 1960s *Star Trek* fiction is based on the same principle as the Royal Navy's policy of never awarding 100 per cent. In the intervening forty years however the idea of failure as a necessary lesson and a spur to further reflection and endeavour has come under significant pressure.

The expansion of education and training across countries and industries has been massive, but along with it have come accusations that certificates don't mean what they once did. Far more people now pass exams than fail them and rates of qualification have increased enormously, but according to employers competence has fallen.

Part of the reason for the massive expansion of education and training has been the growth of regulation. Thanks to a complex web of it—non-fulfilment of which leaves a business wide-open both legally and financially—organisations are locked into hiring people with the appropriate qualifications. And nowhere has this been more acute than in possibly the most regulated industry in the world—shipping. Despite shipping's increasing need for qualified people, and the proliferation of courses, the gap between training which delivers compliance and training which delivers competence, according to ship operators, continues to widen.

The response from the UK government to increasing dissatisfaction amongst employers has been to try and inject more rigour into the school examinations process, which in a roundabout way means the reintroduction of failure. But it isn't just governments which are reassessing the merits of failure.

In 2013 the Oxford High School for Girls in the UK launched a test for its pupils in which it is impossible to get 100 per cent, the purpose of which, according to Helen Fraser, the chief executive of the Girls' Day School Trust, is to help girls grasp that "being perfect is the enemy of learning". This attitude is reflected in another initiative from Wimbledon High School for girls which now holds a 'failure week', where successful women are invited to the school to discuss their own failures with pupils.

Fraser told the British Sunday Times, "What is important in this context isn't whether the girls get 100 per cent but that they learn that failure is not fatal—what counts is what you learn from the experience and how you bounce back from it."

The suggestion from Wimbledon and Oxford High School is that by aiming high in tests and tasks which are just beyond them, pupils will frequently reach further than they imagined possible and develop a much-needed resilience. But fashionable as failure might be in this context, in shipping sadly it is all too often fatal.

In our industry 85-90 per cent of all accidents are caused by human factors, and our crew fatality rate is ten times that of OECD best practice, and yet seafarers are some of the most regulated, highly-trained and qualified people working today. The inescapable conclusion is that current training in shipping isn't working as well as it needs to. This is a major problem, but it isn't limited to our industry, or our people. And there is evidence that harnessing digital technology to address it can be astonishingly successful.

Non-profit organisation OneBillion which develops computer applications—apps—to reach and educate poor children in developing nations, provides a compelling example. Having developed a maths app designed to boost the education of children in Malawi, OneBillion partnered with the University of Nottingham School of Psychology's Dr Nikki Pitchford whose researchers carried out extensive field-testing to assess its effectiveness.

According to the researchers, as children in Malawi often only receive a very basic education with classes of 90 pupils or more to one teacher, the results of the randomised controlled trial were significant. "We found the app boosted the children's maths knowledge to a much greater extent than we expected," says Dr Pitchford. "Indeed it was so effective in Malawi that it begged a comparative test on children in the UK. Dunkirk Primary in Nottingham agreed to take part and allow us to carry out an identical study. What was so incredible was that in both countries we saw the same gain. One week of working on the tablets for 30 minutes a day equalled three months of formal education. We were amazed at the results."

The implications of these results are indeed significant. In just six weeks a computer maths app on personal tablets used for only 30 minutes per day enabled children with wildly different personal circumstances, life experiences, teaching support and teaching environments to make as much progress as would be expected in 12-18 months of class teaching.

What marks out the OneBillion app is its similarity to a simple computer game; one that's based on the national curriculum for maths. Children are encouraged in their success by large yellow ticks and congratulatory certificates when they complete a level. For a video report by the BBC Click programme showing the app in action visit the Futurenautics website.

It is tempting to assume that because this app uses lots of big yellow ticks, badges and certificates, it is designed for children. But to do so is to miss the point entirely. The real lesson that this and other apps are teaching us is that what works for children is not necessarily childish. It works every bit as well for adults too.

It is precisely the same sequence of badges, certificates and levels which form the core of the Deloitte Leadership Academy (DLA) training programme which, since 2008, has had over 20,000 executive users. What underlies both is the potential power of Connectivism - what its proponents describe as "a learning theory for the digital age". Focussed on the relationship between work experience, learning and knowledge, Connectivism values evidence-based and adaptive learning, and places heavy emphasis on the use of technology to influence how people communicate and learn.

It's these principles which also underpin the Massive Open Online Courses (MOOCs) which have been enjoying such hype in recent years.

"Training is a funny thing," James Sanders, Manager of Innovation at Deloitte Consulting, told the Harvard Business Review. "No matter how easy you make it to access, or how brilliant the learning programs are, training is simply not the first thing people think of doing when they have some free time. Let's face it, for most people, on a typical Sunday morning, if given the choice between 'Am I gonna watch ESPN, or am I gonna do some training?' training will not win out."

DLA designed its online program, which trains both its own employees and its clients, to address this. By embedding missions, badges and leaderboards it has driven unexpectedly strong engagement and training outcomes. Even the DLA leaderboards are carefully designed to maximise engagement. "Traditional leaderboards are, in fact, counter-productive," Sanders says. "The same consistent top users, with astronomic scores, turn off everyone who knows they have no chance of beating them."

The DLA model is different though. "Every week you have a new chance to be the best learner on the site." So those executives travelling, or on leave aren't discouraged from visiting the site just because they've missed a few weeks and fallen behind in their scores. Badges and certificates are the LOL, OMG smiley face of the OneBillion app and the DLA, but these conceal the real transformational meat of this new digital training.

Because the OneBillion app differs from most classroom, distance learning or indeed any current teaching in another very fundamental way. Like most good computer games, in order to progress to the next level users have to score full marks. 100 per cent.

It may sound insignificant, but the implications for training are truly transformational. Traditional teaching and testing techniques, whether classroom or computer-based, are by definition geared to the average. One teacher can't possibly respond to each individual's learning requirements. Quicker studies often lose interest, whilst slower trainees frequently don't get it at all.

Where the OneBillion app and the underlying principles of Connectivism differ is in deploying rapidly advancing AI technology to create an adaptive learning environment. The OneBillion app simply won't allow children to move onto more complicated concepts until they've demonstrated they really understand the basic one. And they use the principles of gamification to keep them engaged while they do it. Ironically, OneBillion's adaptive learning algorithm designed to ensure 100 per cent scores is just the same as the one being deployed by the Oxford School for Girls to ensure no-one ever gets 100 per cent: it's just doing the opposite job.

Of course, our collective acknowledgment of the fundamental

inability of traditional teaching and learning to give everyone an adequately tailored learning experience has become embedded in our qualification and certification systems. The result is that in shipping—one of the most dangerous and regulated in the world—a trainee usually only needs a mark of around 70 per cent in an examination or test to be considered qualified.

For example, the SIGTTO LNG Cargo Operations Management Level administered by the Warsash Maritime Academy requires a 70 per cent pass mark. Taken another way, it is possible for an officer aboard an LNG carrier to hold that qualification having failed to grasp almost a third of everything he or she has been taught. By any standard in a hazardous environment that represents a potentially dangerous competency gap.

Stop for a moment and consider the impact on maritime safety across the board if the requirement wasn't 70 per cent but 100 per cent. If there's anything which has the potential to dramatically change and improve the industry's safety and efficiency, this has to be it. It would permanently close the gap between box-ticking compliance and real competency.

It requires an entirely new approach to training though. One which blends the power of connectivity, AI and algorithms to provide personalised, ongoing, multi-faceted learning experiences which deliver real understanding and competence. One which harnesses our enjoyment of, and willingness to play, compete, succeed and crucially, to fail, and does so in a safe environment. In short, failure is indeed the key. But getting there doesn't just mean more failure, it means failure on a massive, industrial scale. Failure has to become an unavoidable constant rather than an occasional aberration, and it has to be rapid and followed immediately by the chance to learn from it and try again. Not met with the phrase, "failure to pass the assessment will result in no certificate being issued."

If this sounds vaguely familiar to sharp-eyed readers of Futurenautics that's because I'm describing in essence, what a learning algorithm and astute digital businesses do with such success. Iteration, the constant failure, and acquisition of knowledge based on that failure is the basis of the success of digital behemoths like

Amazon, and algorithms which are already better than humans at reading road signs and interpreting cancerous biopsies.

In the digital age algorithms and businesses are leveraging the incredible power of failure, and if they are allowed to, then frankly, shipping people should be too. Iteration and failure is the heart of success in the digital environment and Shipping 3.0 will be no exception. Failure has to be the engine which moves us forward rather than the brake which stops us in our tracks. Our objective should be failure, because we won't get to 100 per cent without it.

So let's put this in some kind of context for shipping and Shipping 3.0. At the moment a shore-side quality broadband connection with a vessel is affordable and getting cheaper. The advent of HTS services mean that picture is only going to improve.

According to the Crew Communications 2014 Survey, the vast majority (77%) of respondents said that the ship was a good place to undertake training, and yet online training materials are only available to 25 per cent of seafarers. 42 per cent of respondents had undertaken some form of Computer Based Training (CBT) on their last vessel, which typically related to either safety or security. The Offshore and Passenger sectors provided least CBT to their crew members with only 22 per cent of Passenger ship crew given any form of CBT—mostly basic language training.

In the Offshore sector this figure was 32 per cent and consisted mainly of compliance related safety training. The desire to be trained ashore at a training centre is lowest amongst the youngest, Millennial (18-24) age group.

Put together the opportunity is clear. And the industry is beginning to align to capitalise. The acquisition of major training provider Videotel in June by KVH with its IP Mobilecast connectivity and the recent connection of two simulators as part of the MonaLisa project with the involvement of Transas amongst others, are two significant steps along the way. The next one is for them all to get together and start failing. Collectively and spectacularly.

Of course there is a big difference between failing safely and constructively in a digital environment and failing with dire and fatal consequences at sea. With the best will in the world not every disaster can be averted, but seafarers and the maritime industry have always understood that in the midst of grief and loss, the lessons we learn from failure can be used to protect future ships and seafarers. In that respect we are the masters of iteration, of turning failure to our ultimate, collective advantage.

Going to sea isn't a game, and no training is failsafe. But that shouldn't stop us from failing safely. To waste the opportunity would be the worst failure of all.

London, October 2014.

23

DON'T PANIC

The *HitchHiker's Guide To The Galaxy* describes how a race of hyper-intelligent, pan-dimensional beings build a supercomputer called Deep Thought which runs a 7.5 million year program to come up with the answer to life, the universe and everything. Eventually it tells them that the answer is 42.

When its creators rail at Deep Thought that the answer is meaningless, it responds that the answer is only meaningless because the beings that programmed it never actually understood the question.

Maritime had its own Deep Thought moment last month. As part of its ongoing 150 year program, DNV GL chose Posidonia to give us the answer to shipping's future. And it's connectivity.

The Future of Shipping report is important, timely and valuable and I urge you to read it—you'll find it echoes an awful lot of what you'll find in Futurenautics every quarter—but the upshot is, connectivity is the one crucial element that is going to provide the gateway to every improvement from operational efficiency and safety right the way to the autonomous or unmanned ship.

Which is kind of ironic when you consider that until now connectivity, far from being front of mind for ship operators, has been hovering somewhere around mid-calf. If you're lucky.

Evidence of this—were it needed—came from research undertaken by InterManager and network operator Inmarsat in 2013 in an effort to try and quantify the return on investment of fitting broadband on vessels.

Having crunched through a considerable amount of data the research found that communications represented around 1% of the operating expenditure for the average ship operator. According to Inmarsat that translates to the average merchant ship in its portfolio spending US$50 per day.

It is against this backdrop that maritime satellite communications is entering what many are calling a new era. High Throughput Satellites are creating a buzz everywhere, with talk of speeds up to 50Mbps, 'fibre-like' connections, and much more bandwidth for your buck. But even as the first dedicated maritime HTS service—Inmarsat's Global Xpress—successfully entered partial service last month, the response from most ship operators has been at best lukewarm.

At the SingTel ship efficiency roundtable at the end of 2013 a range of senior ship operators were asked about new technology and connectivity. The unanimous response was that they aren't even using the technology they've got now to anywhere near its full potential. Communications technology is something you adopt late, when the costs have come down and when someone else has gone out and discovered what's wrong with it first. "I don't like it," said one, "but I'm going to have it."

So on the one hand we have connectivity providers making investments in the billions of dollars in order to deliver the door to shipping's future, and on the other ship operators who haven't yet learnt how to work the handle.

Of course it's a good deal more nuanced than that and to appreciate why, it's important to understand how we got here.

A potted history of maritime satellite communications goes like this: Inmarsat; VSAT. Yes it's an oversimplification but not by much. Inmarsat was formed to supply GMDSS communications under a regulatory mandate which was focussed solely upon the safety of seafarers and their ships at sea. That mandate grew into a monopoly position in the maritime satellite communications market which was only challenged, comparatively recently, by the advent of TDMA (Time Division Multiple Access) VSAT networks.

Maritime satcoms was difficult and expensive and, worst of all, mandatory. Little wonder then in an environment where there was no choice, and a regulatory requirement to carry it, price became the key and overriding factor. Everything which could be done to hold down costs, was done. Jim Dodez, Senior VP of Marketing & Strategic Planning at KVH Industries puts it best. "For the first 30 years of the maritime satellite industry all the technology innovations we saw were designed to figure out how not to use the service."

But then maritime suddenly got choice, and encouraged by multiple projections by numerous researchers about the size and value of the maritime market, new suppliers piled in to get their share.

Using virtual network operator platforms and bundling together modems, antenna, hardware and space segment, companies with no experience of, or in some cases particular interest in, shipping were able to get offerings out into the market. Nothing wrong with that per se, but lack of maritime domain knowledge led to other things, which were wrong.

"We put one particular supplier on board and we asked them to walk the talk. And they failed. They failed miserably. They told us we'd have a broadband, and we said fine, excellent! So we put this on board, our guys started using it, and it failed, chock-blocked," explains Captain Kuba Szymanski, Secretary-General of InterManager. "Then the suppliers came and said, 'yeah but you didn't tell us you want this capacity, you have to buy this. Well that's $15,000 a month'. This is not what we were prepared for. And immediately we could see that our expectations were false, and they could not deliver."

"The problem maritime VSAT faced at the outset was twofold:

at the supply side you had some cowboys in for a quick win who sold consumer grade solutions at high end prices, while at the demand side you faced people who did not really understand IP—and VSAT is an IP product," says Filip Vanheer, Global Business Development Manager Maritime Satellite Solutions for Orange Business Services.

"There was overpromising and underachieving, customer expectations weren't met at all resulting in a lot of frustration on both sides, including for the serious VSAT providers, because they were tarred with the same brush. On top of that the services offered could be significantly different, revolutionary in maritime satcom used to the closed Inmarsat world."

A brief review of the maritime satcoms supplier market would tend to support that view. At the time of writing there are more than 250 different suppliers in the market all offering dedicated maritime connectivity packages. But most of these suppliers are actually resellers, more than 90 of VSAT, and others of both Inmarsat and VSAT systems.

There are only a finite number of birds up there, and despite the rapid expansion of the services available, there are still only a handful of companies offering maritime satcom solutions which actually own the satellite which is at the core of the equation. So when we talk about ship operators having choice, the reality is that they have lots of choice when it comes to suppliers, but nowhere near that level of choice when it comes to the network. The bottom line is that most services will use either Inmarsat, Intelsat or Iridium, and in broadly that order.

But does that matter? And will the wave of HTS entering the market alter it in the revolutionary manner that some are predicting? For a start, what exactly is HTS?

Northern Sky Research (NSR) coined the term and define it as a satellite or satellite payload that has at least twice the throughput of a traditional FSS satellite for the same amount of allocated frequency on orbit, can use any frequency and almost exclusively makes use of frequency reuse and multiple spot beams to increase throughput and reduce the price per bit delivered.

These services include Inmarsat's Global Xpress, Intelsat's EPIC, Telenor's THOR 7, and the new O3b solution.

"New HTS services are a good thing for the maritime world as they will drive competition, but their capabilities are available already," says Tore Morten Olsen, Head of Maritime Satellite Communications in Airbus Defence and Space, one of the largest maritime satellite communications suppliers. "For instance, we can provide global connectivity with VSAT bandwidth that offers 12mb/s data upload. But should a customer want to move to HTS in the future, it's easy because AuroraGlobal services are designed to be technology agnostic."

And 'technology-agnostic' is key phrase when it comes to maritime satcom connectivity, both now and in the future.

The war between Apple's iOS and Android on mobile phones has divided brother from brother, but it's nothing compared to the fratricidal spleen vented about the relative merits of Inmarsat and VSAT. In fact the war of words which continues to rage around the topic has been intensified by the next-generation HTS services coming online.

All HTS services conform to the given NSR definition, but over and above that they diverge considerably. Firstly, in terms of the bands they use. The suitability and robustness of Ka- versus Ku-band is not a technical discussion for these pages, suffice to say that it's unlikely any operator investing billions into a service isn't going to be pretty confident that modulation techniques and hybrid network designs are going to mitigate those impacts to a suitable degree. The real meat is what are referred to as 'open' versus 'closed' architectures, put simply the VSAT model as opposed to the Inmarsat one. Intelsat's EPIC platform is the former where service providers control system elements and therefore can incorporate high-throughput capacity without having to replace existing network hardware.

"This means maritime users will see improvements in throughput and cost-per-bit while leveraging their current network investments. This leads to lower total cost of ownership for the end user," says James Collett, Director of Mobility Services for Intelsat.

"Open architecture puts choice and control into the hands of the users. The communication demands placed on modern vessels will continue to grow, and as fleet operators scale up their communications networks, we believe the advantages of an open-architecture approach will become even more apparent."

In the context of cloud and increasing digitisation, an open approach would appear to be absolutely correct, but does the failure of VSAT to meet the expectations of a significant number of ship operators suggest otherwise?

Many struggled to understand the service offerings and various service element providers, and the patchwork nature of the bundled solutions were often responsible.

It's no accident that the most successful VSAT provider by market share—KVH Industries—took a different route. Unlike its VSAT competitors KVH focussed on delivering what was essentially an Inmarsat model for VSAT, and it's proved an extremely smart move.

"We had a great opportunity to get into the marketplace back in 2007, because although Inmarsat is a great company with great solutions, it was a monopoly and most people were complaining about the price," says KVH's Jim Dodez. "We wanted to create a simple, affordable, end-to-end VSAT solution that was simple for dealers to install and we had a distribution network to take advantage of, just like Inmarsat."

KVH, like Airbus Defence and Space is technology-agnostic, "we're talking to HTS providers and we will take advantage of whatever bandwidth is out there, whether it comes from Google or whoever, we will design the capability in our systems," says Dodez. But KVH maintain that in terms of innovation, the closed architectures of its and Inmarsat's offering have the capacity to be far more innovative.

"People who object to the end-to-end closed system are the people doing the modular architecture. In the VNO (Virtual Network Operator) model, Intelsat does most of customer management and technical management of their network, and allows Service Providers to tap in and use it. As a Service Provider it means you don't get an opportunity to engage your customer and develop solutions to their problems which offer something different in the market. A lot of the noise on this is coming from those who don't have the ability to do end-to-end, and so they paint it as bad."

It's an interesting point, particularly when you look at the nature of the new offerings from both Inmarsat and KVH. Global Xpress will offer each ship its own CISCO server linked to cloud computing and what Inmarsat describes as a 'state-of-the-art' satellite applications Service Enablement Platform.

The GX SEP will allow the application itself to dynamically request additional bandwidth just for the period of time its needed, before returning to normal levels. This could be a game-changer for operators who have shied away from data-heavy services because of the need to upgrade their subscriptions to have capacity on standby.

But what it really indicates is that Inmarsat is recognising that just supplying connectivity isn't enough. Connectivity is the gateway, but, as Shane Rossbacher, Director of Maritime Market Development at Inmarsat says, "Inmarsat's future strategy is to offer services beyond pure satellite connectivity. Our task is to deliver solutions that help improve our customers' business, driving operational efficiencies between shore and ship."

That's why applications are at the heart of GX, and also why they're the backbone of KVH's new IP Mobilecast product. Using multicast technology and bandwidth management KVH are enabling application providers to deliver new types of services to users, which cost barely, if anything, in bandwidth.

"The trend towards applications is a good one and, yes, the IP Mobilecast concept is basically similar to the SEP," says Dodez. "We're having ongoing conversations with all the leading applications providers in the industry, those conversations are definitely happening."

It's a vision of the future where the cat-fight between Inmarsat and VSAT should melt into the background—particularly considering that GX is actually a VSAT service. The focus on applications speaks to a wider trend in technology to reduce complexity for the user, and it's one which Airbus' Olsen is well aware of.

"I think, yes, the level of knowledge of what the market offers today is pretty good. I don't mean to say that most vessel operators need an in-depth understanding of the scientific intricacies of satellite communications. But I believe this is not necessary, either. Shipowners shouldn't need to worry about all the technical details and challenges. They need a satcoms supplier that takes care of the technology, packages the best of what's available in a smart and easy to operate way, ensures seamless usage and offers that package at an affordable rate. Much like how we all use our mobile phones in fact."

"The introduction of new HTS bandwidth will benefit those in market sectors for whom such solutions are relevant," says Mary Ellen Kramer, CEO of Maritime Broadband. "Commercial shipping with truly global and relatively low bandwidth communications requirements is not likely to be impacted."

Rashid Baba, Director of Products at Thuraya takes a similar view. "For Thuraya, the opportunity lies in providing a better standard experience than is currently available to customers for whom an investment in VSAT or future HTS services is beyond their budget or requirement. Those owners want the kind of reliable communications that we can provide together with added value applications from its partners."

Between Airbus Defence and Space's AuroraGlobal Network, Inmarsat's SEP, and KVH's Mobilecast it seems that the message from every part of the maritime satellite communications ecosystem is—as was written in large, friendly letters on the front of the *HitchHikers Guide to the Galaxy*—Don't Panic.

Well, it's the wrong one, and here's why. Connectivity is going to enable just about everything your shipping company wants to do in the future and to continue in the comparative ignorance of its technology in which most operators currently dwell, is untenable and dangerous.

HTS is going to change what's possible and it is essential ship operators take advantage of it sooner rather than later. In short, HTS should have 'Panic Now' written in large unfriendly letters up and down both sides and across the front for good measure.

"In this age of big data it is not about optimising the connectivity to the vessel so much as a focus on implementing applications that utilize the connectivity to optimise business operations. Far too often ship operators look to purchase a communications platform and then figure out what to do with it," says Brian Pemberton, Executive Director for Iridium's Maritime Business.

"This has grown out of the service provider distribution model for communications where they would sell marked up airtime, and it was up to the ship operator to figure out what to use the service for. With broadband connectivity now available to nearly all ship operators, it is more about identifying which applications are going to improve business operations and the purchase of those applications will include the communications technology and charges as a bundled package."

He's absolutely right. And that's why HTS should be the shove ship operators need to fully engage with connectivity.

"It has always been our ambition to offer the same kind of solutions to our customers, irrelevant of the fact if the connection they are using is DSL, fibre, satellite or whatever. HTS brings this ambition closer," says Orange's Vanheer. "For some applications, due to their bandwidth consumption, it makes no economic sense. HTS will change that. HTS will allow us to bring our complete portfolio of solutions to the vessels, at a reasonable cost."

It is a step change, and in order to take advantage of it ship operators have to take some responsibility. Relying on the maritime satcom providers to do the work for us isn't viable in the long term.

Ship operators have to engage with connectivity on an enterprise level, and focus their talent to do so. Bandwidth is never going to be the commodity service at sea that everybody hopes it will. The amount of data that ship operators are going to start sending is going to overwhelm the capacity of networks to carry it very quickly.

Yet in many shipping IT departments there's still a belief that making a satellite operator guarantee a specified data rate and SLA, and optimising and controlling the flow of data down the pipe is going to solve that problem. It's a view which is increasingly naive.

The only way shipping can truly capitalise on this step change is by understanding its own requirements for data and the how much capacity it needs in order to adequately deliver its effective transport.

This is the data which will build completely different organisations, will allow closer integration between charterers and operators, allow ship managers to demonstrate their value to ship owners and drive savings and productivity. We can't any longer leave all that prize in the hands of the maritime satcoms suppliers to deliver to us. We have to take it.

The idea of connectivity nicely bundled and delivered to us in a beautiful and intuitive interface is very attractive, and if you want an example of just how powerful a proposition that is, then take a look at Apple and how incredibly successful its closed architecture has been. But that model has limitations, as the deal between Apple and IBM this month illustrates.

Closed architectures in a competitive market work well in the first phase as audiences get used to a new technology, but as soon as the customers become familiar with the technology and gain confidence they begin to look for their own solution. Apple's deal with IBM allows them to extend their reach beyond the maximum potential of their closed business model.

Of course, that's only happened in a mature market. In maritime connectivity we're far from that point, so the likelihood is that closed architecture has a good deal of mileage in it yet. But in the long term open architectures should become the norm—and if they don't then we will have failed as an industry.

Things are changing and according to Frank Coles of Inmarsat, "This will demand a change in mind-set for shipowners, who tend to fight every communications penny without considering the value to be gained." And in the end that's what this comes down to. Value creation. In a word, business. But not just any business. Your business.

The number 42 is 101010 in binary code. It is the average number of lines on an average page of an average paperback, and it is the number of laws in cricket. Light requires 10^{-42} seconds to cross the diameter of a proton and 42 is the number of degrees by which light refracts off water to create a rainbow. It is also, of course, the answer to life, the universe and everything.

42 is the answer to an awful lot of different questions, but not shipping's future. That's connectivity, and the questions it answers are different for every ship operator. It's like Jeopardy!, only more so.

Jeopardy. Now there's a word.

London, July 2014.

24

BREAKFAST OF CHAMPIONS

Not so long ago an irate father walked into a Minnesota Target store—the second biggest discount retailer in the US—and he was angry. Very angry.

The man demanded to know from the manager of the store why it was sending his teenage daughter, who was still in high school, brochures with coupons for baby clothes and cribs. Was Target trying to encourage his daughter to get pregnant? The manager checked the mailing and saw it had the girl's name and address on it and contained nothing but baby products. He then apologised profusely and assured the man that was not Target's intention.

The incident obviously caused some concern in the store because a few days later the manager called the father again to apologise. This time however, he found the man rather embarrassed. "It turns out there's been some activities in my house I haven't been completely aware of," he informed the manager. "She's due in August. I owe you an apology."

That man's daughter had become a victim of Target's pregnancy prediction algorithm which, just by analysing a woman's shopping habits and data, can predict their delivery date with some 83 percent accuracy. And she isn't alone.

You will probably also have seen the slew of sensational head-lines about the Amazon Prime Air service. Using unmanned aerial vehicles—drones—the aim of the service will be to get goods into the eager hands of consumers within 30 minutes.

It was a interesting sleight of hand. Because whilst we all obe-diently watched the video footage of the drones with their Amazon logos and carry pouches landing on people's doorsteps and chatted about it at the water cooler, Amazon was quietly being granted a patent which was far more significant, and has potentially far reaching implications.

The patent is for what it calls 'anticipatory shipping', which is basically a method whereby the retailer begins the process of deliv-ering a package to you before you've even bought it.

Amazon plans to box and ship products it expects customers in a specific area are going to order, but haven't yet done so. In de-ciding what to ship, Amazon said it may consider previous orders, product searches, wish lists, shopping-cart contents, returns and even how long your cursor hovers over an item.

"Based on all the things they know about their customers they could predict demand based on a variety of factors," said Sucharita Mulpuru, a Forrester Research analyst. "It appears Amazon is taking advantage of their copious data."

So is the UK retailer Tesco, and not just their customer data. The 70 million data points generated by the cheap, internet-con-nected sensors embedded into the chillers in its 1,800 stores led to the discovery that they'd been running at too low a temperature. That translated into a saving on the company's electricity bill of 20%.

Welcome to the world of big data, that buzziest of buzz words. In fact the hype surrounding that phrase is becoming so toxic that I hesitate to even use it.

It's in part the reason that many senior people are dismissing it as purely a technology wave. But to do so is a serious misjudge-ment. Big data is not a technology wave, it is a business transfor-mation wave, and shipping and maritime companies just like every other business, have to ride it, or they're going to get flattened.

First let's establish what it is. Big data is characterised by the four 'V's. The first of those—and what marks big data out from the data of the past—is volume. There is one heck of a lot of it. To try and get an idea of scale, the US chain store Walmart harvests around 2.5 million gigabytes of data each hour from its customer transactions alone. GE and companies like it are harvesting similar levels from M2M industrial sensors.

The second is velocity, the ability to analyse that data in real-time means that businesses can predict demand and dynamically adjust their operations based on current data, not prior performance. Sales figures in large shopping centres can be predicted quite accurately by monitoring the activity of mobile phones in the car park before shoppers have even entered the complex.

Variety is the third characteristic of big data, and that means anything and everything. Location data, web browsing, purchases, credit cards, stock values, weather data, customer purchases, the list is endless.

But what is causing the most difficulty, and controversy, is the final characteristic of big data, and that is value. It has to create value. For leaders, that has to be the area of tightest focus. With all that infinite variety of data out there, how do we identify the meaningful bits?

There are five key areas of application for big data, and they are, revenue generation and business model development; cost containment in real-time; real-time forecasting; tracking of physical items; and reinventing business processes. What you will immediately see from that list is that none of these are IT functions. They are business functions.

Many businesses today are being encouraged to develop big data strategies, but that's really missing the point. Big data is the emergence of a new opportunity to base management decisions on objective insight and unprecedented detail, and that requires more than a strategy.

Connectivity is a key enabler of big data, and for shipping and maritime—as you will understand if you read this issue's feature article—it is a transformative one. Connectivity is the answer to shipping's future, but the really important thing is to ask the right questions. It's the same with big data.

Big data has been on the high seas for some time in the passenger sector. Royal Caribbean Cruises Limited, one of the biggest cruise operators in the world was reportedly one of the first to get a data scientist involved. So it should be no surprise that it's also in the process of rolling out new state-of-the-art connectivity for its vessels.

RCCL transitioned its services away from MTN in favour of Harris CapRock and the new O3b constellation, with one core objective.

"Our objective was to dramatically enhance our communications capability by modernizing the approach. The Harris transition increased our resulting capacity by roughly 8 fold," explains Bill Martin CIO at RCCL.

"This was a great start, but the modernization also prepared us for the revolutionary step in our plan, O3b. The connectivity on the O3b enabled vessels will have more than 100 times more capacity and 4 times lower latency. For the first time, we will truly have shore-like connectivity, with no shore in sight."

Martin admits that their goal has been an audacious one, their aim to reinvent the onboard experience for guests and end the decades old concern about being disconnected whilst at sea. But there are also very significant operational benefits driven by this 'land-like' connectivity.

With reports of incremental ROI of 241% for enterprises using big data, how is RCCL leveraging the possibilities associated with it? "I can't speak to the 241%, but I do know that whenever we build business intelligence around a business process, we see significantly better returns," confirms Martin. "We introduced an on board revenue analytics platform a few years back and the on board revenue performance has improved every year since. That's not a coincidence."

Martin cites a more connected crew as an immediate operational benefit, "Our crew has always been at the forefront of everything we do onboard. As the old adage goes, Happy Crew, Happy Guests!"

But there have been other unexpected benefits, including large groups requiring high speed connectivity while travelling which can now consider cruising as an option. "We have already seen inquiries from a number of travel sellers that are interested in exploiting this new capability, including travel blogging groups! We didn't see that one coming."

It's an example of how the cruise industry has grasped the potential of connectivity to profoundly alter businesses, but it's when you talk to Martin about the future that the difference between RCCL and the average commercial operator becomes clear.

"Longer term, we also believe this type of connectivity will dynamically change the way we operate our vessels, from new types of entertainment and new services enabled by the high speed connectivity," he says. "But probably the most exciting things are those that we haven't thought of yet."

Contrast that with the attitudes on show at a panel discussion entitled, *"Growth opportunities in the dry bulk sector"*, at this year's Posidonia.

According to the grim faced selection of dry bulk company CEO's, there aren't any. Aside from waiting for the market to pick up—which despite their predictions it hadn't—moving vessels from fixed to spot, and controlling costs, we were told there was nothing they could do. Much like Bill Martin's guests, they're just passengers.

There is a problem here, and it isn't one that a big data strategy on its own is going to solve. This is a culture problem, and, as the old management adage goes, culture eats strategy for breakfast.

Einstein said, "We cannot solve our problems with the same thinking we used when we created them." But even if the thinking is there—in this case connectivity and big data—without a wholesale cultural change shipping will not be able to capitalise on it.

Going on gut feeling is rapidly becoming an unnecessary risk, but in order to make evidence-based decisions you have to actually trust the data, and more than that, you have to generate the data in the first place.

"The analysts can tell you everything about the market but deep down shipping is not just a set of numbers," says Anthony Zolotas, chief executive of Eurofin. There's your cultural problem right there. Shipping is a set of numbers, the same way every business is, but you have to have enough of them to turn them into insight.

The reason that some sectors of shipping have remained untroubled by private equity is because there simply isn't enough data for them to make the kind of evidence-based investment decisions which are their stock-in-trade.

The fact that the CEO's of such major dry bulk companies can all get the performance of their companies and the market so wrong is an indication that they don't understand it as well as they could. From technical and commercial data from their ships to market and world news and customer data, big data represents a massive business transformation that could change that.

And change is the key word here, because this transformation is as much about the management of change within your company's culture as it is about new analytics competencies and IT infrastructure.

There are digital natives and digital immigrants—all of shipping and maritime's leaders are likely to be the latter. We didn't grow up with the Internet and in a world filled with volatility, uncertainty, complexity and ambiguity, the challenge of leading businesses into their digital future is enormous. Agility, both in thought and action, will be key as the world changes exponentially. Those who win will win big, but they will also be removed from the top of the tree faster.

So it's crucial that shipping and maritime leaders engage with this cultural shift now, and make it stick. Because it takes between 3-5 years to gather datasets significant enough to really operationalise. Leaving it in the inbox for your successor is not an option.

It's also important that the culture change comes from the top because this new big data paradigm changes a lot of assumptions in businesses which make people very jumpy.

We've lived in a corporate world of gut-feel for a long time, but research is beginning to demonstrate just what a handicap that has been.

For example, a variety of studies are showing how statistics and predictive analytics in football could make a better job of judging talent than the expert intuition and gut feel of coaches and scouts.

Whilst the focus has always been on strikers and goals, the biggest performance boost comes when teams address their weakest links, normally in defensive positions. Not conceding goals is more performance-enhancing than scoring goals, which inverts much of the received wisdom in the sport. Apply that to the kind of entrenched beliefs we have in business and consider the impact.

Big data is already changing shipping, but it's starting with the supply side. Algorithms like ShipServ's matching engine and the VesselsValue algos are just two of them, and they will be at the heart of Shipping 3.0.

But these algorithms don't appear in isolation, they come from a culture with technology and data at its heart. And it isn't something you can fabricate, or pay lip-service to if you want to make big data work.

"When the rate of change outside your organization outpaces the change within the organization, the end is near," said Jack Welch, former CEO of GE.

Change is the key to big data.

You don't need a big data strategy. What you need is a data culture, embedded in the corporate DNA. Otherwise your shiny big data strategy will get chewed up and spat out.

Success depends on living and breathing data, for breakfast, lunch and dinner. And failure to do so runs the risk that your organisation ends up as toast.

London, April 2014.

25

THE WEAKEST LINK

At the time of writing the mystery of Malaysian Airlines Flight MH370 remains unsolved. Any speculation as to the fate of that jet and the 239 souls aboard is above Futurenautics' pay grade. But what the intense focus around MH370's disappearance has exposed is the extent to which Industry 4.0 is already with us.

Whilst the aircraft's satellite tracking and other transponders were switched off—deliberately or otherwise—the sensors buried in its two Rolls-Royce Trent 800 engines were not. According to reports these sensors continued to transmit a variety of data which was being monitored by engineers back in Derby, UK in the firm's Service Operations Room.

In fact, that Service Operations Room monitors all Rolls-Royce engines currently in service, as do similar operations rooms run by the likes of General Electric (GE) and others supporting a huge range of components making up complex machinery from aircraft to manufacturing plants.

It goes by a variety of names, but whether you call it the Industrial Internet, Internet of All Things, or Machine to Machine

(M2M), doesn't change the magnitude of its implications. And it is one of a group of technology trends which are forming the basis of a new industrial revolution, one which could fundamentally alter the way that goods are conceived, how and where they are manufactured, and the journeys they make both as component parts, and finished products, across the world.

"We are at the precipice of a major technological shift at the intersection of the cyber and physical worlds, one with broad implications that will lead to substantial benefits, not just for any one organization, but for humanity," said Janos Sztipanovits, E. Bronson Ingram distinguished professor of engineering and director of the Institute for Software Integrated Systems at Vanderbilt University, in a statement recently.

In isolation that statement is in danger of sounding like hyperbole, but when you begin to identify the practical ramifications of this technology shift and concurrent generational trends—examples of which are manifold—it's hard not to agree. It has to be fairly profound in order to be labelled the next industrial revolution. Industry 4.0 is a term originally coined by German manufacturing giant Siemens, and other German industry leaders and follows the steam engine, the conveyor belt, and the first phase of IT and automation technology. Manufacturing 3.0 is part of it, what some call a renaissance in that sector which has traditionally been seen as the bedrock out of which economies evolve service industries.

Now the technological shift which Sztipanovits is talking about is opening up a new era for manufacturers, but with it comes massive new challenges.

You may wonder why Industry 4.0 should be of interest to shipping and maritime. The short answer would be because its implications and benefits apply to humanity, and by the commonly accepted definition of humanity, at least most of the shipping and maritime industry qualify. The more pointed answer is that the business of shipping rests upon moving raw materials, components and finished goods around the world on behalf of their manufacturers and owners. The implications for our customers of Industry 4.0, the new challenges it poses, and the changes it will bring to the way they need to operate, have to be appreciated, understood and—ideally—anticipated by the shipping industry. Because the truth is that we're struggling to support them adequately now, and things are about to get far, far more complex.

We've called this article the weakest link, and that's not a reference to a quiz show, it's how one major auto manufacturer described shipping and it's part in their supply chain. We're fond of telling everyone how shipping transports 90 percent of everything, but where we're slightly more reticent is in admitting how much of everything that gets shipped gets there on time, or at all. Current manufacturing depends upon long, and tightly integrated supply chains, but these supply chains are going to become an even more crucial area of competitive advantage for manufacturers in the future and there are some very good reasons why.

With approximately 3 billion new consumers expected to enter the consuming middle-class by 2030 demand is going in only one direction, but technological advances like the industrial internet, digital manufacturing and factory digitisation, new materials, advanced robotics, 3D printing, or additive manufacturing, plus the new energy landscape are changing the goalposts for manufacturers. The result is that traditional manufacturing strategies which focus on long supply chains and low-cost labour in cheap countries are unlikely to be optimal in the future.

Having cycled through 'offshoring' and 're-shoring' where certain business functions were first sent offshore and then brought back to be located close to consumer markets, McKinsey are dubbing this new phase 'Next-shoring'. According to them, "A next-shoring perspective emphasizes proximity to demand and proximity to innovation. Both are crucial in a world where evolving demand from new markets places a premium on the ability to adapt products to different regions and where emerging technologies that could disrupt costs and processes are making new supply ecosystems a differentiator."

So what are these emerging technologies and why are they proving a catalyst for such major change? One you will most probably have heard a considerable amount of talk about. 3D printing, or additive manufacturing, has been around for some time, but it's only in the past few years that the technology has moved mainstream. This isn't the place for an in-depth description of how it works, more for its implications, which are considerable.

A huge range of items and component parts can be 3D printed now, from aircraft engine parts to human organs without the need for massive factory production line tooling. This opens the way to rapid prototyping, personalisation, single item manufacture or economic short runs. It's also driving innovation. Whereas traditional machining and production techniques favoured certain materials, 3D printing is different. There are some traditional materials with which additive manufacturing struggles, but it's opening up scope to experiment with different types of existing materials, and new ones, which never suited traditional manufacturing, but work with 3D printing.

In short, it means that one auto manufacturer has reduced an 8 month prototyping lead time to just one week, and another manufacturer has dropped their Mexican, low-cost parts supplier, from whom they regularly shipped bulk orders, in favour of a local 3D printing supplier who produces on demand and allows them to carry no inventory. Or shipping costs.

It's also opening up a talent and expertise gap within manufacturers. GE, which already has additive manufacturing competencies, used a crowdsourcing approach to solve its issues with a particular engine bracket problem you can read more about in our *The In-Crowd* article this issue. GE are also going beyond 3D printing developing a new additive technology called 'Direct Write' which involves inking miniaturised sensors directly onto parts of products which were previously unreachable. This, as GE says, "...will allow us to collect new data points to perform real-time analytics and condition monitoring for our customers."

Which brings us neatly to the industrial internet, IoAT, or M2M depending upon your preference. Cisco have a fun widget on their website which counts in real time the number of devices which are connected to the Internet of All Things. But there's nothing flippant about the stats.

According to Cisco in 2012 there were 8.7 billion, today it's over 12 billion and by 2020 they expect it to reach in excess of 50 billion objects. By the way, they believe that more than 50 percent of the connected objects added between 2013-2020 will be added in the last three years of that decade, because that's when the connectivity costs will be lowest, but more of that later.

These objects include everything from coffee makers to cars and even, as already discussed, jet engines. Utilising tiny, low-power chips—and thanks to GE, now inked sensors—these devices are able to send us streams of real-time performance and environmental data about everything from their location to their temperature, speed and altitude. But they are evolving to do more than that. Combined with actuators, advanced robotics and algorithms they are part of what is possibly the most science fiction part of Industry 4.0, the Cyberphysical System.

One kind of cyberphysical system is the robot which, rather than being programmed can actually be trained by humans on the factory floor. It is the deep learning algorithms which make this possible. But from the supply chain point of view it is even more profound. It is here that the 'intersection of the cyber and physical worlds' which Janos Sztipanovits talks about finds its expression. At Robert Bosch GmbH, they've tried to capture the concept of fusing the digital and physical worlds in a slogan, "process2device".

Siegfried Dais, the former deputy chairman of the board of management described what that translates to in practice, "For example, a piece of metal or raw material will say, "*I am the block that will be made into product X for customer Y.*" In an extreme vision, this unfinished material already knows for which customer it is intended and carries with it all the information about where and when it will be processed. Once the material is in the machine, the material itself records any deviations from the standard process, determines when it's "done," and knows how to get to its customer."

The advent of these cyberphysical systems and the real time data they provide will mean that manufacturers will have an unprecedented window into, and opportunity to optimise, every area of their operations. Particularly as advances in communications continue.

The new generation of high throughput satellites are making even remote areas accessible to the industrial internet. Recent advances in battery-free wireless communications like 'ambient backscatter' devices which communicate with each other and exchange data without a battery by either absorbing or reflecting ambient signal, like those from a TV tower, will extend that reach even further.

These and other steady increases in communications quality, speed and reach, together with cloud technologies delivering increasingly powerful software, is allowing collaboration and digital manufacturing on a previously unthinkable scale. Micro manufacturer Local Motors which developed the world's first crowdsourced military vehicle (see *The In Crowd*) relies upon a high-end CAD system called Solid Edge from Siemens. Whereas collaboration in the past may have involved 100 people, now that could be a dynamic crowdsourced team of tens of thousands of people working on different CAD systems.

The Siemens system enables the Local Motors platform hub to import non-native formats, and offer professional grade CAD services to any member on a rental basis. The software can also be downloaded rapidly and used to work offline—an essential feature for the Local Motors community. It's also worth recording that GE have recently starting working with Local Motors to translate this approach into developing consumer appliances. Crowdsourced ideas will become prototypes in dedicated GE micro-factories—about 20,000 sq ft employing around 50 people, as opposed to current appliance factories at 1 million sq ft and employing 7,000—and sold in small quantities.

Siemens isn't just working with auto manufacturers though. Its Shipbuilding Catalyst is designed to enable shipyards to accelerate the digital transformation of the enterprise, optimising productivity with preconfigured elements for key processes. The objective is to allow operators to improve fleet support and achieve greater availability and reliability while reducing the total ownership cost.

Current customers include Hyundai Heavy Industries, Fincantieri and IHC Merwede which announced earlier this month that it was standardising on Siemens' Product Lifecycle Management (PLM) software as part of its "One IHC" initiative. "Our business strategy is based on four pillars—growth, internationalisation, innovation and co-operation," said IHC CFO Dave Vander Heyde in a statement. "This strategy led us to the creation of our One IHC initiative with the aim of increasing value for our customers by striving for harmony and operational excellence in all our processes. Having instant access to all product data from any location will increase efficiency, reduce costs, enhance quality and help us make smart product development decisions more quickly."

At its recent press conference at the Hanover Messe Siemens revealed a variety of new technical innovations designed to support the transition to Manufacturing 3.0 and Industry 4.0, but it also recognises that overcoming the decline in productivity gains is key.

Looking at the reasons behind that decline offers an insight which contextualises just why Industry 4.0 is badly needed. The year 2000 marked a turning point for the global economy, at which the rise in the real prices of natural resources began to wipe out a century's worth of real-price declines. Not even the global economic downturn has halted that trend and resource prices have continued to rise faster than global output.

Resource scarcity means that for the first time since the first industrial revolution the linear economic model which sees us take virgin natural resources, make something from them, sell them and then throw the lot away, is under severe pressure. Rising and volatile resource costs are forcing manufacturers to look again at how the economic model works.

The result is the concept of the 'Circular Economy', where the emphasis is on re-use and regeneration which has the potential to de-couple the economy from resource constraints. Already major companies including Renault, Philips, B&Q, and others are aiming to reduce waste, which in the fast moving consumer goods sector (FMCG) alone, accounts for 80 percent of the $3.2 trillion worth of materials it uses each year.

Moves towards leasing rather than purchasing, use cycles rather than life cycles and cost of ownership rather than purchase price give manufacturers the opportunities to embed deep relationships with customers, gain powerful data about their usage and habits, and eventually ensure that equipment is returned to them to be refurbished or re-used.

The results so far indicate that the benefits of the circular economy could be huge, capturing opportunities to increase margin, reduce costs and re-think businesses. With strategies designed to minimise the use and extend the re-use of virgin materials, a recent report about the potential impact of this trend by the Ellen MacArthur Foundation says, "If applied to steel consumption in the automotive, machining, and transport sectors, a circular transformation could achieve global net materials savings equivalent to between 110 million and 170 million metric tons of iron ore a year in 2025." Something that shipping should be particularly alert to, see *A Bigger Boat* to learn why.

But there's another reason that the circular economy should and will gain more traction, and that is because it sits neatly alongside the mindset of the Millennial generation. Collaboration, sustainability, crowdsourcing, digital rather than physical, access rather than ownership adds up to a different kind of consumer than that which has gone before.

Whereas the current generation buy cars which spend 96 percent of their time idle, and drive on roads which are poorly utilised, the Millennials and their children, increasingly won't. That means not only are resource scarcity issues challenging the traditional linear economy, so are consumers. The days of mass produced consumer goods making a one way trip from the Far East to the US and Europe look to be numbered. The mass market is fragmenting rapidly.

No one can be certain how fast or how deeply these changes are going to make themselves felt, but already major manufacturers are trying to prepare for and make sense of how they'll deal with the new order. What is absolutely clear though is that economies of scale, reputation and heritage are no match for agility, innovation and the ability to add value to products, supply chains or consumers.

Manufacturers, shipping's customers, are beginning to wrestle with a whole new range of technological and strategic questions. Questions which shipping should at least understand, and begin to actively help them solve. But a brief survey of some of our big customers sends a stark message: shipping is already the weak link in many operations.

As we wrote in our launch issue shipping has been described as operating in the stone age, and when one compares the level of connectivity, digital operations, insight, data and intelligence involved in our customers' businesses, as compared to the average ship operator it's hard to dispute that. But we do have the opportunity to change. Maritime connectivity has advanced massively, and that opens the doors to closer digital integration and adding value of which shipping hasn't always been capable in the past.

Industry 4.0 could radically change shipping as a business, and there is an urgent need to technologically upskill to remain competitive.

But we can't start to do that until we appreciate the challenges our customers are facing, and our part in both addressing and solving them. We need to innovate with them, collaborate with them and potentially far more broadly with each other. We too need to be looking at smart materials, sensors and data, but not just from shipping's side. "The thinking really has to expand. It has to expand beyond the traditional industry that you're in," says Stefan Heck, co-author of *Resource Revolution: How to Capture the Biggest Business Opportunity in a Century.*

It's an area where shipping is weak. The rest of industry are looking at strategies to add value as suppliers both to businesses and consumers, taking advantage of new technologies to help them. Shipping is still stuck in the linear economy mindset, focussed on any kind of money it can get, when what we need to work out is how our ships can become part of the cyberphysical systems of the future.

Despite the best efforts of Rolls Royce and Inmarsat, not to mention the hundreds of vessels, both surface and underwater, military airplanes, and the men and women who crew them, there has still been no trace of flight MH370. It has, we can only assume, been swallowed up by the ocean. The awesome power of nature is nowhere clearer than at sea, and there is a tacit acceptance by those who ship their goods across the oceans that some things are beyond anyone's control.

But if Industry 4.0 is about anything it is about optimisation, using technology to improve wherever possible. Shipping will always be under extra strain in the supply chain because of the environment in which it operates, but if the industry which carries 90 percent of everything could just improve its performance by percentage points, the effect on our customers, and the world, could be massive.

And when you put that way, doesn't it feels like a really tantalising prospect?

London, April 2014.

26

A BIGGER BOAT

If you haven't read our feature article this issue, *The Weakest Link,* then you might find it beneficial to do so before you continue. The reason I encourage you towards it is because it examines the drivers behind, and the implications of, what is described as Manufacturing 3.0 and Industry 4.0. What it illustrates is that shipping's customers are entering an era where many of the established rules of business are being changed—permanently—by a range of technology-enabled trends which are already forcing them to adopt radically different approaches to the way they operate.

You may ask why a shipping and maritime publication thinks it's worth focussing on such a subject. The fact that we have to acknowledge those views exist in the first place indicates we have a problem.

To be clear, the reason this is important is that shipping relies on selling its services to customers, and understanding the new challenges they face is an essential part of structuring profitable shipping and maritime companies for the future. But it isn't just ship operators who need to understand the seismic shifts in industry which are likely in the near future.

For generations maritime equipment and service suppliers have relied upon their unique competencies in developing products for a highly regulated industry which operates in one of the harshest environments on earth. The importance of being big, globally resourced, highly reputable, and having worldwide presence has been as important to maritime suppliers, as the ability to invest in increasingly large ships has been for operators.

If the experience and the predictions of some of the largest manufacturing organisations on earth are to be relied upon however, comforting things like reputation, economies of scale, and heritage are shortly going to be at best, of little competitive benefit, and at worst, a source of handicap.

To recap for those who haven't managed the feature article yet, there are several trends which are converging to drive Industry 4.0, what Siemens and others are calling the new industrial revolution.

The first is the Industrial Internet, also known as the Internet of All Things or M2M, an integral part of sophisticated digital manufacturing, where advances in robotics are contributing to the development of cyberphysical systems.

Together with these trends come the rise of new types of high-tech, smart materials, and new processes such as 3D printing, or additive manufacturing, which is allowing the use of existing materials in new ways and for new purposes. At the same time the increasing power and speed of connectivity and communications is delivering opportunities for efficiencies and collaboration both within and between companies, and with external crowdsourcing communities, whilst advances in augmented reality solutions combined with big data and it's insights are changing when and how equipment is monitored, maintained and even fixed.

Finally, what may be the elephant in the room, is the increasing scarcity of virgin resources which is likely to require the best of the world's technological ingenuity and creativity, and all the advances already mentioned, to adequately address. It could however—if it leads to the creation of the so-called 'Circular Economy'—be a catalyst for massive savings, efficiencies and increased profits. Now, whilst we wait for all the people who didn't read the feature article to go and check they really understand what all those thing are, why don't we sit back and watch a movie?

Back in 1975 a rookie film director named Spielberg decided to turn a bestselling book by Peter Benchley, into a movie. *Jaws*—for anyone who by some weird fluke has never heard of it—is the tale of a uniquely grumpy Great White Shark which terrorises the beachgoers of Amity Island by attempting to eat as many of them as possible. It is—as a friend of mine is fond of saying—not so much a movie as a process of elimination. In order to rid the ocean of the man-eater, a professional shark hunter, the local police chief and a marine biologist set out on a little tuna fishing boat in order to catch and kill Jaws.

The movie has us bobbing around in the open sea on the boat with the three men, the suspense palpable as we await the first glimpse of Jaws. The sheer size and viciousness of the creature, when it makes an appearance utterly shocks everyone and leads to one of the most famous movie lines of all time. Chief Brody backs into the wheelhouse, looks at the shark hunter and says, "You're gonna need a bigger boat." And he doesn't even drop his cheroot.

As it turned out a bigger boat wasn't necessary. What saved the day was lateral thinking, i.e. stuffing a compressed gas cannister in the beast's mouth and blowing its head into something resembling dog chow.

But Brody's was a perfectly natural reaction for anyone faced with a major problem. It's been the same in industry for the better part of 200 years. Big has been better, and bigger than that better still. Whether by organic growth or M&A up until now the goal has always been to get big enough that you reach a critical mass allowing you to start controlling forces rather than being at their mercy.

It is a paradigm under which economies of scale rule and it has formed the successful basis of dealing with, or becoming, a corporate shark for generations. It is the reason that shipping has a powerful tier of mega-ship operators, and why they're now operating fleets of mega-ships. It is also the reason that maritime equipment and service supply has evolved in the way it has, targeting its services at the big guys where a few contracts can make a business, whilst reluctantly servicing the expensive long-tail. Technology, however, and the trends already mentioned are about to profoundly change the nature of markets and competition for shipping and it's maritime supply industry.

Let's start with ship operators. The message from the majority of shipping's customers—and certainly many we spoke to who understandably didn't necessarily want to go on the record—appears to be that they are underwhelmed. When they are dealing with the complexities outlined in *The Weakest Link*—which, by the way is how one major shipping customer described our shipping industry—they find it hard to understand how shipping can not only fail to add any value whatsoever to their operations, but persistently fail to successfully complete the most basic of service expectations, namely, getting goods where they're supposed to go reliably, safely and on time.

The industry's response to increasing homogenisation, overcapacity, lack of service differentiation and falling rates has been slow steaming, bigger ships and the creation of even bigger alliances like the P3. In the light of what's already changing, it suggests a profound lack of insight into what businesses in other industries are already recognising they have to do to remain competitive. Shipping has of course long recognised that there is a problem. What it hasn't yet grasped is that the problem is shipping.

In a recent report McKinsey quotes the example of a major manufacturer who discovered that switching from a low cost parts supplier in Mexico to a new local supplier with advanced 3D printing capabilities meant it lowered stocking costs, as parts are made on demand, and created opportunities to develop prototypes more quickly. It also, of course eliminated its shipping costs, and the risk that the manufacturer would be adversely affected by a shipment not turning up on time, or at all. That manufacturer was a customer. It could have been yours. One day soon it will be yours.

Even the apparently bright spots are beginning to cast long shadows. The trans-Atlantic containerised auto parts trade, according to recent reports, is 'booming'. "There is a big recovery coming in Europe", Nissan CEO Carlos Ghosn said at the opening of a Nissan plant in Brazil earlier this month. There are "lots of bright spots in 2014, and without any doubt you are going to have a lot of car manufacturers preparing for the future."

But the future they're preparing for may not be what shipping is expecting. 'Nextshoring' is changing the traditional tactics of locating your factories in areas of low-cost labour and then shipping the final product to your markets. Digital manufacturing, 3D printing, or additive manufacturing, and the need to develop innovative supply ecosystems means that in future manufacturers are far more likely to consider locating factories closer to their markets and sources of highly skilled suppliers with whom they can collaborate. Supply chains are identified as a source of real competitive advantage as digital operations intensify and McKinsey recognises that, "As information flows among partners become more robust, they will usher in a range of improvements, from surer logistics to better payment systems."

Of course the most certain way to achieve 'surer logistics' is not to ship anything in the first place, and as we've already seen, there are those who will try to do that. But it won't be a solution for everyone. Goods will still need to be shipped, and shipping needs to realise the damage it inflicts upon tightly integrated supply chains. A major motor manufacturer explained how the lean manufacturing—and indeed the zero-inventory manufacturing to which every manufacturer aspires—can be completely de-railed by shipping's inability to keep up.

A late shipment can mean the manufacturer being forced to send parts by air, a massive extra cost and strain on a complex logistics chain. These costs and more importantly the damage to the manufacturer's operations have led some to predict that the massive container ships currently plying the oceans aren't going to be around in any kind of number for that much longer. The prospect has led to somewhat unkind mutterings that it's a good job Maersk's new Triple E's are so easy to recycle.

As Filip VanHeer of Orange Business Services said in last

quarter's issue, customers aren't prepared to lose track of their goods for days or weeks. With the industrial internet growing daily even ship operators are beginning to see the value in getting technical and commercial data on and off a ship. But there still hasn't been a recognition that customers need exactly the same kind of data and information flow about their shipments. Cyberphysical systems rely upon components being sentient enough to know what they are and where they need to go in the manufacturing process, but despite having highly robust and functional satellite links shipping is turning the ocean into the equivalent of the dark side of the moon.

If it feels as though it's only the box ship operators who are in trouble then think again. The circular economy which is already gaining traction with really big manufacturers, has at its heart a focus on minimising the use and extending the re-use of virgin materials. A recent report about the potential impact of this trend by the Ellen MacArthur Foundation says, "If applied to steel consumption in the automotive, machining, and transport sectors, a circular transformation could achieve global net materials savings equivalent to between 110 million and 170 million metric tons of iron ore a year in 2025." That's up to 170 million metric tons of iron ore per year that won't need to be shipped any longer, and the projection only covers a few, though major, sectors.

Then there are the broader trends and attitudes at interplay likely to alter consumer demands, expectations and behaviours. The circular economy is one facet of a broader collaborative economy which rejects waste and is looking to digitisation to increase yield and utilisation of the goods we create. Self-driving cars are effectively possible, as are the complex algorithms required to take the huge streams of environmental data from the industrial and wider internet, make sense of it and take optimum decisions on that basis.

Add to this the fact that the average car is utilised less than 4 percent of its lifetime, whilst roads only perform at minimum efficiency, and some are already envisaging a radically different approach to car use. Combining the Millennial preference for access over ownership, and the ability of the city transport authorities to take data and make real time provision for car availability and sharing. The days when people bought new cars which sat on their drives or outside their offices for 95 percent of their lives before being scrapped may soon seem criminally wasteful.

With 3D printing and increased computing power the possibilities of maintaining older cars also changes, as does creating new ones. The move to personalisation, rapid prototyping and crowdsourcing are already leading manufacturers like GE to look at the Local Motors model. Local Motors crowdsources auto designs and then uses its micro-manufacturing facilities to produce them using 3D printing among other technologies. The company already knows what the demand is likely to be for its models before it begins to micro-manufacture them, unlike traditional auto manufacturers who invest a billion dollars in a model and produce it on a massive scale, with no guarantee it will be successful.

Access over ownership is extending to other areas like consumer white goods where the tradition has always been to buy the product. New leasing models are being proposed for everything from televisions to washing machines which focus on total cost of ownership rather than purchase price. It's been suggested that such models will save money for consumers and manufacturers, allow deep, data rich, ongoing relationships, and mean the goods can be returned and re-furbished or recycled at the end of their lives.

None of these things are far-fetched, but taken together the impact upon shipping will be far-reaching, even transformative. Are shipping leaders confident they understand the potential impacts on their organisations? Are we in good shape to start addressing these issues? In truth it doesn't feel that way, and that's a problem, not just because there are threats to us, but because there are some emerging opportunities.

With the circular economy focussing on reducing the demand for virgin materials, new business models create new requirements. Take Ricoh's GreenLine brand of office copiers and printers which are leased, returned, dismantled, extensively refurbished and then re-enter the market.

For those which can't be re-used Ricoh harvests the components and recycles them at local facilities, but the longer term plan is to return some of the recycled materials to its manufacturing plants in Asia for use in making new components.

According to them, "After factoring in the price differences between virgin components and the cost of Asia-bound container shipping, Ricoh estimates it could save up to 30 percent on the cost of materials of these components."

So what the circular economy is taking with one hand, it has the capacity to give back with the other. Customers like Ricoh are now facing new challenges, thinking about 'reverse-network' activities, turning products back into components and materials, and where and how it's best to do that.

Decisions will be based on the economics of whether refurbishment should happen in the place of usage, or that of manufacture. These are difficult calls, and shipping could be playing its part in helping its customers to make them, and facilitate them. A strategic approach to service delivery and pricing for this type of emerging segment could grow it considerably. And this is just one example.

But in order to really add value to its customers shipping has to start looking at the emerging technologies, particularly connectivity and data, and—crucially—implementing and leveraging the technology it already has.

What came out loud and clear from the SingTel Ship Efficiency Roundtable late last year (*download the whitepaper from the Futurenautics website*) was that ship operators know they aren't using the technology they have properly, and as far as many are concerned, it's too complex a job to start.

And that's where we have to look to the maritime equipment manufacturers and suppliers, and question how ship operators, their customers, come to be in that kind of position. Interviewed recently a senior GE executive said, "Complexity is free." It neatly sums up a big part of the problem in maritime.

Necessity, as they say, is the mother of invention and it's a widely acknowledged truth that maritime has been the poster-boy for regulation-driven product and service development. It's proved to be damaging, in a number of respects.

Suppliers aren't meeting customer requirements, so much as

regulatory ones, and the focus is more about ticking and selling boxes than solving operational problems.

In the fight to sell against each other suppliers develop ever longer lists of features making products more and more complex, but—as proprietary designs, parts and code are included in order to lock ship operators into a relationship which is too expensive, or too much hassle to change—less and less interoperable. The result is that the majority of ship operators have an awful lot of extremely expensive, highly complex boxes of kit, which comply with regulations, but don't add anywhere near the value they should and could.

The bottom line is that maritime has to stop selling complex products and start developing elegant solutions. Using technology will help them to do that, but first of all, the same way ship operators have to understand their customers, maritime suppliers have to understand theirs. It is remarkable how very little the vast majority of suppliers really know about the economics of running a shipping business.

There is a great scene in the movie *Sneakers*, where Robert Redford is trying to break into a building. He comes up against an entry keypad and speaks on his earpiece to his geeks in the van around the corner and asks them how he defeats the electronic keypad.

He listens for a moment to the reply, and then says, "I'll try that then." And he kicks the door in. The point is that they identified the problem wasn't beating the electronic keypad, it was getting into the building. Too many maritime suppliers still think they have to beat the electronic keypad.

Understanding the problem and the customer is only the first step though. What manufacturing 3.0 and Industry 4.0 is already showing is that collaboration, even pre-competitive collaboration between suppliers, is essential to overcoming complexity. The traditional corporate paradigm of developing, testing and manufacturing products in a vacuum is untenable. Maritime has to start leveraging the power of the global brain via crowdsourcing to start innovating and solving some of the intractable issues ship operators face.

New models for leasing equipment, or cloud-based as-a-service products which streamline and simplify procurement, maintenance and end-of-life recycling could make a real impact upon shipping.

The acceleration of augmented reality solutions for maintenance, training, healthcare, are all needed, but not in isolation. Unless real dialogue and collaboration takes place, complexity will only increase.

It has been an interesting experience putting together this issue more from what we haven't been told by maritime companies, than what we have.

We have asked about the possibilities of 3D printing fabs—fabrication hubs—being created at ports in order to locally print ship spares; we've asked about how far augmented reality solutions for marine maintenance are progressing and to what extent the new wearables like google glass are going to be a part of that; we've also asked how the industrial internet is being leveraged to create better, cheaper, less complex maritime products and services, and make servicing the long-tail cheaper and more profitable.

There don't seem to be many answers. There are a couple of possible reasons: one being that people just didn't think we were worth talking to, a view to which they are perfectly entitled. But actually it may be something deeper than that.

Some of those we asked one suspects had little understanding and certainly no strategic response to the trends and technologies we're talking about. The remainder undoubtedly do, but are still rigidly stuck in that competitive, secretive, rut which says that telling anyone what you're doing is a dangerous mistake. And I'm not entirely sure which of those groups has the bigger problem.

There are 'Moments of Truth' in business where crossroads are faced and often long and solid relationships fracture. But the genesis of those fractures is often in an escalating series of small failures to deliver. Shipping isn't going away, but it is going to change, and we have to not only prepare for that, but understand and capitalise upon it. If we don't others will.

Shipping and maritime companies have always aspired to be big sharks, but the time is approaching when the smaller, faster tuna fish who know that to stop swimming is to die, are gaining the advantage. Bigger boats and bigger sharks are not the answer. What we have to do is to start swimming for our lives.

Those that don't are in real danger of getting canned.

London, April 2014.

27

THE MEN IN THE GREY SUITS

In 1951 Ealing Studios released a satirical comedy, *The Man In The White Suit,* starring Alec Guinness as Sidney Stratton, a brilliant research chemist. When Stratton accidentally invents an astonishingly strong, dirt-repellent, mildly radioactive, white fabric which never wears out, he is first hailed as a genius.

However, when the consequences of offering consumers a fabric which once purchased never needs to be replaced are fully realised by textile industry bosses, trades unions and textile workers, he is hounded through the streets by a mob, desperate to destroy his fabric before it destroys their industry. The film was a hugely successful and typically British story about the little man pitted against the establishment.

But Sidney Stratton wasn't only up against the British establishment, his fabric was challenging the built-in obsolescence of products which has been an integral part of the linear, one-way production model that has dominated for almost 200 years.

Of course in the early 1950's there was little appreciation of just how ultimately unsustainable that model would become, but by the year 2000 when a rise in the real prices of natural resources began to wipe out a century's worth of real-price declines, the cracks in the system began to show. Even the economic downturn has failed to halt the problems, with resource price increases still rising faster than global output.

The likely addition of three billion middle-class consumers from the developing world by 2030, and the rise in commodity prices mean this 'take-make-dispose' approach to products is now under pressure.

The solution it seems lies in addressing the very built-in obsolescence, that Stratton's white suit challenged. This means a change in emphasis from disposability to reuse which recognises existing natural resources as finite, and too valuable to use only once, together with the development of new, innovative, smart materials which can perform multiple roles better.

At the same time products are designed and optimised for multiple cycles of disassembly and re-manufacturing, their respective materials reclaimed and recycled across not life cycles but use cycles. This radical sounding model is known as the 'Circular Economy', and although it shares some of the green overtones of recycling, it is a far more fundamental and innovative concept. To give some idea of scale, around 80 percent of the $3.2 trillion worth of materials used each year in the Fast Moving Consumer Goods (FMCG) industry are not recovered.

Little surprise then that according to a 2012 report the projected net savings from a circular economy in the European Union alone for durable products with moderate lifespans could reach $630 billion per year, and could reach $1 trillion per year globally.

Although these figures are projections, the circular economy is far from an abstract concept. There are major companies committed to realising its principles and already demonstrating real returns. Helping to drive their message home is former yachtswoman and multiple record holder Ellen MacArthur. Following her retirement from competitive yacht racing in 2010 she set up the Ellen MacArthur Foundation, which runs the world's first dedicated circular economy innovation programme, the Circular Economy 100.

Its purpose is to provide a 'unique forum for businesses to build circular capabilities, address common barriers to progress and pilot circular practices in a collaborative environment'. It was the time spent at sea which, according to MacArthur, opened her eyes to the resource scarcity issue.

"When you set off around the world on a boat, you know that you only have so much food, so much diesel. And you become incredibly connected to those resources," explains MacArthur. "As you watch those resources go down, you understand just what "finite" means because you're two and a half thousand miles from the nearest town. I realized that our global economy is no different—powered by resources that are ultimately finite—and that there is a much greater challenge out there than sailing around the world."

Of course for the shipping industry sailing around the world—and doing it profitably—is quite sufficiently challenging in the current economic climate. But unlike most green-sounding initiatives which ship operators tend to find merely translate into higher costs, there are a couple of reasons why the circular economy and its principles could be economically attractive.

The first reason why shipping could capitalise is simply because the ships upon which it relies represent massive material costs in themselves. DNV GL last year announced a project to repurpose phased out tank ships into offshore treatment plants handling waste and water for coastal cities. According to DNV GL a fifteen year old product tanker could treat the wastewater from a city of 250,000 inhabitants.

"There are many problems and the challenges are large and global," admits Bjorn K Haughland, Group Chief Sustainability Officer for DNV GL, but also points out that converting a tanker for this purpose could add 20 years to its lifecycle.

Perhaps the most widely known example of circular economy principles within shipping though is Maersk Line. Featuring as one of the Ellen MacArthur Foundation's principal case studies the development of the 'cradle-to-cradle' passport for the 20 new generation Triple E's was a first for the industry. Effectively the passport is a detailed online inventory which is maintained across the 30 year lifecycle of the ship and used to identify and recycle the components to a higher quality than currently possible.

According to Maersk the ultimate vision would be to manufacture new hulls from old ones, but for now the revenues from higher quality scrap metals was enough to give the initiative the green light. So far, so good, and it's all welcome in an industry plagued by footage of ships being run up beaches and slowly picked to nothing by dirt poor scavengers who risk their lives working at dizzying height with jagged steel and toxic chemicals, in a pair of shorts and sandals. But smarter recycling is only one aspect of the 'cradle-to cradle' philosophy.

It is in the potential for innovation that the circular economy should also really deliver. Redesigning materials, systems and products is a 'fundamental requirement' according to McKinsey, and it's one which shipping and maritime could really do with. But whereas Maersk Line have achieved an impressive industry first with their passports, all they've actually done is to document what's gone into making the Triple E. The more fundamental requirement, to evaluate the materials, design and systems of the ship in the first place, they not only failed to do, but it seems they flatly refused to do.

The Ellen MacArthur Foundation Maersk Line case study delicately points this out. "Those familiar with the Cradle to Cradle philosophy will be aware that emphasis is placed on materials choice and product design," it says on its website. "However, this hasn't been a priority for Maersk Line at this stage. Sterling (Jacob Sterling, Head of Climate and Sustainability at Maersk Line) sees understanding the materials currently used in the shipping industry as an essential step before thinking about substituting materials or re-thinking design."

Really? If you're having a hard time accepting that Maersk don't actually understand what they've been making their ships out of, then the explanation comes later in the Foundation write-up. According to them 'stakeholder engagement' with the project was an early barrier which Sterling and his team faced. "There was a perception that the Cradle to Cradle Passport meant redesigning the entire ship, using new technologies or alternative materials, requiring significant research and R&D investment," the Foundation says. "However, when key parties were made aware of the gains that could be realised simply taking the practical step of recording the composition of the ship, the initiative received greater internal enthusiasm."

So the Triple E passports represent Maersk grabbing the low-hanging fruit of the circular economy, and kicking the real opportunity into the long grass. It's an attitude which, much like the linear economy, is rapidly becoming unsustainable. Whereas one of the biggest container lines on the planet are still trying to understand what they're making their ships out of, the revolutionary materials which are destined to replace them are already undergoing research and development by other industries.

You may remember in the Sentient Ship article in the launch issue of Futurenautics in October 2013 we wrote about Buckypaper. This feather-light sheet made of carbon nanotubes is being tested in electronics, energy, medicine, space and transportation. Researchers at Florida State University's High Performance Materials Institute were recently awarded more than $1.4m to develop a system which can produce large amounts of the material. The project will involve transforming carbon nanotube thin films from a lab-scale demonstration material into 'commercially viable products with superior properties potentially surpassing the current state-of-the-art material in quality and production rate.'

"The goal is clear—to show industry the ability to use this in large-scale quantities," said Richard Liang, director of FSU's High-Performance Materials Institute (HPMI) and a professor for the FAMU-FSU College of Engineering. "We're looking at a more efficient, cost effective way to do this."

The key phrase here is 'commercially viable', and Boeing already get it. They've tested buckypaper, and projected that it could replace metal shielding in the Boeing 787, currently made up of 60 miles of cable. Engineers believe that replacing the cable with buckypaper could reduce the weight of the Boeing 787 by as much as 25 percent.

That weight reduction is going to have major implications for fuel efficiency, but add to that the wider savings on the manufacture, installation and maintenance of 60 miles of cabling.

Translate that to a ship and consider for a moment. Steel makes up approximately 98 percent of the volume of a Triple E. And it suffers from significant price volatility. How much of the current cabling which costs money to make, install, survey, maintain and replace could a ship potentially rid itself of by using buckypaper instead?

Shipping and maritime is seeing the beginnings of next generation materials—read our interview with metamaterial antenna company Kymeta's CEO Vern Fotheringham this issue for an example—but if a giant like Maersk has put this kind of circular economy R&D on the 'too difficult' pile then how are these innovative materials, product designs and systems going to find their way in?

No one disputes that implementing the principles of the circular economy is a complex business, but there are tools out there that shipping and maritime aren't taking full advantage of. In our *The In Crowd* article this issue we describe how GE recognised that it's lack of expertise in 3D printing, or additive manufacturing, was a problem it could solve by using crowdsourcing to tap the global brain. Engaging online communities and building links to other industries both broaden horizons and cross-fertilise ideas. The belief that shipping or maritime domain specific features, experience or qualifications are essential has to be dispelled. GE found their aeronautical engineering problem solved by a man with no aero experience whatsoever.

But far more can also be done by engaging the smart minds within companies. Philips CEO Frans Van Houten readily admits that the manufacturer's move towards circular thinking hasn't been simple, but says, "People become resourceful and inventive when you challenge them."

But that challenge has to come from the top where the biggest danger is what McKinsey describes as the 'Curse of the Status Quo.' Ingrained habits and the worry of higher capital investments and R&D are real issues. But with examples like Renault—whose remanufacturing operations use 80 percent less energy, generate almost 90 percent less waste, 70 percent less oil and detergent waste and deliver higher operating margins than Renault as a whole can boast—Philips, and Ricoh out there, not to mention Boeing and buckypaper, shipping and maritime's leaders have to try.

The Man In The White Suit, Sidney Stratton, and his white suit came to a sticky end. Having refused various tricks and bribes to sign away the rights to his amazing fabric, by the end of the film Stratton is running through the streets in his luminous white suit, pursued by an angry mob. As they close in the chemical structure of the fibre reveals its weakness and breaks down, allowing them to triumphantly tear the white suit off him. Stratton is left standing in the street in his underpants.

Fast forward sixty or so years and the men in white suits are creating genuinely revolutionary materials, while the world is running low on the old ones. Far from being the shipping industry's nemesis, they could well be one of its saviours.

And if shipping's men in grey suits don't start taking a serious interest in them shortly, it'll be them caught with their pants down.

London, April 2014.

28

THE IN CROWD

In 2012 the Oxford English Dictionary (third edition) included an entry relating to Godwin's Law. Created by American attorney and author Mike Godwin the law is an Internet adage which asserts that, "As an online discussion grows longer, the probability of a comparison involving Nazis or Hitler approaches—that is, if an online discussion (regardless of topic or scope) goes on long enough, sooner or later someone will compare someone or something to Hitler or Nazism."

A cursory review of comments sections and message boards, tweets and wall posts suggests that Mr Godwin has a point. The level of bile in certain sectors online, what is known as 'trolling', is quite shocking and has already led in some cases to criminal convictions. For many people it's a reason not to engage online, and for many businesses it represents a concrete justification as to why they don't want to expose their company and their brand to the dangers of reputational damage that an online community can pose.

Until now the more forward thinking shipping and maritime businesses have experimented with extending their digital footprint outside their website, creating Twitter feeds, Facebook and

LinkedIn pages, and Instagram and Pinterest accounts. The focus has been on brand, PR and awareness. For others, the prospect of spending time, energy and money managing social networking accounts with no particular ROI, has been deterrent enough.

But look beyond the people telling you what they had for breakfast on Twitter and there are other, far more interesting communities, made up of engineers, designers and materials experts amongst others. And where there is very little mention of Nazis. Although shipping and maritime haven't really engaged with them yet, they could be the key to solving some major challenges, from ship design and efficiencies, to maritime domain awareness and navigational safety.

One such community, GrabCAD, comprises more than a million engineers and designers, and it was to them that General Electric (GE) decided to turn in what has become a widely reported crowdsourcing success story. For those not familiar with the term, Crowdsourcing Week describe it as, "…the practice of engaging a 'crowd' or group for a common goal—often innovation, problem solving, or efficiency. Crowdsourcing can take place on many different levels and across various industries. Thanks to our growing connectivity, it is now easier than ever for individuals to collectively contribute—whether with ideas, time, expertise, or funds—to a project or cause. This collective mobilization is crowdsourcing."

With the Internet, social networking and cloud technologies (read January's cloud issue of Futurenautics for more) bringing organisations closer to their customers and stakeholders, crowdsourcing represents one facet of a new approach to collaboration and value creation.

The phenomenon can provide organisations with "access to new ideas and solutions, deeper consumer engagement, opportunities for co-creation, optimization of tasks, and reduced costs," and GE is a solid example of precisely how, and why it's becoming so important.

GE's aviation engineers were wrestling with a problem. A jet engine weighs around 13,000 pounds, and in order to keep them and their components securely in place, engine brackets are required. The way to create very strong, very stiff brackets was using moulded titanium alloy, but the resulting parts weighed 4.48 pounds each.

In an industry even more rigorously focussed on fuel consumption than shipping, GE worked out that if they could reduce the weight of these brackets, perhaps by 3D printing them, the lighter engine could result in millions of dollars worth of annual fuel savings. GE's problem however, was that they didn't have the time, or the advanced manufacturing knowledge, to significantly reduce the weight themselves.

Enter GrabCAD, to which GE presented its engine bracket challenge. Offering a prize of $7,000 to whoever could redesign a bracket that reduced the most weight whilst still safely supporting the engine, GE received over 1,000 entries. A young Indonesian engineer by the name of M Arie Kurniawan won by managing to reduce the weight of the bracket by a massive 84 percent, to just .72 of a pound.

M Arie Kurniawan took home $7,000 but what GE took away was more profound. The new, featherlight bracket was a vindication of an innovation strategy into which it has reportedly invested a major portion of its annual $6 billion R&D budget. That strategy is a very simple one—using all the collaborative tools and Internet connectivity at its disposal, to tap the global brain, and using it to solve problems.

Steve Liguori, GE's executive director of global innovation & new models, describes taking M Arie Kurniawan's bracket to Jeff Immelt, GE's Chairman and CEO. "He was like, 'Where did you find this kid, and how much aviation experience does he have?' And you know the answer to that question? Zero."

In short, this is an individual who, without crowdsourcing, would probably never have appeared on GE's corporate radar, and yet his design has solved an issue for them which they would most likely have paid an experienced aeronautical engineer many tens of thousands of dollars over a prolonged period of time to do likewise.

But what's almost more interesting about the GE example, is how the company has cut through the traditional inheritance of a 20th century manufacturer with secrecy, competition, patents and privacy in its DNA, and embraced the transparency and collaboration required by crowdsourcing. Not only did GE admit that it didn't have the 3D printing, or additive manufacturing, expertise in house to solve the problem, it recognised that expertise probably did exist elsewhere.

Steve Liguori is the first to admit that, "For all of the smart engineers at GE, we sure don't have a lock on all of the smart engineers in the world." But it's still a massive leap from there to putting parts of your intellectual property out into cyberspace to allow design challenges to be solved by anyone who cares to.

In light of that, it seems even more incredible that crowdsourcing recently produced the XC2V, the world's first crowd-derived combat-support vehicle, for the Defense Advanced Research Projects Agency (DARPA), part of the office of the US Secretary of State for Defense. The company they turned to for help is Local Motors, which, at less than six years old, has pioneered bringing crowdsourcing—or co-creation as it prefers to call it—to vehicle manufacturing.

Run by former US Marine and McKinsey Consultant John B Rogers, Local Motors is based in Phoenix, Arizona, and is notable for producing the first ever crowdsourced production car. The Rally Fighter, with its 6.2 litre engine and 430 brake horsepower, was built by incentivising the crowd and then tapping its knowledge and creativity.

Managed by the Local Motors team, individuals would work either alone, or within competing groups focussed on particular challenges. The result appears to be a dramatic acceleration in the design and development of the complex system which is a modern automobile. News of this rapid and efficient formula for turning ideas into industrial, manufactured products attracted DARPA to this comparatively tiny company.

"The reason is that a non-traditional business can break into any field where there is a great need that is not being met," John Rogers explained in a recent article. "Not only did we show DARPA that a troop transporter could be built on schedule and under budget, but we gave them a process by means of which this could be done over and over again." With even President Obama referring to the XC2V as an example of how collaboration between the military—one of the most secretive institutions on earth—and industry can enhance the competitiveness of US manufacturing, the reasons for the huge success of these projects, and the willingness of giants like GE and the US Military to try them, has to lie in something greater. That something is the convergence of the forces which are driving us towards Manufacturing 3.0 and Industry 4.0.

3D printing, or additive manufacturing is allowing rapid proto-typing, individualisation and product diversity, but there are other technological developments including simulation, collaborative software tools, scanning and high speed communications which are driving digital manufacturing towards the revolution. Read our feature article *The Weakest Link* for more detail. Combined with increasing resource scarcity and the moves towards the circular economy (see *The Men In The Grey Suits*) the world is becoming sufficiently complex that even behemoths like GE know they have to concentrate to stay current.

"You pretty quickly start to understand, you can't do it all," says Beth Comstock, GE's senior vice president and CMO, who is reportedly in charge of GE's open innovation push.

As a result GE is trying to think more like the highly social, transparent, collaborative start-ups which are proving week after week that the power of the crowd can be converted into hard cash if properly harnessed.

But with 300,000 employees worldwide, $16.9 billion in 2013 earnings and a 130 year heritage, GE is more like the big, venerable ship operators and maritime manufacturers than a Local Motors. So if they can do it, why can't we?

Shipping and maritime has always been insular, and the attitude that anyone who hasn't worked in the industry, and doesn't have the relevant qualifications and experience cannot play in our sandpit, persists. But the experience of GE and many others like them is signposting that there are huge opportunities to solve problems, enhance efficiencies, accelerate growth and increase margin by utilising crowdsourcing. And it isn't as though we couldn't benefit from all of those things. With the increasing burden of regulation the costs associated with compliance are ever increasing, but the solutions—from ballast water treatment to ECDIS systems—are all routinely developed in highly secretive, closed R&D groups with the focus on proprietary hardware and software delivering ongoing revenue.

Worse still, the level of pre-development customer research undertaken in the maritime industry is woefully small compared to others. The result is a host of competing systems each trying to outdo each other in terms of features and functionality, at least some of which ship operators neither want nor need, but lacking any interoperability with other shipboard systems, which they do.

E-navigation highlights one specific area where this traditional, adversarial commercial approach is handicapping the industry. The new Millennial 'Internet' generation finding their way onboard as Navigation Officers don't suffer from any wariness about trusting what's on the computer screen, rather than their own charts. But that exposes a deeper issue. "Such users may not realise that the source data may very well be quite old," says former Rear Admiral Nick Lambert.

But why should that data be old? Most likely because of the extreme reluctance of the various stakeholders in the chart data ecosystem to share what they consider to be their proprietary product and service information. It's the same problem which has plagued AIS and other initiatives. It is an area where Nick Lambert sees a very practical crowdsourcing application.

"It's up to the hydrographer to address this issue. We need better data," he recently told Hydro International, "meaning that the hydrographer should embrace new techniques to create modern surveys more quickly: for instance, the use of satellite derived bathymetry and crowdsourcing."

It was a sentiment shared by former Singaporean Navy man Kuet Ee Yoon, now Deputy General Manager at Pacific Radiance Ltd, during the SingTel Ship Efficiency Roundtable late last year. (You can download the full whitepaper now on the Futurenautics website.) On a broader maritime domain safety and security theme he identified the immense potential of the world's commercial fleet routinely sharing the information they gather in the course of their normal activities.

"Can you imagine that every single ship out there is an eye? And that picture can be shared through the central portal," said Kuet during the discussion. "That will completely change the whole maritime situation awareness picture, security and how we respond to it."

Maritime stakeholders may be reluctant to 'pre-compete', and share ideas and data, but the benefits to them could far outweigh any downside. Using crowdsourcing techniques allows the development of products you already know your market wants, and gets the global brain to help you create the features they like. Together with a shift to initial 'minimum viable' products offering just the core features required, this approach could transform maritime equipment supply and deliver the promise of enhanced efficiencies, accelerated growth, increased margins and, crucially, happier customers.

But getting there is going to require a wholesale rejection of the prevailing business paradigm in shipping and maritime: that you conceive, design, manufacture and innovate in a vacuum, only making contact with your market in the shape of a finished product.

As our January 2014 cloud issue identified, the cloud and the new business models it enables is really a mindset. It isn't necessarily dependent upon age, but it does require an appreciation, if not an understanding, of the Millennial generation who are our future employees, customers and stakeholders, and the wider trends which are shaping them.

We need to be more transparent, more accessible, and, like GE, perhaps a little more humble about what we can and can't achieve as individuals and companies in an age of increasing technological complexity. And put more faith in what we can achieve as part of the Millennial crowd.

For as Adolf Hitler once said, "He alone, who owns the youth, gains the future." And there, Ladies and Gentlemen, is Godwin's Law in action.

London, April 2014.

29

CLOUD CAPITAL

In a dark and musty corner of the Internet which one suspects probably smells of cold pizza and disappointment, there are a bunch of anonymous guys locked in a titanic struggle. They are wrestling to discover a truth which, on the face of it, seems unimportant set against the travails of the world. What occupies these committed individuals and their increasingly irate Q&A forum, is the correct capitalisation of 'The Cloud'. For the sake of editorial balance we should point out that other capitalisations are available including 'the Cloud' and 'the cloud'. Oh, and capitalisation should possibly have a 'z' in it depending upon where you're reading this.

The reason they, and the rest of the world, are having such a hard time deciding how to capitalise the cloud, is because it's all about context. The cloud is, at a tactical level, about computing resources, but at a strategic level it is about far more. Scalable, flexible and cheaper access to computing resources level commercial playing fields. Cloud architectures built on an 'outside-in' approach (of which more later) fundamentally change the way that businesses can interact with each other, their employees and customers.

Mirroring as it does the hopes, beliefs and aspirations of 'Gen C' and the Millennials of which they are a constituent part, underpinning trends such as Collaborative Consumption, the cloud can also be viewed as a technological facilitator of a new philosophy.

In short, when the cloud has such a broad range of impacts, it's no wonder punctuators are having difficulty deciding whether it's the definite article. It is however, the real deal.

If you want a definition then the US National Institute of Standards and Technology's is as good as any. They state that the cloud is, "a model for enabling convenient, on-demand network access to a shared pool of configurable computing resources (e.g., networks, servers, storage, applications and services) that can be rapidly provisioned and released with minimal management effort or service provider interaction."

In fact the cloud has been around since the 1960s, the name developed from the graphical representation of the internet on network diagrams. According to John Hagel, and John Seely Brown, of the Deloitte Center for the Edge, its current manifestation is part of a third wave of technology disruption which started with the personal computer in the 1970s and led to the advent of the publicly accessible internet ten years later. Cloud computing, they believe, could be just as disruptive, transforming institutional architectures and management practices in a range of industries.

And its use is growing fast. Gartner say that by 2016 cloud will form the bulk of all new IT spend, and by the end of 2017 nearly half of all large enterprises will have hybrid cloud deployments. But we're not there yet. A survey of 300 CIOs and senior IT decision makers by NTT Communications suggests that, in Europe at least, cloud has reached a crossroads. "To use the language from Gartner's Hype Cycle models for technology, the cloud has passed the 'peak of inflated expectations' and is heading into the 'trough of disillusionment'," they tell us. The results show that, "adoption of cloud services is largely tactical in nature. IT leaders are wary about placing their strategic ICT platforms – the business engine, if you will – into the cloud."

So is the focus by IT providers on the tactical/delivery side of cloud obscuring the real strategic business implications? Sylvain Quief, Cloud Computing Marketing Director at Orange Business Services, disagrees. "Although a couple of years ago this may have been true—the cloud was looked at from a very technological standpoint—customers today are very educated when it comes to the cloud and the CxOs understand perfectly the implications of using cloud-based solutions, from the CFO looking at the financial side to the legal offices interested in data privacy concerns."

If there is a 'trough of disillusionment' presumably Orange would be well placed to see it. The business services arm of Orange S.A., Orange Business Services provides integrated communications solutions and services to global enterprises in cloud computing, unified communications and collaboration. Within the shipping and maritime market they supply both ICT services and VSAT connectivity to vessels, counting four of the world's top five, and sixteen out of the top twenty container shipping companies as customers, and three of the top five tanker operators.

Focussing on their cloud activities under their umbrella 'Flexible Computing' range of products Orange is primarily active in IaaS (Infrastructure as a Service). Computing and Storage solutions are provided in a Public mode, (shared resources accessed via the Internet), in Virtual Private mode (secured shared resources accessed through a VPN), Private mode (a resource pool dedicated to a customer/community), and increasingly, in a Hybrid mode where "a little bit of everything" is managed through a single pane of glass console. They're also a strong SaaS (Software as a Service) player with collaboration services such as Unified Communications as a Service with Cisco or Microsoft, Contact Centres deployed in the cloud and even Security as a Service.

For Quief the cloud is a business model, a new way of consuming IT made popular by the current investment difficulties faced by businesses, i.e. OPEX rather than CAPEX. "This definition is actually very close to the DNA of a network operator like Orange, who for decades has been investing in bandwidth capacity throughout the world and selling it as a service. We are very proud of that, so it has been very natural for us to extend our playground a little bit, from the network to the cloud."

In terms of the type of companies and customers deploying these varying cloud solutions, that's difficult to pin down. "With regard to customer segmentation, the cloud again blurs the boundaries," Quief tells us. "While it is true to say that very small companies tend to adopt SaaS much more than IaaS, larger companies are really using a bit of everything, from public SaaS for full elasticity to private IaaS when they are processing sensitive data, for example."

The belief at Orange is that the cloud represents a very fundamental shift in the way companies are looking at IT. Customers are now expecting "auto-adaptation of their IT infrastructures based on the actual need expressed by their business units/users," and as a result the entire definition of the IT department, and how it chooses the best solutions in real time, based on price, SLAs, regulation, privacy and security concerns etc, is being re-written. The results are enabling businesses to be more efficient than ever.

Quief is "profoundly convinced" of the advantages citing three main areas in which businesses can capitalise. Firstly, in shortening time-to-market. With implementation phases reduced to days or weeks rather than months, sales and marketing have a better shot at matching market expectations. Secondly, the ability to experiment without high entry costs. The 'as-a-service' model enables businesses to test a new market or product without a huge upfront investment. As a result the innovation cycle becomes more agile, and any failure less painful. The third area Quief identifies as the ability of businesses to "positively answer to the new Gen Y and Gen C of employees who are expecting high flexibility in the way they work." With the cloud IT departments can facilitate new usage including virtual workspaces, BYOD (Bring Your Own Device) and ATA-WAD (AnyTime, AnyWhere, AnyDevice).

This interaction with employees and also customers and wider groups has traditionally been underpinned by legacy IT systems. Like the businesses they're supporting most legacy IT systems are based on an 'inside-out' approach. In a nutshell the inside-out approach means you start with the problem, the pain points within the company, and you try to solve them. An 'outside-in' approach begins and ends with the customer. The decision is initiated in response to strategic needs that exist outside the company, and the decision-making process focuses on how it will enable an improved customer experience.

Whilst outside-in approaches are possible with legacy IT systems, they are far more efficiently deployed via cloud computing, and their adoption is far from theoretical. Already there are many companies beginning to harness the 'outside-in' way of thinking, and they are encouraging their customers and supply chain partners to do the same. The NTT Europe study shows over half of CIOs (53%) say launching new services and applications more quickly is a key request. In the transport and logistics sector—our sector— 80% of CIOs confirmed this as their most important business focus. Sitting at the heart of so many transport and logistics chains and relationships, how can shipping respond to and take advantage of the cloud, it's challenges and it's opportunities?

ESRG, provider of leading-edge data analysis and remote monitoring technology via its OstiaEdge product, produced a whitepaper on the subject last year. *"Bringing the industrial internet to the marine industry and ships into the cloud,"* puts the opportunity for asset owners, operators and managers to reduce costs, improve fuel efficiency, and increase uptime and reliability at approximately 20 billion dollars today, exceeding 50 billion dollars by 2030. For individual ships they calculate potential annual value creation could be as high as $1 million or greater when considering po-tential fuel savings, optimising maintenance, decreasing downtime and increasing utilisation.

So how do you define a ship which is in the cloud? "It's not that black and white, it's more of a spectrum," says Rob Bradenham, General Manager of ESRG. "Different shipping segments are going to prioritise different applications and uses and will fall out on different points on that spectrum of pure cloud one end and not connected at the other."

Andrew Faiola, Senior Global Accounts Director for Intel-sat says, "A wise man recently remarked to me, 'You've got to get through the cloud to get to the Cloud'. This comment reinforces the need to make the right decisions for communications technology in shipping, or any other sector where enterprise-grade, mission-critical connectivity is a must-have. I'm a big believer that "Big Data" will help to drive more efficient vessel operations, ultimately lifting profits by reducing downtime, saving on fuel costs, and compliance. Most of this data and processing power will reside in the Cloud. But, even such small things as the ability to reliably multicast an FA Cup final will have a positive impact on things like crew welfare as shipping companies start to come to grips with MLC2006."

So how do ship operators view it? "We define the cloud as any applications, storage or services provided by an external company with globally distributed infrastructure," says Rob Grool, President of Seaspan Ship Management, one of the leading independent containership owners in the world. And where does Grool see the cloud having the most significant impact on the shipping and maritime industry? "On the core business of shipping, the actual ships, there will be minimal impact. One of the core requirements for a cloud solution is a permanent, high quality internet connection. Since a ship at sea only gets internet via satellite, there are inherent physical limitations to the quality of the connection."

Is connectivity the key challenge then? Veson Nautical develop and deliver some of the most advanced, user-friendly, commercial maritime management and trading software solutions on the market. With the announcement late last year of a cloud version of their IMOSLive product, Veson can now offer a fully cloud-based solution. With ERP applications such as theirs consistently reported as a top driver for the fitting of IP satellite systems, how important is the connection?

"Highly functional ERP can't deploy over a slow connection, but some bits work," says Sean Riley, COO of Veson. So presumably Inmarsat's Global Xpress and its promised speeds of 50Mbps and satellite-ready Skype apps is a game changer. Not necessarily. "People are surprised what already can be done," Filip Vanheer, Global Business Development Manager, Maritime Satellite Solutions, at Orange tells us. "It is perfectly feasible today to run Skype over our VSAT connection—given sufficient bandwidth. We have no Fair Use Policy in place that forbids that."

So if the connection speeds are only part of the issue, why is there general agreement that cloud adoption within shipping and maritime is—depending upon whom you speak to—between five and fifteen years behind other comparable industries. Perhaps because it's more than a model, it's a mindset.

"Cloud is actually only one of the aspects of a global change in our society," says Sylvain Quief of Orange. "We are now mixing our personal and professional lives; we are always socially connected; we expect instantaneity; we refuse to use software or business apps that require training. All this is more related to a "mind-set" than an approach to IT, even if ultimately it turns into some IT solutions."

But is it a mindset which is rarer in shipping? And if it is, could that be because, in the past ship operators have been exposed to potentially very expensive IT mistakes? Complex, bespoke in-house legacy systems are creaking under the pressure to be more flexible, and in terms of satellite, the great hopes that many attached to the VSAT systems they invested in haven't borne the fruit they anticipated. There's no doubt that as the number of providers in the market increased, the likelihood of operators ending up with systems which didn't do what they needed them to do, did likewise.

But as Captain Kuba Szymanski, Secretary General of Inter-Manager has already pointed out, the operators have to bear a degree of responsibility, for failing to adequately specify what they wanted. The problem of course is that very few of them knew how.

"VSAT or Inmarsat, anyone comes to you and asks, what are your priorities, and we would say, 'communication'," says Szymanski. "This is an extremely broad term. We needed to specify that, but the shipping industry management side is ignorant. We are ship Masters, we are Chief Engineers; we do not understand it."

It's an area where analysts see major opportunities developing. As the cloud starts to stitch together more and more complex offerings, possibilities will open up for consultants focussed not on technology and integration, but on deep domain knowledge to help clients adopt the correct mix of services and applications in order to get the maximum value from these platforms. At the moment though, that role is inevitably falling to the providers.

"Any good software company serves as a consultant to its clients, balancing the cutting edge of what's available and the client's requirements," says Veson's Riley. "You can kill an ant with a grenade, but a fly-swatter works just as well. If you're a good supplier you don't sell the grenade."

The evidence suggests though, that shipping may need that bomb put under it as a failure to move quickly on this core strategic issue could easily blow up in its face. According to Deloitte's Centre for the Edge, it "...cannot be left to the chief information officer alone, as it traditionally has. That is because flexible, constantly shifting architecture is set to fuel the business models of tomorrow."

Already some organisations are creating Chief Digital Officer positions to interpret analytics, mobile and social technologies, the introduction of which will fundamentally change business planning. But the CDOs ability to manipulate applications and data depends on having a cloud model for ICT.

"It takes a certain attitude to grow from a grocery store to a supermarket, but it requires another attitude to lift that to the level of a supermarket chain. Meaning, the current generation of shipping tycoons absolutely has its merits, but the world has changed and so has the technology," says Orange's Vanheer.

"The new generation that is taking over control of these companies is much more open towards technology changes than the current ones. But above all, their customers expect new services; they don't want to lose track of their goods for weeks."

It's a sobering point. When it comes to satisfying customers, shipping's performance is far from stellar and with manufacturing gearing up for cyberphysical systems and zero-inventory, it is only by deploying 'outside-in' approaches that shipping has a chance to stay with them.

Filip Vanheer is clear about the potential consequences. "If they don't adapt, the others who will, will take their place. And here is where cloud comes in, because it is so much easier to create an environment to interact with your customer in a cloud-based solution due to its flexibility. The companies who are open to integrate IT in their business will be best placed to fulfil the customer's requirements."

It is a warning which applies more widely in maritime than just ship operators and their end customers. Maritime software and equipment suppliers are just as vulnerable to new, innovative technology-centric start ups that will identify and fulfil their customers' needs more seamlessly. In an industry where big has always been better, the traditional economies of scale are diminishing, whilst legacy IT systems and big overheads are a drag on innovation.

As the Millennials occupy more and more influential positions, both as leaders and consumers, bringing with them their desire for sharing, partnership, sustainability, and cutting-edge technology, the cloud will be the basis for the businesses they create, interact with and the way they live their lives.

"By 2020, Cloud will have disappeared. It will have disappeared simply because it will be everywhere," says Sylvain Quief with a smile. "Cloud will be the "default" IT deployment model, and everything that we currently call "legacy" will have been more or less replaced. We are not there yet—still a long journey to go, but the trend is inevitable."

Looking at the three waves of computing disruption, it's possible to draw a comparison with Stephen Covey's description of the three stages of human development in his book, "The 7 Habits of Highly Successful People." Covey believed that humans moved from Dependence: the paradigm under which we are born, relying upon others to take care of us; to Independence: the paradigm under which we can make our own decisions and take care of ourselves, and finally to Interdependence: the paradigm under which we cooperate to achieve something that cannot be achieved independently.

From the personal computer to the cloud, technology has demonstrated an uncannily similar journey. In this context, the cloud is perhaps more of a reflection of a maturing society than it is a technological phenomenon. And perhaps that is the best way for shipping and maritime leaders approach the cloud strategically—as a generational mindset, an adequate grasp of which is essential to the development of an organisation fit for the future.

"It is impossible to foresee all the advantages the Cloud can give the shipping industry", says Lena Göthberg, Secretary-General of the Institute of Shipping Analysis, "but it will definitely give us the power to become a more attractive industry for young people to work in."

Back in that sweaty, emoticon-fuelled corner of the internet the punctuators continue to slug it out with no end in sight. Of course the truth about the cloud is that how you capitalise it doesn't matter. But how you capitalise upon it could just be shipping's defining challenge of this decade.

London, January 2014.

30

CLOUDED JUDGMENT

Shipping is a truly international business. As a result most of the people working in it are seasoned travellers, and we spend a lot of time in hotel rooms. Until a few years ago, unless you were fortunate enough to have friends or business colleagues ready to put you up in the city to which you were headed, your most likely bed for the night would be a hotel. Now however, there is an alternative.

Airbnb is only a few years old, but it is in the vanguard of an economic revolution in the accommodation business. Built on a cloud-based platform it allows those with a spare bedroom, apartment, castle or boat, to sell a night in it online. It even has camper vans and treehouses. Combining an intuitive user experience with a community-based approach to recommendation and reviews, Airbnb's growth has been nothing short of exponential. To put it in context, the Intercontinental group books approximately 100 million nights per year. Airbnb is already booking 55 million, and it's currently doubling in size every six months. The company trades entirely online, holds no large assets and, due to its utilisation of cloud technology, hasn't even had to make major capital investments in the technology infrastructure which it buys as a service. It charges between 6% and 12% of the value of the transaction as a fee.

Part of the reason for Airbnb's success has been attributed to the homogeneous, unreliable and all too frequently disappointing performance of the big hotel chains. Since the comparison websites appeared and brought transparency to their previously arcane room pricing practices, cost has become such a prime driver for consumers that hotels in response have become less and less differentiated. No wonder a site which offers the possibility of a treehouse for the night, or a clean, friendly bedroom, for far less money, is so refreshing.

Airbnb has found an incredibly sweet spot. They have pointed out to all those people—like your friends who offer to put you up for the night—that they have an under-utilised asset, be that a sofa, a spare room, a wing or a guest cottage. They are by the same token offering them a safe, fast and convenient way to monetise it. And on the other hand they are providing a travelling public sick of expensive, soulless, disappointing hotels, an enjoyable and usually cheaper alternative.

That this revolution has happened in the travel industry is significant. Shipping may transport 90% of everything but travel accounts for 10% of global GDP. In the biggest industry in the world the seemingly inexorable consolidation into fewer and fewer major chains has been driven by economies of scale and service delivery, but in many sectors has led to overcapacity. The capital investments necessary to build and operate hotels are so massive that challenging their dominance was impossible. It took Airbnb to do it. But it also took the cloud.

It's easy to say things like, the cloud offers scalability and flexibility and levels the technology playing field, but the example of Airbnb and the hotel industry is a far better way to illustrate it. It's also useful because you can see clearly that, although it was the cloud technology which allowed Airbnb to deliver its offering in the way it has, on its own the technology was just an enabler. It would have been nothing without the idea itself. An idea which actually, any of the really big hotel chains could have had at any time. But they didn't.

You're smart people so you will already have noticed that there are some very significant parallels to be drawn between the current state of shipping—and the liner industry in particular—and the hotel business pre-Airbnb. Consolidation, homogeneity, overcapacity, unreliability, and unhappy customers.

The advent of the comparison and review websites was the first stage in the erosion of the hotel chains' stranglehold. Opaque pricing, awkward policies, optimistic descriptions and the fact that, once you'd turned up at seven in the evening and weren't happy, going somewhere else cost you a fortune, were all challenged by the internet model. Transparency was the first thing that technology gave the hotel's customers. An alternative was what it went on to enable.

Shipping is still dealing with transparency. Featured as this issue's Futurenaut is Patrik Berglund, CEO of Xeneta. The cloud-based software-as-a-service collects container price information directly from freight buyers and feeds back real-time price benchmarks. To quote Patrik, "Utilizing the principles of crowd-sourcing and big-data analytics Xeneta delivers transparency in a highly volatile and opaque sea-freight industry – allowing companies to measure and monitor their performance, which forms the basis for improvements."

There are other disruptive, technology start-ups too. Take Ocean Insights, which offers container sailing schedules, tracking and on-time performance in real-time. Or Freightos whose patent-pending Freightos Routing Engine can 'filter billions of multi-leg door-to-door routes and find the most efficient routes for shipping freight between any two points on our planet.' Their pricing engine meanwhile claims to cope 'accurately with charges based on origin, destination, lane, subcharges, seasonal fees, overweight and out-of-gauge fees, volumetric ratios, weight and volume breaks, and every other fee in our complex industry.' The service costs nothing in hardware, backup, setup or admin, it's all included in a monthly fee.

These companies and others like them are already bringing the transparency which was the precursor for such rapid change in the travel industry. Where they win is in their rigid focus on the customer. One major facet of cloud architecture is its ability to support an 'outside-in' approach to the business. This approach begins and ends with the customer. The decision is initiated in response to strategic needs that exist outside the company, and the decision-making process focusses on how it will enable an improved customer experience.

But on the face of it the customer experience is a way down the priority list in the liner trade. According to Drewry box ship on-time reliability dropped 1.4%, declining to 69.5% in the third quarter of 2013. Lengthier than scheduled transit times is the explanation, which is another way of describing slow steaming to reduce costs.

As the transparency grows questions are even being raised about the reliability of these figures, as more and more sailings are cancelled and therefore never get counted as late or otherwise. For a customer though, they are equally inconvenient.

There's no question that the market is tough, but the response by operators is more consolidation. The P3 network is, at time of writing, still awaiting regulatory approval, but apparently confident it will open for business in the second quarter of 2014. The G6 alliance has been around for some time, but where the P3 is significantly different is not necessarily in the market share it has, but in the way it will be structured. The three partners, Maersk, CMA-CGM and MSC, intend to outsource their entire operational effort to the P3 Network Centre. London based and headed by Maersk man Lars Michael Jensen, the centre will handle 255 ships and around 2.6 million TEU per year.

Jensen has been clear in interviews that the centre will operate completely independently from the companies which make up the alliance. In fact he has already stated that when there is a conflict of interest, it will be the Network Centre which makes the operational decisions, not the individual carriers.

There is a lot of talk about how the P3 will reduce competition for shippers, but the dangers for the three carriers involved in taking this strategic direction, have the potential to be far greater.

In our cloud-enabled world the economies of scale which have traditionally ruled in shipping are likely to diminish, whilst cumbersome legacy IT systems, inside-out processes, and the harsh difficulties of changing anything, act as an anchor on innovation. Becoming utterly customer focussed and responsive, obsessively gathering and using data to analyse how to do so and utilising cloud-based IT approaches to deliver seamless services runs completely counter to handing over your entire operations to a centre which, by its CEO's own admission, will do "what's best for the common good." One isn't entirely clear whether he's including customers in that.

When these carriers hand over the operations of their vessels to Jensen and his very capable team in London in the next few months, one wonders where the lines of ownership will begin and end. Two leading data analytics companies speaking to us in this issue - one technical and one commercial - are quite clear that both the technical data from the vessel and commercial data from the business, is going to be of critical value and importance to shipping. And at some stage, the two are going to have to come together.

In order to run operations, the Network Centre will require much of that data. So who will own it? The Network Centre, or the alliance partners? It's a question which, unless it's carefully considered now, may just come back to haunt them. The sharing economy may be a buzzword, but there's a difference between sharing and giving it all away. The trend is clear, integration and analysis of technical and commercial data is going to be a huge part of competitive advantage going forward, but whilst others are trying to bring it together the P3 is resolutely splitting it apart—reportedly for the next 10 years.

Drewry point out that the P3, "will contribute to the trend towards lack of service differentiation in container shipping." That's putting it mildly. Meanwhile, the transparency which has brought us to the shipping 2.0 we're currently dealing with, continues to shine a light into the dark corners where money can be made. Highlighting dissatisfaction, inefficiencies and processes which algorithms, automation and cloud technology—which is the warp and weft of bright, innovative ideas-men like Xeneta's Berglund and his ilk—have the capacity to turn into the big businesses of tomorrow.

Between private equity—already taking a serious interest in shipping—and tiring of the chase for the next big app in favour of ideas which will solve real-world needs, and these tech-smart innovators there is a growing realisation that our industry is fertile and lucrative territory, ripe for disruption.

The cloud will almost inevitably be the platform which enables shipping's 'Airbnb' from which will emerge the new Shipping 3.0. But where the idea will come from isn't set in stone. Cloud is more than technology, it is mindset, and it is judgment. The opportunities are still there for the incumbents, if they just allow theirs to be clouded.

London, January 2014.

31

E-NAUTICS
SHIPPING'S TECHNOLOGY-ENABLED FUTURE

Hindsight has 20:20 vision, so the old adage goes. Which is probably the case for embattled German shipping lender HSH Nordbank. According to a report by Reuters, HSH is on its way back to the European Commission regretting its decision to repay its original post-crisis bailout and asking for the majority of it back.

Explaining the EUR3 billion hole caused by its shipping portfolio in 2009 a HSH source says, "The shipping industry deteriorated surprisingly. The regulatory requirements changed, not in a way the industry expected, the hurdles went up. Based on the information at the time, the chances of what happened happening were very low."

Whilst one appreciates that there's a difference between a bad decision and a bad outcome, can it really be credible that shipping and its wider maritime stakeholders can be that bad at predicting the future of their industry? In an environment where ratification and introduction of regulations are measured in terms of years, can this really be, even in part, an explanation for the worst downturn in shipping in living memory?

The development of future scenarios and stochastic modelling is quite fashionable of late in shipping circles. In a joint venture earlier this year Lloyd's, Qinetiq and the University of Strathclyde produced the "Global Marine Trends 2030" report designed to map out a range of potential future scenarios and stimulate reflection and discussion. In a similar but more focussed vein DNV produced the Shipping 2020 report, trying to identify what shipping will look like in 2020.

Both of these are very accomplished and fascinating reports and tell us a lot about the maritime industry. Unfortunately—certainly in the case of the Lloyd's report—the primary thing they tell us is that when it comes to its future, shipping doesn't even have its hand on the tiller. The idea that shipping's cyclical bi-polar economic rollercoaster is beyond its control is simply being reinforced. Like Socrates' description of the male libido, shipping is destined to remain shackled to the madman that is the global economy, just a passive reactor to world circumstances and by 2030 exhibiting no significant innovation or change.

But change and innovation are two things the industry badly needs. The prolonged downturn has exposed the soft underbelly of archaic business attitudes and opaque practices still entrenched in some shipping and maritime quarters. One analyst has already described the industry as operating 'in the stone age', but if shipping is struggling now it's difficult to know how it will cope with what is on the horizon.

Global Marine Trends 2030 focusses exclusively on the global drivers external to maritime—geopolitical, economic, environmental and demographic. But perhaps the most crucial—technology—the report doesn't touch. Describing technology as enabler, not driver; disruptive but unforeseeable, its impact upon shipping—including 3D printing, robotics and artificial intelligence—is rated alongside global economic collapse.

The report is correct to be scared because the potential threats are manifold, but its analysis is flawed in two crucial respects. Firstly, the technological future is, at least partly, foreseeable. Secondly, it offers as many opportunities as it does threats. Shipping finally has an opportunity to—if not entirely divest itself of the economic madman—at least loosen the chains sufficiently to give it unprecedented room for manoeuvre. The key to this seismic change is technology, and whether you like it or not, it's not only coming—it's already here.

On July 1st 2012 this new era really began. The introduction of IMO's ECDIS mandate marked the first concrete implementation of its e-navigation agenda. Although nominally a navigation issue, the actual scope of the e-navigation agenda in practice is much wider. It is designed to bring about increased safety and security in commercial shipping through better organisation of data on ships and on shore, and better data exchange and communication between the two. And that goes far deeper than a simple IT change.

Taken together with the glass bridge and IP satellite communications systems IMO's mandate supports a wider convergence of maritime technologies. The transition to new, digital and technological-based standards of operation and monitoring within the maritime space is something we term 'e-nautics'. Driven by regulation, commercial necessity and global change, together with IMO's agenda, it includes the increasing use of voyage optimisation and routing software to reduce fuel costs, the rising implementation of applications designed to streamline operations and integrate better with customer requirements and systems, and the response to future mandates which can increasingly only be met by the intelligent deployment of technology solutions.

To date regulation has been the prime driver of innovation within shipping, but both external and internal market pressures are conspiring to make that status quo untenable. The environmental impact of shipping at present monopolises any discussion about the future of the industry, but 'green ships' represent at best a tiny part of the picture and at worst a blind cross-alleyway. The relentless obsession with emissions reduction has meant that 'technology' is still shorthand for 'engineering' when in fact it needs to become shorthand for 'business'.

Increasing technology convergence and IT enabled trends mean that in order to be successful those at the helm of shipping and maritime companies need to be looking across their businesses at the impacts, threats and opportunities from a technology paradigm. The importance of—and the profits to be made from—transitioning technology from a cost-centre to an enabler of intelligence and innovation at the heart of the business cannot be overestimated.

Considering the huge importance of shipping to the world economy, it is surprising that more innovation isn't visible. Other transportation industries, aeronautical in particular, are actively investing in new technologies which will allow them to cut costs, improve efficiency and deliver better customer experiences.

Just as importantly they are recognising the way that business itself is evolving in the digital age. For an object lesson in how costly miscalculating the impact of new digital technology, products, customer attitudes and competitors can be just take a brief look at the music industry or the publishing industry. In both long-established sectors the prevailing wisdom held that disruption would be minor. Both have been devastated by technology companies who understand digital, data, marketing and customers.

Digital models scythe through margins and middle-men slashing costs and disintermediating whole layers of business process and professional services. Don't think shipping is immune. Take Xeneta for example, an online repository of container rates which claims its users are saving 30% and more on their budgets. It is the first, but it will not be the last. Add to that the rise of 3D printing which on the face of it has the potential to decimate the container shipping model and suddenly you begin to get people's attention.

If you pay a short visit to the Futurenautics website you can see a brief video of water bouncing. It was produced by GE's advanced technologies division which encompasses nanotechnology. The manipulation of matter on an atomic and molecular scale is creating science fiction materials which could revolutionise marine operations. Hydrophobic nanotech coatings available now could produce dry decks, oilskins which never get wet, boots which repel water and hulls which glide through the water perpetually un-fouled. Engineering components which never rust and need no oil, water which bounces and liquid with memory will transform the marine supply chain and lifetime costs of ship operation.

Carbon nanotubes are creating new materials like buckypaper, one tenth the weight yet potentially 500 times stronger than steel, the lightness of which means a vehicle built from it offers improved structural integrity and allows wireless data transfer through the composite material. Already airlines are investigating it for the aeroplanes of the future, what about ships? Combined with the new high throughput satellite systems such as Inmarsat GlobalXpress and Intelsat EPIC smart ships could pump data into corporate networks via applications routinely held in the cloud, taking advantage of secure, reliable and scalable infrastructure, communicated via the very fabric of the vessels.

With a reputation for conservatism, insularity and—without putting too fine a point on it—having short arms and deep pockets, perhaps it has been assumed that shipping and maritime leaders simply didn't want to hear all this. Certainly it is difficult to find much coherent coverage of these technological developments which puts them in any context for shipping and maritime leaders. But there are already signs that assumptions about the 'technophobe' shipping and maritime leadership may have been wide of the mark. A recent project by InterManager focussing on the return on investment of broadband showed clearly that shipping's senior management have already grasped that the intangible cross-business benefits of uprated communications capability were far more significant than the tangible ones—even though they are currently difficult to quantify. Similar opinions were voiced at the recent SingTel maritime communications roundtable in Singapore (see more of that later in this issue).

Whilst there are most certainly many for whom M2M, the cloud, learning algorithms, Manufacturing 3.0, disintermediation, big data and nanotechnology all feels slightly overwhelming, the shipping industry didn't get built by people who liked nine to five desk work with no heavy lifting and a nice cup of cocoa before bed. This is an industry built on risk, which intimately understands the relationship between that and the potential reward. The key to getting shipping and maritime leaders to invest in their future via technology is to give them the tools, information and context that allow them to properly evaluate both and take suitably informed decisions. Because whilst the threats can't be overstated, there's also money to be made.

There is evidence that shipping may be about to emerge from the deepest trough in its collective memory. In recent years it has been understandable that many companies have just battened down the hatches and focussed on surviving.

In those fortunate sectors such as LNG where rates have been buoyant there are already companies who are making investments in technologies which are providing measurable competitive advantage. With better times in sight it's essential that every shipping and maritime leader begins to understand the new skill-sets they, their employees and stakeholders will require to remain competitive, how new consumer and customer expectations will threaten established industry structures, and the potential consequences of a failure to innovate laying the way open to aggressive new cross-industry competitors.

Whether Reuters' source at HSH Nordbank really speaks for it no one can be sure, but in the context of the technological onslaught shipping is about to experience his words are the unacceptable face of complacency. In the future things *will* happen which the industry does not expect. Hurdles *will* continue to go up. Information about what is likely to happen *can* and *must* improve.

There are a plethora of shipping-themed metaphors I could use at this point: we're facing choppy seas, long voyages, heavy weather. But this is Futurenautics and we like to cut to the chase. The bottom line is that this will be hard, there will be big challenges along the way, but it has to be done.

Because if we get this wrong, in the future when it says "shipped by Amazon", they really won't be kidding.

London, October 2013.

Lightning Source UK Ltd.
Milton Keynes UK
UKOW04f0604190917
309457UK00001B/24/P